Never Too Late

ADETOUN A. AFOLABI

Copyright © 2023 Adetoun A. Afolabi
All rights reserved
First Edition

Fulton Books
Meadville, PA

Published by Fulton Books 2023

ISBN 979-8-88731-216-3 (paperback)
ISBN 979-8-88982-164-9 (hardcover)
ISBN 979-8-88731-217-0 (digital)

Printed in the United States of America

CHAPTER 1

Bungled Opportunities

School started at 8:00 a.m. this Monday. It was already 7:45 a.m., and students were rushing through the gate to beat the bell. Francine walked briskly toward her classroom to drop her bag in her locker before rushing to the assembly. Georgina was in the same shoes as Francine. Many students were already at the assembly hall. The teachers, senior prefect, and assistant senior prefect were already on the podium waiting for all students to converge. Morning assembly started in earnest. The process went smoothly from the National Anthem to the Pledge of Allegiance and announcements. The teacher on duty started a song (a quote that turned into a song), and the students chorused it. They sang happily. The students started marching toward their various classes, singing the song with lyrics to ponder upon.

> I shall pass through this earth but once
> Any good thing I can do
> Any kindness I can show
> To any woman

Or man on earth
Let me do it now

Chorus:
Let me not deter
Let me not neglect it
For I shall never (3ce)
Pass this way again

(Stephen Grellet)

Francine settled into her seat in the classroom. English language was the first subject of the day, and the teacher just walked in, an amiable teacher, compassionate, and always willing to help. A review of the last lesson was soon over with high participation from the students. The lesson for the day began. Students, including Francine, were active. Her active participation did not deter the teacher from seeing a pain well masked by her. She invited Francine out for a brief discussion. Her mother was not feeling well. She was up all night, and she just had another miscarriage. Her mother, Francisca, already had three previous miscarriages. She wanted Francine to have a sibling at all costs, but all her trials led to miscarriages. Francine and Francisca wanted a girl while her father, Francis, wanted a son. By the time she was leaving the house in the morning, she decided to discuss with her mum when she returned home that she had tried enough and should forget about having more children. She already had a conversation with her father during the night.

The mathematics teacher walked into the classroom. She noticed Francine was not in her seat. She started the review when she entered. A student was answering a question while she turned to see who came in. Francine did not look like her regular happy-go-lucky self. She noticed it immediately but said nothing. The next question was for Francine. She answered it so perfectly. The whole class was amazed by the admiration of the teacher. The day went so fast, and it was time to go home. As Francine was about to exit her class, the mathematics teacher, Ms. Davis, called her for a chat. It was over in a few minutes, and Francine left for the day. Ms. Davis looked puzzled. The English teacher noticed it as she entered and asked if she noticed Francine's absentmindedness (despite her active participation) in class, which she confirmed. Discussions by both teachers had yielded nothing. It became a source of concern for them.

Francine was an intelligent, all-around, all-A student, and a good sprinter that had represented the school with immense success. She was also a force reckoned with within the school's debating society and would be the senior prefect in her senior year. She had great leadership traits and qualities. Everything was working well for her in everybody's view. She had grown into a beautiful, mature, understanding, compassionate, studious, and brilliant young lady—beauty and brain personified! The week ran by without much ado until Friday when Francine was conspicuously absent from school. She was to lead her team in representing her school in debating a volatile political topic with another high school for the County Cup. Her absence affected the group and cost her school the esteemed cup. Francine was in school on Thursday, and nothing seemed to be out of the ordinary. She seemed a bit withdrawn, but nobody attributed much to it.

Francine's debating skill was unmatched in the County. Several scholarships were awaiting her high school completion. Francine was outright forthright, principled, outspoken (yet an introvert), and brilliant. At her youthful age, she had integrity, the key to a fruitful and effortless life, always holding on to whatever is true and not minding anyone. To her, "truth" was sacred. Her absence was a rude shock. The debating society members and debaters struggled to fill her spot; her vacant shoes were difficult to fill. The group did the best they could and were in the top three. The leadership effort and skill of Francine rubbed on them. They drew inspiration from her skill and pulled the second spot. The members tried to reach her but to no avail. Her phone was off. The phone of her mother, Francisca, rang but, the voice mail was full and no longer accepting messages. The situation made tensions high. No one was sure of what had happened. The school's administrative department and debating tutor tried to contact Francine and her family, also at a dead end. Everyone had to wait till Monday for information on Francine's whereabouts and welfare. She had never missed school, always punctual with perfect attendance.

At the morning assembly on Monday, everyone was disappointed when Francine was absent again. Tongues started wagging especially from the notorious group that Georgina belonged to. Gina was a bully to the core, a proud, self-centered, arrogant, self-conceited, and rude individual at such an early age. Georgina had two jealousy-ridden friends, who had formed a clique with her, highly domineering to even her friends, bullied them to submit to her will, worshipped the grounds she trod upon, and were envious of Francine to the heavenly. Francine's offense to this notorious group was her brilliance and good heart. Did I also mention her beauty, warmth, nice-fitted clothes, and an aura of friendliness that addressed Francine? Classy, well-mannered, graceful, and audacious rolled into one was not enough to describe Francine. She had the right answers to questions, the right attitude to situations, contributed intelligently to conversations, had the best solutions to challenges, and never looked down on anyone even when outrightly visible that the person was stupid. Students who detested Georgina's ugly disposition toward Francine were too afraid to talk because they would find themselves in the bad books of this notorious clique.

The school's admin department called the numbers on her admission card to inquire about her welfare—no response. Around noon, a call came from her mother who reported that Francine was in an auto accident on Thursday night and admitted to the children's hospital fighting for her life. Francine's father returned home early on the evening of the faithful day and was happy to give his daughter a treat by taking her to the ice-cream parlor close to the house. Her father dotted so much on his perfect child. She had done nothing but gave him joy. He spared nothing in his ability to spoil her silly with clothes, books, and anything she asked for no matter the price if he could afford it. In return, Francine brought home excellent report cards and enviable attestations from school and families in the community they lived in and represented the school at state and county levels. Her honorable deeds made her parents proud, and it gave them good name recognition. A distracted driver on the phone T-boned Francis's car as they left the ice-cream place. The airbag deployed, and Francine was severely injured. She was in an induced coma since the accident. Her father was also injured, but his situation was not as bad as Francine's. He responded well to treatment and was discharged. The hospital refused visitations because she was in the intensive care unit. She promised to keep the school informed of her progress. As the news of Francine's accident and hospitalization filtered into the school, sadness enveloped the school community, except for Gina. The announcement was made at the assembly the following day, and the school asked students to pray for her speedy recovery.

Exactly one week after the accident, Francine woke up from a coma. The swelling in her brain had gone down. She did not realize where she was. Her discharged father and her mother were by her side when she woke up. Disoriented but happy to see her parents, her journey to recovery would be long according to her physician, and she was moved to the ward from the intensive care unit. Francine was a dogged fighter and fought all odds to cut the recovery period short. She attended her physical therapy sessions with determination and recovered faster than expected. Her fractured bone, which was a cause of concern, responded well to treatment. She was discharged after three weeks with instruction to use crutches for two months. Her parents insisted that she stayed at home for one more week after her discharge before resuming to school. Francine was out of school for four weeks. She returned with crutches, was happy to be back to school, and had lost four weeks of academic instructions. She was determined to catch up as soon as she could. She met with her teachers individually to inquire about assignments and notes to read on her own. Her parents were of immense help. Francisca took time off work to support her around the house although Francine asked her not to. Her father returned home every day, assisted her with assignments, and read her teacher's notes when needed. The session would be over in about five weeks. She had to race against time to catch up with her classmates. She studied hard, spent more time at the library, researched more on topics, finished her assignments on time, and worked hard on past assignments. She was very much on track; her parents and teachers were impressed with her commitment to excel at such a youthful age. She showed dedication, commitment, determination, and embraced her situation without complaining.

*****

Georgina and her friends tried to make her life unbearable, but she ignored them. Though she was using crutches, they tried to pick fights with her but to no avail. She refused to respond to all their tricks and antics. They tried to have open confrontations with her on two occasions, but she kept mute. Georgina was from an upscale family; her father was the most popular attorney in the community while her mother was a company executive. They lived in a big mansion and owned other commercial and residential properties scattered all over the community and state and had name recognition in the community. Georgina bragged about her affluence and affluent parents all the time. She was a spoiled brat, disrespectful, and rude even to her parents who, in fact, had no time for her. Her parents were always absent from home because of their positions, professions, businesses, and time-consuming jobs. Money took the place of parenting. Georgina was virtually raising herself. She spent money as she wanted. Her parents were very generous to her. They gave her more than she needed at any given time. They employed chefs, cleaners, and gardeners to keep the home. The employees dared not chastise Gina or report her to her parents. She had free time—freedom to do whatever she liked, utilized her freedom negatively to her advantage, to roam the streets, and foment trouble.

Georgina had everything she wanted and got by force what her parents termed as excessive. Francine was not from an affluent family but had the best of everything. Francine never envied Gina for what she had or who she was. Francine's parents were middle class, comfortable in their own way, and she was their main priority. Their lives revolved around their only daughter and were bent on giving her the best education. They provided all she needed in accordance with what they could afford. She was not a spoiled or overpampered child. They provided her necessities and trained her to be contented with what they could afford. She had nice clothes that enhanced her appearance and beauty. Her clothes fitted her nice gait and stature, and her beautiful skin color brought radiance to her outward appearance. She looked like a million-dollar child from an affluent parent. Her choice of clothes was appropriate for every occasion, a beauty to behold. Georgina hated that so much! She wanted to be the only center of attraction! She perceived Francine as stealing her *show* and *shine*! To her, Francine had too much *swagger* and *ginger* and hated her the more. Besides, her academic prowess, sportsmanship, debating, and leadership skills were of great concern to her. She became utterly jealous; it birthed more indignation. Francine's good heart and articulation endeared her to all teachers and students. Why should Francine be so brilliant with good command of affection? A zillion questions bombarded her brain, so much disdain! Jealousy was the poison she drank and expected Francine to die! Georgina was poisoning herself with hate and jealousy that she was pulling herself down the drain daily. She got depressed anytime Francine excelled in something. Incidentally, Francine excelled in something new frequently. Gina's academic performance dropped significantly. She no longer cared for herself. Why should she? Francine looked better no matter how she tried.

*****

Francine was able to catch up with all that she lost academically during the time she was hospitalized, one week to the end of the school year; she was in better shape academically than before the accident. She surpassed all expectations both in her studies and in health. Her physical therapy sessions were over, and the crutches were finally gone. Her teachers, physicians, physical therapists, and her parents were all proud of her progress. Francine was fully back with more fire and vigor. No one knew she could pull herself up so fast. She got recognition for her performance. The principal called her out at the morning assembly and showered encomiums on her for what she achieved despite the challenges she faced earlier. Gina rolled her eyes and made eye contact with her friends. She hated the principal's comment and unhappy with Francine's academic and health recognition. On the last day of the school year, hopes were high for the long holiday, goodbyes by friends and acquaintances, and there was a meeting with the principal, departmental heads, and the newly elected student leaders—Francine being the new senior prefect—was in attendance. She was the most suited candidate for the position among the nominees. She had all the leadership skills needed. Georgina and her friends were mad they were not nominated and talk less of being elected. They became superlative haters. Francine automatically became their number one enemy all over again. They would deal with her. They waited and waited with their plan for Francine to exit the meeting so they could bully and fight her. Unfortunately for them, the mathematics teacher, Ms. Davis, offered to give Francine a ride home. They were disappointed. Their hatched plan failed woefully!

*****

Georgina's (Gina) friends, Elizabeth and Ella, were wannabes who adored Gina for the wrong reasons. They were also from rich backgrounds, but to them, Gina was the rich kid with the golden spoon! She called all the shots, had the money, and had the connections! The trio felt they belonged to the class of the rich. Classism was their watchword. They looked down on those without so-called rich parents. Gina was the first wheel in the group. With Gina, they called all the shots. They could do and undo. They were, however, empty vessels making the most noise, empty barrels, no brains, never willing to study, no positive impact to themselves or other people. To the trio, classism was the in-thing. Only the affluent can belong to their clique. They had no regard for authority or people around them, always had issues with the law, engrossed with the spirit of entitlement. Whatever their parents/guardian refused to give, they took it by force. "Money answered all things" was their slogan. With too much money and attitudinal problems, they started experimenting with drugs and alcohol. Marijuana, the gateway drug, was the first. It started as recreational, spiraled out of hands in no time, and led to other drugs—opioids, benzodiazepines, alcohol, cocaine, heroin, and others. They had the means to acquire drugs and alcohol. Without adequate family structure, boundary, discipline, and supervision, their dysfunctional settings became obvious. They had all the time and opportunity needed to enjoy the substances without anyone prying on them.

Ella's mother gave birth to her when she was a teenager. She was in and out of jail, also in jail while pregnant with Ella, gave birth in jail, and was sentenced thereafter. She had been absent from Ella's life from almost day one. Amelia, Ella's grandmother, raised her from the day she was discharged at birth. Carol was a spoiled child growing up.

Amelia was an absentee mother who allowed Carol to roam the streets unabated, and without motherly supervision, Carol eased effortlessly into the evils the world had to offer. Amelia had not deviated from playing the same game with Ella, spoiled, unattended like her mother. Her late grandfather was rich, an international business mogul who dealt in gold, diamonds, and mineral resources. He made so much money but died mysteriously, his death a mystery till date. Carol's father wanted the best for his family and worked hard. His wife took advantage of his international travels negatively to mingle with the wrong crowd. She partied hard, notorious with men of shady characters. At his death, he left so much money for Amelia, and Carol, his only daughter, who was highly undisciplined and always in trouble with the law. She grew up with absolutely no supervision. Amelia was supposed to be a stay-at-home mum, but the reverse was the case. She gallivanted with her friends while her husband traveled the world. With no supervision, Carol became a drug mule for the drug dealers in the community. They started by sending her on errands to the corner store to buy soda and snacks and later to deliver drugs. She was young, naive, and innocent. Nobody would suspect her.

She adored the men on the streets in her neighborhood and respectfully did whatever they instructed her to do. They were the father figure she knew, but they took advantage of her due to her mother's incessant absence from the home. After every delivery, they applauded and gave her gifts. She loved it. When they realized how rich her parents were, they started taking her money, enticed her more, introduced her to drugs, and then took undue advantage of her. She was introduced to drugs at an early age. They taught her how to pretend and fake it when her mother was around, preyed on her without her mother's knowledge, and they were present when her parents were not.

They had access to her house, abused her, and stole from her home. She was apprehended while delivering drugs. Her mother got her off the hook. She lied that she was not aware of the content, that she innocently picked it up by the side of the road. Despite the brush with the law, her mother did not change, always away. Carol learned fast and perfected her game until she landed in more serious trouble. Ella's father had never been in the picture. Her mother had no clue who her father could be. Ella's upbringing had always been on the move. Her grandmother moved from city to city, town to town, and anytime Carol was transferred from one prison to another, her grandmother would move. The way her grandmother raised her was not different from the way she raised Carol. Grandma was a functional alcoholic who cared less about Ella. She belonged to the superrich club who called the shots. Ella's life had no structure. Her grandmother was her role model and loved to call the shots like her. Ella felt privileged to be called Gina's friend, a member of Gina's circle of clique.

Elizabeth's supposedly stepfather was a stay-at-home live-in lover of her VIP (very important personality) single mother. Bethena was a vice president in one of the big mortgage banks in the country. The live-in was her mother's third "husband." Her stepfather cared less about her whereabout or academic performance. He was dependent on Bethena's money and cared for nothing else. It was never a true love story. Bethena needed a male and father figure in the home for the sake of her daughter but was never useful to himself or Elizabeth. He was milking Bethena of her income and inheritance from her late father who was a rich stockbroker. Her mother died less than a year after her father's demise and left her all the enormous family wealth. Elizabeth's father was never in the picture. She had no knowledge of him, and her mother had never discussed who he was or whether he was dead or alive. Elizabeth had little or no supervision like the others. In all the homes of Gina, Elizabeth, and Ella, there were no fixed boundaries or adequate adult supervision. The girls did whatever they liked, whenever they liked, and however they liked it, unlike Francine.

Francine had everything going for her, a loving home filled with love, care, and adequate supervision, a naturally disciplined girl, who always kept her cool and well-behaved. She was an only child like the other girls, but the difference between them was like day and night. Her parents' lives were wrapped around her; she was also the apple of her maternal grandmother's eyes. Her grandmother loved her to death and would do anything for her. Her maternal grandfather and paternal grandparents were all late. They all had college funds and inheritances set up for her whenever she gained admission into college or got married. Despite the inheritance from her lineage which would be substantial, she was humble, unassuming, and down to earth. The accident was an unfortunate incident and had become old news. During the long holiday, Francine ran into Gina at the mall. They lived in a small city with one mall. The encounter was an unpleasant experience, but Francine managed it well. Gina was in the company of her two notorious friends. They giggled and rolled their eyes at Francine. She looked at them and said hello (they refused to answer) with a broad smile and walked out of the store. She sensed they were out to humiliate and intimidate her and left quickly.

They followed her spewing uncomplimentary words at her. The store attendant saw all that transpired, and the store camera recorded everything. Francine felt humiliated but unperturbed. She brushed it off as if it never happened. A few weeks later, there was another incident. Francine was on a shopping spree with her parents. While they were in a store, she told them she would be in the next store to check on an item. Lo and behold, the trio were inside the store. The attendant from the former store was on a part-time rotation at the new store and recognized the three of them from the previous incident. As she saw them, Francine also entered. When the trio saw her, their countenance and body language changed and walked to the back aisle where Francine went to. She did not see them and was busy checking an item. They surrounded her with the intent to start an altercation.

The attendant knew what they were capable of doing, kept watching them, and quickly notified her supervisor. Francine dropped the item, ready to leave. They blocked her. She smiled and calmly told them to let her leave. Gina pulled her hair and jerked Francine's head backward. She felt totally violated, and the attendant quickly stepped in. Francine's parents walked inside the store in the nick of time. The mall security was at hand, and the sheriff's department was involved. The store attendant did not even allow Francine to say a word. She explained everything and backed it up with the store's security footage and promised to provide the footage from the previous incident. Francine left the store with her dignity but felt humiliated and violated. She was happy with the praises showered on her by the sheriff, the supervisor, and the attendant for her good behavior and composure during both incidents. Her parents were happy that the attendant had the camera footage to buttress her report and gave a glowing report of their daughter's levelheadedness. The trio had a date at the sheriffs' detention center and bailed by their families after writing undertakings never to bother Francine again. The experience did not deter the trio from their notorious ways, still nurtured plans to deal with Francine.

The new school year started. Francine was in high spirits and ready to begin school. On the first day of school, Francine was on the podium with the principal and other staff members. She was the school's senior prefect, the number one student citizen, a position of envy, serious headache to the number one Francine haters! The first day's morning assembly went fast and smooth to the amazement of the staff and students. Running the school's student affairs was an easy task for Francine. It was as if she was born for the task, a born leader. The school had peace, undiluted and unquantifiable. Daily, group, sporting, and other events all ran smoothly without a hitch. The debating society, with Francine at the helm of affairs, won the County's Prestigious Cup. All the different sports excelled. The school was on a roll. Favor smiled on the school in a marvelous and big way. All hail to Francine, her period of leadership brought new grace, favor, and prominence to the school!

Gina and her group are dying silently of hate and jealousy. All their plans to bring down Francine had failed either at inception or the point of execution. They tried different criminal methods. They were audacious, brazen, and brash, but Francine exhibited strategic patience. Prejudice had a hold of them and placed them on a wide dangerous road of destruction. They spread their tentacles to other gullible friends both inside and outside the school, but Francine's popularity surged and was on the increase daily. She was recognized not only in the schools in the county but in all schools statewide. She became a household name for the right reasons and was interviewed by major news networks for her accomplishments and school activities. Other parents used her as a positive source of counseling for their children. Her name became synonymous with brilliance, winning, goodness, kindness, good works, and good deeds. Patience was a virtue Francine had in abundance. She exhibited empathy and strategic patience and does not get angry under severe humiliation or annoyance. She had every right and opportunity to quarrel and/or fight with Gina and her cohort for their behavior toward her, but she never did. On several occasions, she would even go out of her way to offer support academically and otherwise, but they rebuffed her. She passed all her college aptitude tests with flying colors and organized extra hours to teach her mates, including her so-called enemies, techniques to pass the SAT (Scholastic Aptitude Test), which prepares students for college admission. She was unperturbed even when she saw them rolling eyes at her and was never moved by their insolence. She loved to help her classmates—help she rendered and offered!

Francine was highly opinionated, never ready to be pulled down nor reneged on her zeal to be kind by extending her knowledge and abilities to others. She was zealous to pull up as many people as possible academically. She had the zeal to have brilliance and performance run in her class, but some saw her instinct as proud. Being highly opinionated made the trio backbite and assassinate her character to whoever was willing to listen. They shared that she was proud and showing off her knowledge and nice clothes. Francine had nice clothes no doubt, but they were not as expensive as Gina's. Clothes fitted perfectly on Francine than Gina, her inexpensive clothes were always neat, well-fitted, and outstanding on her body. Her color and shape brought out the best in any material she wore. Her inexpensive clothes made Gina's expensive clothes look "inferior" and "cheap." What Gina did not realize was the fact that expensive clothes do not translate to perfect fitting. Francine knew they were problematic because of their dysfunctional family settings and pitied them. She identified their peculiar situation from a documentary she watched on TV. Being a rich kid does not mean a person would be well-grounded and morally upright. Beautiful clothes, fashion sense, and riches could never cover the arrogance, ignorance, lack of character, cheeky, overconfident, disrespectful, discourteous, and ill-mannered behaviors they exhibited.

All was not well with the trio. In fact, Francine was kind to a fault most especially to the trio. She identified that they needed professional help. She was a good listener, coolheaded, never raised her voice even in the wake of high provocation. She never rushed a decision, always handy, helpful to everyone, and never argumentative. She sensed they were on drugs though she does not know what drugs they abused. She smelled alcohol once in the classroom and once at the mall on the day of their second encounter. They had issues with the law outside of the school. Among them were public intoxication, open container, and petty theft. They stole items in the malls though they could afford the items. They saw stealing as being smart. On all occasions, their parents came to their aid with the full force of their wealth and personal recognition. The school was never involved on those occasions. They were lucky that the local news outlets were also not involved. Their atrocities were under wrap. The parents/guardian never sought professional help for them. They gradually became more tenacious in their ways and forgot that one day they would glaringly come into the open.

After lunch on a terrible day, they went behind the cafeteria, smoked weed, and drank vodka that Gina brought from home. They became belligerent, had altercations with classmates. The principal informed the school's resource officer who realized they were high on something and transferred them to the County's Juvenile Assessment Center (JAC), where their parents picked them up after they were booked. The school gave each a two-week out-of-school suspension and must provide a letter of best behavior when returning. The trio got no discipline nor was counseled by their parents or professional counselors. Nothing changed in their attitude when they returned. They exhibited no atom of remorsefulness. They carried themselves like goddesses, untouchables! Other students avoided them, except for whose characters were like theirs. It was as if the suspension hardened them. They returned with an evil zeal to torment other students and foment more trouble. They roamed the malls, shopped, and pilfered things of no value, believed they were smart (evil geniuses), twisted egos, and their lives had spiraled into a downward roller-coaster ride without brakes. Francine avoided them like a plague when they returned. They bullied, made dirty passes, and called her names, but it had no effect on her. She had mastered the art of ignoring them and rose above their pettiness but harbored no hatred in her heart toward them.

The school year was rapidly ending when the last straw happened. The honor roll recognition program was held on a Wednesday evening, and parents were to be in attendance. Francine was busy preparing for the event, making last-minute arrangements in the auditorium with other students to be honored when the trio came in. They did not make the honor roll and had no reason to be there. Some parents who arrived early were busy talking to one another. Gina and her friends were poised to cause trouble. They got on the podium and pulled Francine's hair with great force while she backed them. They were ready to fight her for absolutely no reason. The commotion prompted the teachers at the back to rush in and pulled Gina and her group away, but alas, two news networks available to cover the event got everything on tape. The parents in attendance were disappointed; short of words, they pitied Francine who had to seek medical attention at the school clinic. The incident, however, did not deter Francine from performing her duties. She returned to the podium despite the assault and excelled in her presentation. At the end of her speech, she got a standing ovation from everyone in the auditorium, including her parents, Francine's parents were totally embarrassed and insisted on pressing charges. They believed that the trio must be answerable for their insubordinate acts toward their daughter. They've had enough from the trio, especially Gina picking on Francine for no just reason. The trio were whisked away to the Juvenile Assessment Center again by the school's resource officer. He would not have transported them if the parents were able to pick them up after interrogation. All calls to them went unanswered.

News outlets aired the assault all night on prime hour and all day the following day. It was a big shame to the parents and guardian, and a big dent in the school that had enjoyed so much recognition and accolades throughout the academic year. With only weeks to the end of the school year, the school principal and staff deliberated on the best punishment for Gina and her cohorts. At the end of the meeting with the school's board because of the publicity, they were expelled from the school and recommended alternative school programs for them while the case of assault was pending. Gina's parents got a big wake-up call. They had grossly lacked in their responsibilities toward their only child. "Position" occupied the number one spot while the upbringing of Gina was relegated to number two. The damage and disgrace were too enormous to overcome! Their big name rubbed in the mud, exceedingly difficult to clean and wash off. The news channels mentioned their names all night and all day the following day. They were at the assessment center for a long time, trying to secure Gina's release. Reporters were in their faces, bombarding them with questions. They could not even look up or respond. Gina had a long rap sheet that they were ashamed of. Unfortunately, she just turned eighteen. Everything was made public, and for the first time, Gina looked remorseful. She was ashamed and used the hood of her jacket to cover her face. Jealousy, hatred, and insubordination had rubbed shame on her like lotion and makeup, made the public focus on her and her parents.

Elizabeth's mother rushed to the assessment center to secure her release when she heard the news. She was in a board meeting when her personal assistant called her attention to the news on the television and radio stations. Reporters were waiting for her with a barrage of questions. Her live-in partner heard the news but was not bothered. Bethena was ashamed of what she heard on the news about her daughter, too ashamed to answer the reporter's questions. Money, fame, and position had failed her. She bowed her head in shame while going into the center and when she left with Elizabeth. When they got home, her live-in was busy drinking while the incident aired intermittently on television. A big quarrel ensued between them for his lackadaisical and nonchalant attitude toward Elizabeth's welfare.

Intimate partner violence (IPV) had always been a normal occurrence in Elizabeth's home. She was used to the incessant quarrels. Her mother saw nothing wrong in the abuses in her home. She gravitated naturally toward abusive men who used and dump her. She seemed to be enjoying the commotions and kept a good appearance at work while the home front was in shambles. Elizabeth went straight to her room while the two exchanged words. Bethena took time off from work the following day to attend the meeting with the school authority and secure a lawyer to represent her daughter who incidentally just turned eighteen also. She might be charged as an adult. Elizabeth did not see her mother's partner when they left for the meeting. He moved out that night after the quarrel with Bethena over Elizabeth's conduct. To Elizabeth, his move was good riddance of bad rubbish. He left like all the others, had seen so much from the men and live-in partner, an array of abuse: verbal, physical, and emotional including a sexual assault by the live-in. Her mother was aware but felt Elizabeth was at fault, blamed her though she was the victim, sided with the abuser, and instructed Elizabeth never to discuss it with anyone because it would affect her image in the society. Instead, she bought her silence with gifts and a raise in her pocket money. The code in most families with domestic violence was "You can see but not talk." Silence and secrets are paramount, family secrets that could never be discussed, so much glamour outside with severe garbage inside.

Ella's grandmother thought her personal standing and wealth would get Ella out. She was terribly mistaken. She eventually got Ella released at the Juvenile Assessment Center and attended the meeting with the school authorities the following day where her expulsion was handed out. Grandma was undeterred. She took Ella home and believed that was her last attempt at schooling. Ella was adamant, refused to attend an alternative school. Grandma never felt there was a need for education when there was enough money to go around. She never valued education. Grandma was a dropout, and so was Carol, her daughter. Ella's mother had a few years to finish her prison term. Grandma saw nothing, absolutely nothing wrong with Ella's behavior, like mother like daughter, like grandma like granddaughter. Carol dropped out of school when she became pregnant at fifteen and delivered Ella at sixteen while in jail.

Francine remembered the dream she had the night before the honor roll event. She was confused if her dream had a correlation with what happened. She had overworked herself planning for the event. She was a perfectionist and wanted everything to be on point. She got home late and felt tired. She went to bed early because of stress and fatigue, needed rest to get her vigor and stamina back for the D-day. She had an early dinner, watched a documentary on her computer, and went straight to bed. She fell asleep immediately. In the dream, she saw a lot of people in an arena watching a game. Most of the people were in high jubilating spirit. The game became tensed at a point because the winning team began losing, and the underdog was gaining high points.

Three supporters of the winning team got up and started pulling down banners of the underdog. In the process, many people got hurt. When the paramedics and the police arrived, they arrested the culprits and treated the wounded spectators. Those wounded chorused that they wouldn't press charges. "It's just a game they chanted." Sport is all about love. There would always be a winner and a loser. They chorused the release of the culprits. The game continued, and the winning team eventually won. The game ended on a happy note. The supporters of both teams were friendly to one another despite the outcome of the game. As she was leaving the arena, she started humming the song, "I shall pass through this earth but once, any good thing I can do, any kindness…"

Francine woke up sweating profusely, sat up, and pondered over the dream. She shared the dream with her parents. They agreed that expelling the trio would affect their lives forever. Only three weeks to end the academic session.

Expelling them would make her carry the guilt forever. The trio needed a second chance—another chance, a soft landing! Francine wrote a thoughtful, well-worded letter to her school principal and copied the board, booked an appointment to see the principal, and gave her a copy of her letter seeking forgiveness for the trio. She wanted the expulsion reversed to suspension or even nothing. They had only three weeks to their diploma. The principal was amazed and promised to deliver the letter to the board immediately. She also explained to the principal that she would not press charges against them.

Lawyers for the girls met with Francine in view of a mediation instead of a court case. They were amazed when she told them she had forgiven them and would not press charges against them. She informed them of the letter to the principal and board seeking forgiveness and reinstatement of the girls. The lawyers were short of words, in total disbelief. They thought she would be vindictive, but she showed unreserved love, agape love. She was nothing but an angel walking this earth. Gina and her friends were mute throughout the meeting. Their parents heaved a sigh of great relief at the news. The girls were unperturbed and did not know the gravity of the assault case or what expulsion at the point of graduation meant.

The principal had a meeting with her staff and delivered the letter to the board who recommended that the expulsion be replaced with suspension but must stay away from the school premises and its environment for the rest of the school year. They were also barred from walking the stage to receive their diplomas on graduation day where Francine was the valedictorian. The graduation day was impressive. Francine's speech was spectacular and touching. She received a standing ovation that lasted over three minutes. A glorious day for Francine, her parents could not be prouder. The news media were in attendance. The news was all about Francine. They sang her praises to high heavens. She dominated the airwaves for days. The story of her life, beauty, brains, good heart, kindness, and coolheadedness dominated the airwaves. To crown it all, she got offers of admission into several universities and chose one of the best universities in the country armed with scholarships under her belt. Francine resumed at her new college, university environment, and life was different from high school environment. Most of her classmates had college admission and were forever grateful for the impact of Francine's tutorial and support that enabled them to score high marks on their SAT examinations.

*****

The trio had nowhere to go, no admission to any college. Their SAT score was nothing to write home about. Living in their make-believe world, they thought they would pass without studying and forgot that manna no longer falls from heaven. They probably believed that the social standing of their parents/guardian would do it for them. After two attempts at the SAT examination, they gave up.

With nowhere to go, partying, clubbing, and roaming the streets and the malls became the order of the day. As rich kids, menial jobs were never on the horizon. It was taboo to them. The pocket money available to them was far more than whatever income they would get in doing menial jobs. They were never contented with what they had, rather, they mastered the skills of street-smart, mastered the use of alcohol, and drug use. Alcohol and drugs were never a cheap way of life. Their pocket money evaporated as fast as they received it. Maintaining the habit became expensive and unreachable, they resorted to other means of getting money. They stole money at home, jewelry, and valuables and sold them to get cash to augment their habits and sometimes paid in kind. The parents/guardian observed missing items in the home, but the trio lied, feigned ignorance, and quarreled that their parents/guardian lied on them. The signs were glaring about their addictive habits, but the parents were oblivious, ignorant, or turned a blind eye. Life on the street became their passion. Dawn to dusk, they roamed the streets. Nights and weekends, they clubbed. It was not long before they got into profoundly serious trouble.

CHAPTER 2

Reckless Lifestyle

Ella and her grandmother went on a visit to the prison to see Carol. It was a monthly ritual they never missed. While her grandmother was at the eatery to buy a pack of cigarettes and pay money into Carol's commissary account, mother and daughter had time to talk. Carol took time for the first time to come clean on her regrets and escapades while young and told Ella how indisciplined she was. She recounted the story of how she mingled with older adults at a teenage age because both her parents were never around to supervise her. She had no attention from her mother who was to oversee her welfare because her father was always away on business trips. With no attention, she was open to negative attention elsewhere. She took solace in being out of the house and visited friends, or they came to her house. She roamed the neighborhood and became a tool in the hands of the adults who saw her as easy prey.

They sent her to deliver drugs without knowing what she was delivering and would reward her with candy and cookie. They took advantage of her ignorance and vulnerability and eventually became exposed to drugs and alcohol. She was cajoled, lured, and convinced to do the wrong things. She gained their trust. She saw them as the father figure she lacked, but they began to drug and abuse her without any complaint from her because she thought they were truly giving her the right support and protection. In return, she would get drugs and alcohol. Before she knew what was going on, she became initiated into wrong vices by men she looked up to for fatherly protection. They taught her to lie to her mother. Anytime her mother returned home late, she would visit the club, lie about her age, and her physical look gave the impression that she was older than her actual age. She became addicted to drugs, alcohol, and other vices. She stole from her abusers, home, and anywhere possible to support her addiction. Drugs are expensive, could ruin you if you are rich, and make you do things you are not supposed to do if you are poor. She got into brushes with the law and had a long rap sheet, and her mother would bail her out every time without the knowledge of her father. She was lucky not to have gotten pregnant from the age of twelve when it started. She was never on contraceptive pills though her mother used them daily because of her gross infidelity, but she never touched them. She was shocked and astonished when she became pregnant at fifteen.

There was no way to figure out who the father could be. She hid the pregnancy for a few weeks. Her mother was not vigilant and never noticed the changes. She continued with her wayward life without any remorse until her father returned from his trip abroad. He immediately noticed the physical changes that his wife should have noticed. He loved his only child so much, realized something was not right and asked Carol. She lied to her father who vowed to call the family doctor. She came clean and told her father about her escapades and how her mother was never around and how she found companionship in other people. Carol's father was upset. He was enthusiastic about his family. All he did was create generational wealth for his family, which was why he worked hard, always away from home. He expected his wife to fill the gap effectively. Obviously, she did not. A big disagreement ensued between her parents. Her mother was unperturbed and blamed her husband for the situation. She played the victim's card and claimed she was always home alone while her husband gallivanted across the world seeking excess money! Money cannot replace companionship. She needed someone in her life, needed love and affection, not excess money. They took vacations together occasionally, but it was not enough time with him. He threatened to seek a divorce and take full custody of their only daughter. His last will and testament were in favor of his wife and only daughter. He told his wife during an argument that he would strike her off his will. He, however, disappeared mysteriously without a trace after a heated argument on that fateful day. His badly decomposed body was found three weeks later. Grandma was arrested and interrogated. She was not charged, and nobody was. There had been no clue on how he died and no charges to date.

After the funeral, life went back to normal for Amelia and Carol in a matter of weeks, perhaps the best coping skill to mourn their breadwinner's death. The police could not link Carol's mother to her husband's death, though the suspicion was high. Amelia and Carol were persons of interest. The officers released them after interrogation. No evidence to hold on to them. They are still suspects/persons of interest but remained free while the investigation continued. Two months later, while Carol was about three months pregnant, she stabbed a male patron whom she stole drugs from. She was high on drugs despite her pregnancy and had drugs in her possession when arrested. The victim eventually survived the attack while Carol got charges of attempted manslaughter and possession of illicit drugs, remanded in jail, and her mother was not able to secure bail for her even as a teenager.

The judge referred her to treatment and counseling while in jail. She was released when her pregnancy was four months gone with a referral to an outpatient treatment program. She, however, did not follow through and refused antenatal care, which would have limited the risks Ella had at birth. Carol dropped out of school. She went to the court-ordered outpatient treatment program but never followed through. She continued abusing drugs and alcohol, and her amoral orientation did not change; in fact, it got worse. She got into another big fight while under the influence. This time, she stabbed a prostitute to death with a broken bottle while fighting over an older adult and drugs. She was arrested for murder and was in jail for the remaining months of her pregnancy.

Ella was born while she was incarcerated. She went into labor before Ella was full-term. She was severely affected by the severity of Carol's drug use. Ella was at the intensive care unit (ICU) immediately after birth. She was born prematurely at just above twenty-eight weeks. Ella had neonatal abstinence syndrome (NAS). She was diagnosed as soon as she was born. Carol was exposed to several drugs. She used anything she was able to lay her hands on. Whatever her partners used, she used. She sometimes used two to three different drugs/alcohol in one day and developed a high tolerance to drugs. Ella had a lot of withdrawal symptoms when she was born due to exposure while in the womb. Her symptoms were not as severe as expected for a full-term child. Carol cared less about the side effects of drugs and alcohol while pregnant. She only cared about her enjoyment and freedom.

She, however, lost her freedom to addiction and could do nothing about it the moment she became hooked on them. She was counseled at the treatment center on the effect the drugs could have on her child but was too far gone to effect change.

Carol abused heroin, opioids, cocaine, crack, methamphetamines, marijuana, and cigarettes, coupled with alcohol. The effects of the abused substances passed through her bloodstream to the placenta and eventually to her unborn child. Fortunately, incarceration enabled Carol to minimize drug use, but it was not enough to erase the damage already caused to Ella's normal growth in the womb. Ella was in an incubator at the ICU with a high fever, severe trembling, screams, sleeplessness, seizures, and other side effects. Ella's NAS symptoms began immediately after she was delivered—a rude awakening for Carol but were too late. Ella, at her tender age, endured the trauma while Carol was helpless. She was sorry for the havoc she caused her newborn baby, but there was no way to undo it. "Sorry" could not fix or take the pain away.

Carol also went through withdrawal symptoms when she arrived in jail and was able to appreciate what her baby was going through. She was privy to trickles of drugs behind bars by those who were able to illegally smuggle them into the system. She went through some level of detoxification because of her pregnancy. The withdrawal symptoms led to the early delivery of Ella. When she returned to jail after the delivery, the trauma of her newborn had a tremendous impact on her conscience and gave birth to her journey to abstinence. Carol was unable to nurse her baby after Ella's discharged from the hospital. She returned to jail while her mother got custody of the baby. Amelia immediately employed two nannies to care for the baby day and night, 24-7.

Money was not an issue to Amelia. She had an abundance of it. She inherited a fortune from her late husband that would last her lifetime, even outlive Carol and Ella. She was not a homely grandmother who would stay at home to nurse a baby. She was the psychedelic mama who enjoyed her life and freedom. After the death of her husband, she threw all caution to the wind and cared less how anybody felt. She dated the who is who in the community, men of timber and caliber who also controlled enormous wealth. She sometimes dated younger men and spent lavishly on them.

Grandma got the best lawyer money could buy for Carol whom the state tried as an adult. A twenty-five-year sentence was handed to her without the possibility of parole because she was an unrepentant criminal, a habitual jailbird from an early age with a long rap sheet. She was moved from the city where they lived to a different city to serve her term. Her mother was disappointed and appealed the case but lost again. Grandma sold all the properties owned by her late husband in the city where they lived and moved to the city where Carol was sent to serve her term. That was the beginning of their fluid movement from city to city. When Carol finished her story, Ella was in tears. It was the first time she heard her mother's story, especially from the right source. Her grandmother never told her anything or the offense her mother committed that sent her to prison for such a long time. Grandma never had time to sit with her to have a meaningful conversation. She was always in and out, doing her own thing, always the community show-woman with a deep pocket. Grandma was beautiful, full of life, a go-getter, gaily and expensively dressed daily, but not a family woman or caregiver to her only granddaughter. She visited Carol monthly and spoiled her with money, even in prison. She still lived the life of a rich spoiled kid behind bars. Carol began her incarceration when Ella was only two years old and would be out in less than five years.

Ella left the prison visit emotional and in deep thought. Was change imminent on the horizon? She cried her eyes out and vowed that her story had to be rewritten. She must not end up like her mother. She, however, had to find a way to break her cycle of addiction, waywardness, criminality, and life totally spinning out of control. Ella felt sorry for her mother. She experienced so much at a youthful age, robbed of her innocence by pedophiles because she was unfortunate to have absentee parents. What they did to her mother was child abuse due to Amelia's negligence and carelessness, adults who should be locked behind bars, a young girl whom they were supposed to teach the right way. They knew better but instead abused her vulnerability and loneliness.

Pedophiles are individuals with psychiatric disorders that prey on children and took advantage of them, irrespective of gender. These pedophiles behave like they are sincere, nice, and kind. They would give gifts as baits, familiarize themselves and make the victims respect, feel safe with them, and gain their trust only to inflict pain on them eventually. They employ different tactics from undue exposure, fondling, watching dirty movies, indecent touching, and eventually rape and defilement. Carol was subjected to wicked manipulations from those pedophiles. Ella was lucky to escape what her mother went through but had towed the same path in a different dimension. She needed a change—a fast one. Amelia was not observant with Carol, was nonchalant, and was also not observant of the negative escapades of Ella, her only grandchild. Pedophiles abused Carol right under her nose, in her house, and under her roof, and she was not aware or vigilant nor sensed it. She just did her own thing and enjoyed life to the detriment of her family. Ella wished she could hate her grandmother but could not. She was the only family she knew in the world besides Carol. She vowed to champion a change at all costs, not only for herself but for Grandma too. She knew the steps to change herself, but how to change Grandma would be a tall task. You can only change yourself not another individual. Change is difficult. Easier said than done.

*****

Now adults and out of high school, the trio had become uncontrollable. They had the ammunition to use against their parents and guardian. Their golden statement—"I am an adult"—became their idiolect and new-formed sentence. Out of control, the streets and bars became their new abode. The impact of Carol's story lasted days, withdrawn and remorseful initially but jumped right back into the destructive pattern and bandwagon of her friends, unable to do without them. Addiction to substances already had her fully in its grip. Occasionally, when reality kicked in, she would withdraw into her shell and ponder on the need for a change. She felt sorry for her mother and what she had gone through. Her story ruminated in her brain day and night, and she would kick the thought out with more drugs whenever the flashbacks occurred. She remembered the look of regret on her mother's face. It had formed a permanent fixture in her brain, how sorry she was and wished she could roll back the hands of time. Her mother took responsibility for her actions and never for once blamed Amelia for her dysfunctional life that pushed her into all she did. She had matured in prison, had been of good behavior lately, and the officers attested to it.

Addiction is a disease that eats away a person's life and freedom, a fatal disease that makes a person lose control to the mercy of drugs through a change in brain chemistry. Addiction had always been a magnet that magnetizes trouble to people. Did I say trouble? *Yes*, trouble in unquantifiable measures! The trio sought trouble, pulled trouble from its abode, and trouble they got! The trio went clubbing as usual on a Saturday night. They were well-known faces at the club. Alcohol and drugs were in abundance. The men were all over them like ants on sugar because they were always in good supply of drugs. When it came to issue of drugs, "sharing" was a key factor. An addict would give you free drugs but would never buy food for you.

The trio had the means to purchase unadulterated drugs, and the dealers who supplied them the "real thing" knew them as deep pockets, dependable customers, and trusted allies. They left the club close to four in the morning, totally wasted. They were drunk and high but decided to have one last shot for the road. Gina brought out a syringe. They shot heroin in turns. It was a near-fatal shot. They left in Gina's car. Gina pulled into a parking lot two blocks away. She felt dizzy and disoriented but managed to park her car. She passed out as soon as she parked the car with the ignition on. Ella and Elizabeth had already passed out. A store owner who resumed early saw the car with its headlights on, he called 911 when he saw three ladies passed out inside it.

They were unresponsive by the time the paramedics arrived. They had overdosed on adulterated heroin sold by a new dealer, also had other drugs and alcohol in their system. The doctors at the emergency battle to save their lives. The police notified their next of kin and gave them information of the hospital. It was days before they regained vague consciousness with a longer period to fully remember what happened. They were extremely lucky to be alive. Upon discharge, they were arrested and charged. Gina with driving under intoxication (DUI), possession of drugs, drug paraphernalia, and open container while Ella and Elizabeth with possession of drugs, open container, and drug paraphernalia. The judge ordered a thirty-day inpatient drug program and a sixty-day outpatient program for them. It would have been more effective and better to send them to different facilities, but there was only one center in the community.

The treatment program had a hitch from the first day at the facility. Ella started exhibiting severe life-threatening withdrawal symptoms while Gina and Elizabeth followed suit. Their probation officers were notified, and they were transferred to the detoxification center. The three of them had developed great tolerance to ingesting more than one drug at a time and would compete among themselves to know whose tolerance was the highest. At twenty years of age, while their mates were in the second year in college, they had ruined their lives sampling all the various drugs on this planet Earth. They had abused marijuana, cocaine, crack, methamphetamine, heroin, opioids, and more.

The detoxification process went well, a painful experience for the trio. Their withdrawals varied but, at the same time, not an enjoyable experience. They discharged back to the facility for treatment and counseling sessions. After the psychosocial analysis, the therapist developed individualized treatment plans for them, which included daily group therapy sessions, individual sessions, and family therapy sessions. The parents/guardian attended the monthly sessions because it was court-ordered, and all the charges against them were dropped at the completion of the program. The counseling sessions, however, did not deter them. The counseling went through the right ear and exited through the left. It had virtually no impact as they resumed their drug and immoral behavior immediately after the charges were dropped—a story of a leopard never shedding its spots.

*****

The completion coincided with Francine's second-year completion at the university. She read stories of the trio's escapades from the community's newspapers. She felt sorry for the lives they chose and thought of how she could be of help. Francine had gone through two semesters of psychology courses and had a better understanding of what they were going through and how destructive it could lead them. There was no way to meet or talk to them, but luckily for her, she ran into Ella, who seemed sober and remorseful at the library when she came to drop her grandmother off for a community meeting of the rich women's association. Francine expected her to snub as usual but enthused when Ella was the first to say hello with a broad smile.

Francine quickly took advantage of the warm aura to open a channel of positive conversation. Without asking, Ella shared all that had happened since they left school and was so forthcoming that she even shared her mother's story. The thorniest issue for her was that she would never know who her father was as her mother had no clue. Francine, being a good listener, did not disrupt her flow and allowed her to fully verbalize. While narrating, her voice cracked, and she teared up. She shared how she had been codependent on her friends, how they had been envious, hated, and jealous of Francine for no tangible reason. Francine's offense was her brilliance, beauty, good heart, and sense of fashion. Gina envied her for her talents and pulled them into it. She wanted to belong and got involved with the wrong person and group. She was ready to break off the group's grip on her, work on herself, and live a positive life. Her family had failed her. She had no good upbringing. She was willing to sway the family onto the right path by being the positive force to embrace positive change.

Francine did not utter a word. Her inner spirit was joyous, jubilating to say the least. She allowed her to shed tears, which would help her feel better. Verbalization is key in the recovery process. It could lead her to accept the fact that she had a problem. Acceptance is the first step in the recovery process. Francine was empathetic but sympathized with her on her ordeals, showed her compassion and self-respect, and did not judge her. She encouraged her to get an experienced therapist that would offer her counseling sessions privately since she could afford it or have her health insurance pick up the bill. To beat her addiction, she needed to learn new coping skills, avoid things that would arouse her cravings, avoid people she used to be with, and continually mingle with others working on overcoming addiction like her.

For starters, she needed to avoid things that could trigger her desire for drugs, including cigarettes. She promised to support her in any way she needed in her recovery process. Francine explained the positive impact of being clean and how her life could change remarkably for the best. Ella looked at Francine in awe. She could not believe that the same girl she had prejudged could listen attentively and offer advice without any sign of animosity. They discussed for close to one and a half hours. Her attention was rapt, never seemed bored, dismayed, or in a hurry to leave. Her responses were outrightly genuine in her best judgment. They exchanged phone numbers and departed. Francine went into the library, ruminated on all Ella told her, and resolved in her heart to reach out to her and offer as much support as she could; after all, we will only pass this earth, but once, it was paramount to offer all the good in our hearts before we leave this world.

*****

Ella was deep in thought all day and all night. Her encounter with Francine changed her opinion about her. She felt sorry for herself. Francine should have been her friend instead of Gina and Elizabeth. She thought about the desired change Francine talked about and how to achieve it, but her thoughts were short-lived. When she picked up her grandmother, Grandma needed to pick up something on the way home. Ella had to drive past an area where she usually bought drugs. She avoided the area by driving through another route that was longer than usual but unfortunately ran into a dealer on the detour she drove through. Her heart skipped. The urge returned despite the court order for mandatory drug tests.

When she could not sleep that night, she called the dealer and bought crack cocaine. Francine was the first person to call her the following day. Ella was remorseful and ashamed and regretted driving through the area. To fight addiction, you must avoid people, places, and things that could trigger a relapse. She told Francine what happened, as usual, she listened to her attentively and without disparaging, condemning, judging, or belittling her, encouraged her to concentrate on her coping skills. Mistakes do happen. We learn from them and move on. Fighting addiction is a continuous battle, not a onetime battle, a consistent battle fought daily. She offered that she could call her anytime she had an urge and needed someone to talk to, offered her a shoulder to lean on. Francine told her she saw her genuine heart and real identity when they had the encounter and told Ella she was not a bad person but chose bad behavior. If she worked diligently on her behavior, her true person would resurface. The conversation was soothing to Ella who saw the power of compassion, love, humanity, and forgiveness firsthand as exhibited by Francine and coveted to be like her.

Ella had codependent on Gina and Elizabeth for so long. She was ready to break the jinx for good. It had been a journey of destruction. Carol's story kept reverberating in her brain. Time to rewrite her family history was ripe, and she was willing to spearhead it. Her life had been a mistake from inception, an unplanned pregnancy, an unknown father, a drug head who suffered inside and outside of her mother's womb, born prematurely to experience the pains of severe withdrawal symptoms and seizures she recently overcame. The effects drugs had on her brain, health, and physical growth, coupled with a lack of structure and attention on the home front made her underperform academically with the inability to recall or retain things for long. She acted at the spur of the moment without thinking issues out thoroughly, never made good and tenable decisions, never participated in sports, never been good or outstanding in anything, was always a hanger-on, and the list went on and on.

She had always sought someone to depend on to mask her natural flaws, mostly negative, and saw herself toeing the line of her mother. She had tangible doubt that she could do better. No longer ready to doubt, ready to grab the bull by the horn, it would not be easy because nothing good comes easy. Turning the negatives into positives was now up to her. With the opportunity of a mentor in Francine, she could and must do it—now a matter of must. Her family background of wealth and affluence had masked her flaws. "Rich privilege" had failed her woefully. Life had thrown her a lemon for over twenty years now, ready to turn her lemons into lemonade with the right support. She reflected on what to do to change her life for the better. She sat in her room, soliloquizing when her grandma came inside, wondered who she was talking to as the phone was off. They had a short conversation, and she left. Ella got up from the bed, looked at the mirror, and spoke to the image she saw to get ready for the rough road ahead. She affirmed positively to herself that she must free herself from all her demons and become a self-made success with or without the help and support of others. Francine had shown her the power of compassion and redemption. It was left for her to show compassion and redeem herself from her unproductive and destructive life. She was ready for a new lease on life, a clean slate, a scraped tablet, a tabula rasa!

The therapy sessions for the trio were with three different therapists with random weekly drug tests. The judge wanted them separated to break the codependency they had. They had become a nuisance and menace to the community, an understatement that they were psychologically imbalanced in which without quick intervention, they might head for a psychiatric hospital soon. They exhibited anger and traits of severe psychotic outbursts even when not under the influence of drugs and had no atom of moral compass. They failed the first three tests, though Ella used one more time immediately after meeting Francine, but miraculously, lucky that the drug was no longer in her system by the next test, she was negative on all other tests and was discharged.

Gina and Elizabeth failed more drug tests during the ninety-day court-ordered program. The judge was again lenient with them and extended their programs instead of sentencing them to jail. The judge encouraged them that they were not good for one another and should separate for their psychological well-being.

*****

Francine finished her second year at the university with flying colors as usual. For the summer holiday, she took time off for the first summer program to rest and took courses in the second summer. Her first summer was eventful. She met with her former classmates in high school, they had a mini-reunion, and encountering Ella was the icing on the cake. She felt good that she was able to make an impact on her well-being. The reunion with her former mates was amazingly wonderful. They had fun and shared stories of high school and experiences so far in the university. Francine enjoyed every bit of it. Everyone looked up to her for wise counsel and encouragement. She was like the mother hen to her group, not that she was older than them. Her wise counsel and golden heart endeared them to her and accorded her respect. The discussion at the reunion was about the situation with the trio. Francine discouraged them from backbiting and gossiping about them. What the trio needed was for the group to extend a hand of love and support. The following weekday, they visited the school to say hello to the principal, staff, and students. Everyone was happy to see them, most especially the beloved Francine.

*****

The trio had been out of high school for two years, were not gainfully employed, not seeking, lived at home, drove the best cars, shopped the malls during the day, and frequented the different bars and club at night. They lived on the sweat of their parents and guardian who no longer had control over their whereabouts. They had no right to complain, and when they do, the complaints turned on deaf ears. The foundation of their upbringing was faulty. When a foundation is faulty, what can a righteous do? They had access to big weekly/monthly pocket money and ample time to roam the streets. Whenever the parents/guardian complained, they quarreled, disrespected, and cursed them out. The monsters they raised were indirectly raising, intimidating them. They became scared and afraid of the children they bore.

One day, Gina and Elizabeth wandered aimlessly into a car dealership and fell in love with a sports car, a two-door open-roof car, beautiful to behold with a nice array of colors. Gina got home and demanded her father buy the car for her. When he refused, hell descended. She threw a tantrum as if she were a six-year-old child and told him she deserved the car since her parents are rich and could afford it. She claimed she was entitled to whatever she wanted being an only child. After all, she would inherit all their wealth when they die. They rather give her what she asked while alive, or she would get it when they are dead. The statement caused them concern, but they brushed it aside. Her mother tried to make her see the reason but to no avail.

Elizabeth pestered her mother with the same request and got the same response. Gina and Elizabeth afterward disappeared for five days. Their parents were scared. On their return, they made life difficult for their parents. Gina and Elizabeth stole jewelry worth thousands and pawned them for peanuts. They frustrated their parents to the point that they reluctantly gave in to their demands. Two sports cars, and problems solved. Both cars were total write-offs in accidents within one month. They were under the influence. Gina's father was furious and regretted buying the car. He gave in to the pressure from Gina's mother. His auto insurance went up significantly, and the same for Bethena. Gina and Elizabeth never accepted they had a problem with addiction or were remorseful for wreaking the expensive cars. They believed they were just rocking, enjoying their lives to the fullest. Three drug offenses are indicative of a drug problem, the trio already had more than three brushes with the law, involving drugs and alcohol.

"Thank God she was alive" was the response of Gina's mother. She told Benjamin she was ready to add money to whatever the insurance company paid to buy another car. He was infuriated and insisted Gina be grounded and take responsibility for her life by getting a job or better still return to school. If she worked for money, she would value and spend it wisely; after all, money does not grow on trees. Money had to be worked for. Gina was too far gone to accept any of that. She had no intention of doing anything. Her inheritance would last her lifetime. The house they lived in was worth millions when sold at her parents' passing.

She would make a fortune. Not to talk of other properties, choice investments, and money in the bank, she was set for life. Gina's thought process was horrible. She could kill her parents, and they knew it. Their daughter was terrorizing them because of their inability to raise her well. Elizabeth was a total replica of Gina. Though not related, they possessed the same gene. They perfectly matched each other in behavioral patterns. Birds of the same feather flock together, they say. An only child to Bethena, her mother too was always away and gave whatever she demanded to fill the gap in her absence. With her mother's live-in boyfriend gone, Elizabeth became free as the bird in the air. She brought male friends home anytime her mother was out of town on work-related assignments. Elizabeth would become the property owner and did as she pleased. Gina could also bring anyone to Elizabeth's house, had control over the cars, and had access to her mother's accounts and investments. She knew she had no problem economically no matter what happened to her mother. As the only next of kin, she needed no job or further her education. Her mother had done enough for both. To crown it up, her inheritance from her grandparents was still intact.

To Elizabeth's amazement, her mother brought another live-in lover. This time around, he came with appendages. His baggage included two girls and a boy, Jane, Judy, and Jason Jr., all teenagers. Elizabeth's secured life and position seemed threatened. First off, she was not ready to babysit anybody. Second, she needed no stepsisters or stepbrother. She was not ready to share her house or supposed inheritance with the newcomers. What if they eventually get married? She knew her mother was seeing somebody, but he never visited. No wonder her mother's incessant travels. Was he out of state? Who is their mother? Dead or alive? So many questions without answers. She got on the defensive from the moment they stepped foot on her front porch. Her mother did not inform her anyone was coming. She would have refused anyway. Her perfect, stable monogamous life had turned upside down in an instant.

Bethena realized she had hurt her daughter deeply with the living situation. She tried to explain to Elizabeth, but she refused to give her audience. She locked herself up in her room, drinking herself to a stupor. The live-in lover was having fun with Bethena and his children. At dinner, Elizabeth could hear them laughing and giggling. They watched movies afterward and seemed enjoying themselves. "Why would my mother do this to me? Why would she bring in another man? Why would he bring his children? Were they intentionally tormenting me?" Questions bombarded her head, but no answers.

They arrived on Saturday. Elizabeth had been indoors since the introduction. Her mother had an explaining to do. Whatever the situation or explanation, she would never forgive her for this dastardly act. It was late Sunday night when she picked her car keys to go to the club. She contacted Gina about her ordeal, and clubbing on a Sunday night was what they settled for. Her mother and her lover were on the sofa in the living room. She walked past them without a word. Her mother said hi, but she never responded. As she was about to drive off, she realized she had a flat tire. Her mom and Jason offered to help. She shunned them, called triple A, and walked back inside to await the arrival of the agent. When her tire got fixed, she left and did not return home for the night. Elizabeth returned the following day around noon. Her mother had gone to work. Jason and his children were at home. Jason was in the study while the children were in the room. She eyeballed him in disgust, hissed, and without a word proceeded to her room. Another dependent, never-do-well catch by her mother, she thought. Why on earth would her mother settle for a freeloader with baggage?

Elizabeth slept all day. She had too much to drink and used lots of drugs. Gina had no money and was waiting for her ATM card replacement. Elizabeth was too angry to ask her mother for money. Both were out of pocket and depended on the men at the club for alcohol and drugs, and they supplied. There are no free meals in America. You have to pay one way or the other! She was very tired and needed sleep to recuperate. She crashed the moment she entered her room. By the time she woke up, it was past midnight. The house was quiet, and she was famished. She went to the kitchen and fixed a plate from the leftover. She was exiting when her mother appeared and proudly announced to her that Jason prepared the sumptuous dinner she ate. She hated herself and felt like throwing up, but she could not because her body needed food after the last night's jamboree. Her mom told her she wanted to have a word with her. She looked at her with disdain and left for her room.

Jason was the chief executive officer (CEO) of his company, a self-made billionaire who came to live with Bethena while the mansion he recently purchased was under renovation. He had been dating Bethena for close to two years, and they planned to take it to the next level. A widower, he lost his beloved wife a decade ago and had done so well raising his three children by himself. He wanted to give love another chance and had found Bethena to fill that spot in his life. His children adored Bethena and wholeheartedly asked their father to marry her. He loved her so much. He could run his business from anywhere and does not have to be there for his business to run effectively. He had able hands. He needed a change of environment for his children who were gradually getting over the death of their beautiful, dutiful, and beloved mother. His wife was a clinician by profession, but he requested her to be a stay-at-home mum (a home engineer). She dotted so much on her children. Her sudden departure left a big vacuum that no other woman had been able to fill until Bethena came along.

Jason perfectly understood where Elizabeth's negative behavior came from, fear and insecurity. He had run his chain of businesses for a long time and knew how to assess people. He envisaged and expected what happened. His only fear and concern were for his children. He guarded them jealously and would hate to see them hurt psychologically or otherwise. He encouraged Bethena to find a way to break Elizabeth's adamant posture with love and care. Elizabeth seemed troubled by their presence. It was normal to feel that way, ready to make her see them as "good trouble," ready and willing to be a good stepfather to her and shower her with love and good things of life. Besides, Bethena already told him everything about Elizabeth, and they agreed that a father figure might straighten her out.

Luckily for Jason's children, they attended the most expensive private boarding school out of state and would be leaving for school soon. They saw Elizabeth once when they arrived and waited each night before bed to interact with her but were not able to see her. Bethena made it a point of duty to return home early since Jason and his family arrived. The children moved to the boarding school after one week. It was on Bethena's insistence that Jason and his children moved to her place while the mansion he purchased was under renovation. Bethena had agreed to marry him and would move in with him after the wedding. Bethena tried to discuss her relationship with Jason with Elizabeth before their arrival without success. She was either not around, inebriated, or too "high" to comprehend anything. Despite Elizabeth's attitude, Jason still loved her, unperturbed by her character. He was a fantastic employer of labor with great leadership skills. He recognized Elizabeth's body language and facial expressions and could read her as a book. He underestimated her reaction though, but he would eventually decode and win her over because of the great love he had for Bethena. No matter how great the trouble she tried to ferment, Jason was ready to surmount and turn it into good trouble.

Bethena missed the children when they returned to school and had taken a great liking to them. Her daughter was always out of the house doing her own thing. She returned early one day and found Elizabeth's car in the driveway. She quickly went to see her because it was unusual to find her at home at that time of the day. She knocked. Elizabeth snapped and told her to leave. She left but returned a while later and knocked again. This time, she responded and opened the door. She apologized for snapping at her mother and told her she was going through personal issues. Her mother immediately noticed that she looked pale and awful. She touched her forehead and realized she was running a high fever. It was unlike her to be sick. She had never been to a clinic, except for her annual physical. She immediately called the clinic, booked an appointment, got on the way with Elizabeth, and called Jason who was out of town on a business trip to intimate him of the situation.

At the doctor's office, the doctor examined Elizabeth while her mother sat in the reception area. He had been their family doctor for decades. He examined her and placed her on a strong antibiotic and other medications. Due to HIPPA (Health Insurance Portability and Accountability Act) law, the doctor could not disclose Elizabeth's ailment to her mother. She was an adult and needed to sign a consent to disclose. They branched at the pharmacy. Elizabeth gave the prescriptions to her mother to fill while she sat in the car. When her mother saw the prescriptions, she immediately knew what the diagnosis could be. A mother's intuition, instinct, or experience? The time was ripe to sit Elizabeth down for a strict, factual, heart-to-heart discussion. She filled the prescriptions, and Elizabeth started taking them in earnest. The doctor had warned her of the implications of not taking the medications religiously. Her mother tended to her devotedly. Elizabeth was not a sickly child. She enjoyed good health and bounced around, year in and year out, partly why Bethena became an absentee mother.

Jason returned immediately from his trip. After all, Elizabeth would soon become his stepdaughter. He wanted to show that he cared. He had an overflowing genuine love for Bethena and was ready to let it overflow and run on Elizabeth. He showered so much love and care on Elizabeth to the extent that she was embarrassed. Elizabeth was too sick to revolt at this time. She took all they offered because she was at their mercy. Her mother was happy that she could spend quality time with her. She needed the mother-daughter bond so bad. Elizabeth felt better after a week. The prescriptions worked like magic.

Gina came to see her after one week. She was particular about a show at the club and wanted Elizabeth to be there despite her ill health. Her health and stability were not of utmost concern to her and chatted happily about the alcohol, drugs, and men that would be in attendance. Jason heard it all, he did not eavesdrop, Gina was loud, and in her world, to her, clubbing and drugs were the best things invented on earth. Bethena returned early from work, and Jason discussed his concern about the relationship between Elizabeth and Gina. It was unhealthy. They needed to sever the relationship as soon as possible. They had to be tactical in managing the situation to get the best and most appropriate result. Bethena thought of how to handle the situation and needed Elizabeth to get well before they could have their mother/daughter discussion. This time around, she must show tough love to Elizabeth. It was high time she get her acts together. The era of enablement was over. She had been an enabler-in-chief for so long. A change of baton was due. She had supplied all her needs, wants, and excesses without questions. She thought she was being a good mother by providing and giving in to all her undeserving requests. The rottenness needed a fast fix. She must stand her ground on reforming her only child. Yes, the time for a total turnaround had come. Goodbye to enablement.

After a week in bed, Elizabeth felt a little better. Bethena took her to the doctor's appointment. He needed to run some more tests. After the doctor's visit, Bethena drove to the restaurant for lunch with her daughter. They got a table outside from the prying eyes of patrons at the restaurant, ordered their meal, and sat to chitchat. They started by discussing irrelevances. Bethena wanted the right time to discuss Jason. The food was good. They enjoyed it. Elizabeth enjoyed it the most. It was her favorite restaurant, and she ordered her favorite meal. She did not order any alcohol because Bethena would never approve of it. They discussed Jason briefly. Bethena saw that her daughter was not too comfortable discussing him. She resented the supposedly "freeloader." To her, he came to milk her mother like the others, even had the audacity to bring children. How could her mother be so daft not to realize he was there to spend her money and disappear like all the others?

Bethena quickly changed the topic before the outing became ruined. Bethena decided to share her childhood story with Elizabeth. She was enthusiastic and narrated it step by step. Elizabeth was attentive and asked questions about why her grandparents loved Bethena so much. She was an only child, an only daughter just like her. They valued education and believed that for her to inherit all they labored for, she must embrace education. Proper education and knowledge would equip her to manage wisely the wealth she would inherit from them. She was not very brilliant but struggled hard to pass even if it would be a C grade. Her struggles were not in vain. She got As and Bs sometimes but mostly Cs. She got herself friends that were brilliant. They gave her support because they saw the zeal in her. She asked questions, gained a lot from their knowledge, turned her grades around, and began to excel in her academic pursuits. When she became a senior in high school, her parents rewarded her by giving her a car for her tenacity and determination to excel. She was overjoyed.

The joy of her parents knew no bounds when she gained admission into the university to study business administration as a major with health education as a minor. Her four years at the university were her best years. Her parents were proud of her. They showered her with love, money, and anything she wanted. They took her on vacations all around the world. It was as if they knew they would not be around for long. She enrolled for her master's degree thereafter and graduated. Her parents felt accomplished and happy with her successes. Then came the issue of marriage and grandchildren. They were eager to have a grandchild(ren) and pressured her to get married, but all the suitors she had were after her parent's wealth.

They lived in a small city where everybody knew everybody. She would be the biggest "fish" caught by any man. She decided to relocate to a bigger city to find the man of her dream that would steal her heart and love her for who she was and not for her parents' riches. City life was different from that of her small community setting. She got a lucrative job with an oil exploration company, and the pay was fantastic. Her parents visited and immediately bought her a nice townhouse in a posh area close to her place of work. To make her parents happy, she went on a few dates, and most of them were wonderful. She was very close to her parents and never hid anything from them. She was their golden child who shared even her dates with them. They became her relationship therapist though not certified. They told her to study the men she dated, what signs to look for, to keep her eyes and intellect open, and above all, to keep her sanctity.

She bought books on how to find true love and read them back to back. Elizabeth enjoyed the conversation, it was juicy gossip to her, and they laughed and giggled throughout. It was time for her to take her medications. She did, and the storytelling continued. She was eager to hear more. They had not had such quality time in ages. Bethena digressed to discuss her jobs over the years and how she became preoccupied with climbing the managerial cadre, allowing all other things to become secondary, including Elizabeth. She made great strides in her jobs, devoted, hardworking, friendly, personable, and professional with great leadership traits. Her jobs sent her to trainings. She also spent her own money to acquire more trainings that made her stand out above her colleagues and peers. She became distinct and distinguished in high circles and echelon. She got rapid promotions and eventually elevated to a vice president position at below forty years old. She was excellent at her job and a perfect example to others. She brought so much progress, profit, and recognition to her company. She attended conferences, became the spokesperson at most conferences, became an invited guest at different talk shows, gave several television interviews, lectures to university students at college events/talks, and so on. She might become the president of the company when the term of the present one expires.

She became lost in thought for a second, heaved a deep sigh, and thought of how she enveloped herself in her job to fill the great void created in her by what she referred to as "life." She excelled outside and was a total failure at home. All her marriages and relationships collapsed. To make matters worse, her only child was a dropout who could not gain admission to any university and refused all entreaties to attend a community college or find a job. All Elizabeth wanted to do was gallivant around town, engage in unproductive relationships, and spend her hard-earned money. To top it off, she was a drug addict, drunkard, jailbird, and never do well. She looked somber and pensive.

Elizabeth cut into her thought process. She was visibly lost in thought. She jolted and felt like she got woken up from a deep trance when she heard her daughter's voice.

Elizabeth asked her mother, "Did you find love? I want to know."

They both giggled aloud, and patrons looked toward their table. Elizabeth could ask questions about her mother's love life. She was already an adult doing adult things.

Her mother teared up and nodded in affirmation. "Yes, but I found love in the wrong places."

She recounted how she fell head over heels in love with this well-built, handsome tall guy. His name was Emmanuel, which meant "God with us." Bethena loved him so much. Besides God and her parents, Emmanuel was next. He was like a demigod to her. She cherished him, loved him, and had so much faith in him. He worked a few blocks away from her job, seemed hardworking, professional, and always well dressed. He was cute as a button every time she saw him. He was caring, calm, and well-mannered. She fell in love deeply. It was not infatuation. To her, it was love—pure, undiluted love. They went on dates, pleasant ones. She enjoyed being in his company. They looked perfect as a pair. After about six months, his true color erupted like a volcano.

They had a wonderful date on a Saturday night. They had so much fun. He told funny jokes like a comedian. She laughed so hard, almost peed in her pant. He dropped Bethena at home and requested to use the bathroom. She obliged him out of respect. She had never visited his house or invited him to hers. She planned to keep her sanctity like her parents advised. He entered Bethena's house, complimented the beauty of her house, and proceeded to the bathroom.

When he was done, she expected him to leave like the gentleman she thought he was. He moved to give her a soft kiss (so she thought), but he kissed and grabbed her roughly. She stepped back, but he applied more force. She politely asked him to leave. Instead, he became aggressive and threw her on the sofa with a lot of force. She hit her head and had a concussion in the process. She used all her might to free herself, ran to her bedroom, locked the door, and called the police. He was arrested. Fortunately for Bethena and unfortunately for him, his fingerprints matched that of a wanted person for an unsolved rape case.

After his bail, he started stalking Bethena day and night. She had no alternative but to get a restraining order on him. Luck came her way from a job she interviewed for a while ago. She got a juicy position in a mortgage company in another city, sold her townhouse, and moved far away from Mr. Cool-Calm-Looking Rapist. After the incident, she constantly ruminated on the true meaning of love. Love was supposed to be a genuine outpouring of affection, fun, and kindness, devoid of pain and hurt, but she got the opposite. He was selfish, brutish, unkind, and a rapist. The experience made her stay away from dating for a while. She devoted all her time to her new job; she was hardworking and got rapid promotions. Not long after the incident, her parents started pestering her again. She loved them so much and knew they wanted a grandchild so bad. They were all she had and wanted to make them happy being wonderful parents. They were her heartbeat, whole heart. She had turned down many dates, probably about ten. She was beautiful and stood out wherever she went. She gave love a second chance when she met Josh. He worked as a stockbroker, rich, handsome, tall, and soft-spoken. He swept her off her feet at the first sight. She was in her late twenties while he was just thirty. They dated for a year and got married.

The wedding was the talk of the town. Her parents spent money, left no stone unturned, and threw caution to the wind. Money was not their problem but how to spend it. Josh did not invite any of his family and never talked about them. It was a red flag for Bethena and her parents. Bethena asked him severally about his parents and family. He said they reside in Italy and would arrive for the wedding. Bethena never spoke to any of his family member. She was looking forward to meeting them before the wedding day. It was a cause of alarm for Bethena's parents who wanted to meet their in-laws. They did not arrive the day before. There was no trace of them at the end of the day. He came clean that he did not invite anyone. He was an only child. His parents were dead. His uncles were not interested in his success or welfare. He struggled to get to the level he attained all by himself. Bethena and her parents were unhappy that they started their union on a lie. Why he lied was a puzzle they were not able to unravel, he told them as an adult he had the right to invite or disinvite his family or whomever he wanted. Josh came to the United States on his own to seek greener pastures. His coworkers were present. They supported him, and the wedding was a success. Bethena was a well-trained, well-groomed, obedient child. She kept her sanctity till her wedding night. A month after the wedding, she was pregnant, and that was when her problems started. Josh wanted fun, time to travel, club, and enjoy with his friends, not ready for a child. His excuses were lame and many. He wanted to wait at least five years before he became a father. Bethena's view of marriage and her reason for getting married was different from his. She told him the desire of her parents before they got married and never said no to her desire—a second lie.

Everything turned upside down just six weeks after her big, lavish wedding. She became brokenhearted and felt like she was losing her mind. Josh became a different person immediately Bethena became pregnant. He wanted nothing to do with the pregnancy and Bethena if she kept the pregnancy. Bethena would never terminate a life irrespective of the situation. They were always at loggerheads in the home her parents gave to them as a wedding gift. He spent more time outside than at home and eventually stopped coming home, but before then, he had hit her during an argument. He annulled the marriage and left for God knows where and virtually disappeared from Bethena's life.

All efforts to find him proved abortive. She wanted to make her marriage work and searched for him despite the abuse. She was about to start living her dream when it shattered and sank into the deep of the sea. Crises became her middle name. She got plunged into the middle of three crises that were at the same time pulling her to a bottomless pit: her marriage, Josh's disappearance, and the baby in her womb. Josh was nowhere to be found, left his job, and disappeared. Bethena realized he lived a life of fallacy and could not believe if he was who he said he was. Bethena had to endure the nine months of her pregnancy all by herself with the support of her parents. She braced herself up and plunged all her time into her job. Her parents wanted her to return home so they could be more supportive but declined the offer.

She gave birth to a bouncing baby girl named Elizabeth. She looked at her daughter and smiled to acknowledge that she loved and wanted her from inception. Her parents were on top of the moon with the arrival of their granddaughter. They showered her with gifts and supported Bethena to nurse Elizabeth. They got her two nannies. Bethena could afford the nannies, but they insisted and paid for the services. Barely a year after Elizabeth's birth, her father died after a brief illness. It was so sudden and unexpected. Her mother followed suit less than a year later. The pain of losing her husband in a sudden manner was too much for her to bear. She had a heart attack and never recovered from it.

Bethena lost her mind. Her life crumbled right in front of her. Losing both her beloved parents in a spate of one year was too much for her to bear. She was yet to fully recover from her crashed marriage, nursing a baby as a single parent, and now both parents gone in a flash. She was distraught, depressed, lonely, nursing a baby, unable to coordinate or make decisions, and unable to cope with life. She turned to God for succor. It was as if sorrow pitched its tent in her life. She broke down psychologically and was diagnosed with PTSD (post-traumatic stress disorder). Her life turned upside down in an instant. She had gone through so much trauma in less than two years. First, it was her husband who absconded, second was dealing with pregnancy all by herself, and third was her parents' death in succession.

She was happy her parents got to see Elizabeth. It gave her a feeling of fulfillment. They clamored and wanted a grandchild(ren). It was as if they waited for her to arrive before dying. They yearned to have her, see her, carry, and pamper her. They were not particular about the sex of the child. All they wanted was a grandchild. They pampered, kissed, sang to her, and walked her pram around the community. They had Elizabeth for a short memorable time. She was their queen; she was royalty to them, the queen of their heart. Her parents were her life support. If not for the arrival of Elizabeth whom she had to be responsible for, she would not have survived their demise.

They were her rock. She depended on them so much for advice, guidance, and everything, talked on the phone every hour, and suddenly, no one to call or talk to. Her colleagues at work were wonderful. Her boss referred her to the employee assistance program (EAP) at work. She got help professionally by seeing a psychiatrist and later a therapist for counseling. She was prescribed medications that helped her to sleep and advised her to take time off work to care for herself and Elizabeth. Her stay at home made her situation worse. She returned to work two weeks later and plunged herself into work, work, work. Her performance slid, but she worked harder and was able to catch up in no time. Unfortunately for Bethena, she had no support systems to fall back on. Her parents came to the United States as immigrants who escaped from a war in their homeland. They had no relatives, no friends, only acquaintances. The few so-called friends and acquaintances disappeared from her life one after the other immediately after the funeral of her mother despite promises to be there for her. She learned quickly that human beings are available only when the going was good. As soon as things change for the opposite, they vaporize like smoke.

Coming home to a baby after work was emotionally distressing. She felt sad that she was not present enough for Elizabeth, but going to work and drowning herself in it was the only safety net she had. If not, she would lose her sanity and mind. Work became her haven, her coping skill for her losses. Her nannies were wonderful and up to the task. They were incredibly good to her and the baby. They took care of the home front and made sure she came home to a clean house, a delicious meal, and a happy and healthy baby. She needed to bond more with her little bundle of joy and created time as much as she could. Collaborating with other people for long hours every day gave her a level of sanity. Being at home with Elizabeth and the nannies were torture and torment to her psyche. Not that she hated her daughter, but her psyche was still fragile from the traumas she went through. Elizabeth felt sad for her mother. She felt really touched by all she went through in a short span. Why was she telling her all this now? Why had she not verbalized all these years? She looked at Bethena, and tears welled up in their eyes. She felt her mother's pain and could see the deep pain in recounting her life story. She cleared her throat and recounted how she became a vulnerable object in the hands of men who took advantage of her situation and loneliness. Unfortunately for her, she allowed herself to fall prey to them. She sought for love and companionship in the wrong places. The relationships were unhealthy. They abused her financially, materially, and physically. Those were pains she hid from people, even from her daughter. She looked good on the outside, a good leader and role model at work but was in pain and a failure at home.

*****

Francine and her parents arrived at the restaurant for a late lunch. They booked a reserved room to celebrate Francine's accomplishments and accolades. They walked past Bethena and Elizabeth and mouthed hello with broad smiles. Seeing Francine made Elizabeth's blood boil over. Hatred welled up in her. Her heart skipped, and her countenance changed. Her mother saw her uneasiness and gently touched her chin to move her head back to face her. Hatred is a silent killer, her heart and blood pressure rose for no reason, she became tensed and angry. It was healthier to love a person and keep your heart functioning effectively than to wallow in hatred that could give you a raised blood pressure. Hatred, envy, jealousy, and bitterness could send you to an early grave while a smile and laughter are the best engine oil the heart needed for smooth functioning. While Elizabeth was stressing, Francine was bubbling in good health, progressing, on the way to remarkable success. Bethena looked at Elizabeth intently, directly into her eyes, and sent the message that she needed to avoid what she just did. She got the message without a spoken word from her mother. Elizabeth cut into the silence.

"Mum, continue your story. I am with you and enjoying the gist."

Her mother smiled, touched her nose lovingly and gently with her finger, and continued, "As I said before the interruption"—they both laughed—"I looked for love in the wrong places."

She pointed out that she repeated the statement intentionally for emphasis. Love is supposed to be genuine; straight from the heart; does not hurt or inflict pain; does not take advantage of other people; offers help and care; given unconditionally; does not harbor hate, envy, or jealousy; filled with happiness; and above all, not sold or bought. You don't sell what you are supposed to keep, never sell your happiness or grant it to another person. You cannot buy any of these things. You acquire them free of charge with free will. You cannot trade or batter with love. When true love exists, life thrives, and happiness reigns.

The men that came into her life over the years and decades had never really loved her. Some were after her wealth, position, and others after her vulnerability. They needed her as a stepping stone to better themselves and their worth. Her name recognition spoke volumes. She thought she loved them too but can now categorically say it was infatuation. She needed them for her sanity, companionship, and to return home to someone, not an empty nest. Besides, she wanted a good man to fill the void that Elizabeth's father and her parents left. She dated a few men after her health stabilized. She was not a loose woman. She kept her dates platonic. She eventually accepted to give marriage another trial and married Bruce in a low-key ceremony. She thought they complemented each other. He worked in a company but was not an executive and not as financially buoyant as Bethena. He was a great, fun lover. They created time to go out with Elizabeth and vacation when the job permitted Bethena.

Elizabeth was about five years old at the time. She had a vague memory of him. The marriage did not last because of his infidelities. He had amorous relationships and eventually impregnated two ladies at the same time—a lady at his job and one domestic staff in their home. Bethena became brokenhearted a second time. He was a pathetic liar, denied both ladies and pregnancies. He initially told Bethena he had nothing to do with them and that they wanted to break them up. It became an unhealthy relationship. She could not fathom her husband mating with her daughter's live-in babysitter to the extent of impregnating her right under her nose and roof. Bethena filed for divorce. It was a messy divorce because she did not have him sign a prenup. He walked away with part of Bethena's hard-earned money and inheritance.

DNA (deoxyribonucleic acid) after the divorce confirmed that he fathered both children. Bethena felt let down. Why was she always attracted to men who eventually broke her heart into pieces? Was she doing something wrong? Was she cursed? Her parents had a blissful marriage. They loved each other even unto death. Why could she not be happy like her parents? After the divorce, they went their separate ways and never crossed paths again.

After her divorce, she stayed away from men and chose her domestic staff wisely. Her third was a live-in lover named Brandon. She started dating him years after her divorce from Bruce. Brandon was a handsome tall guy with no visible means of livelihood. He had great looks and a well-built body; he could pass for a model. He worked here and there with nothing tangible to show for it. He was a handyman and had been to Bethena's place to fix things. He was very funny and made Bethena laugh. Laughter lightens Bethena's heart. She would invite him even when there was nothing to fix just to make her laugh and feel better. She was never going to try marriage again (so she thought), and a relationship was also not on the horizon. She just loved his company.

Anytime he came around, he would find something to do in the house, and Bethena would handsomely reward him for his services. Bethena was a strong-willed woman who never let her guards down. She was firm and knew how to stand her ground. One thing led to another, and before she knew it, they slept together. She enjoyed but regretted it. She had been celibate since her divorce from Bruce. She avoided Brandon, but he kept coming, and a mutual relationship ensued. She decided that someone without a clear means of livelihood might work for her while Brandon stylishly eased himself into her life. She had vowed never to remarry but tolerated Brandon coming over to keep her company sometimes. Brandon needed a good life without working for it. He needed a lovely place to live or perch. He started staying overnight, on weekends, and on holiday weekends. He started leaving his personal belongings behind and became eventually a live-in. He was useful in the house initially but later became a force to reckon with and stopped the fixing jobs in the house. Bethena began calling other people to do what he usually did. He was a baby daddy to four women without the knowledge of Bethena. He had a smooth, calm, quiet look that could deceive even Lucifer.

Brandon became Bethena's source of strength at home. She viewed him as just a casual friend. She never really loved him as they operated on a different sphere. Their positions in life were as high as heaven and earth. When Bethena was around, he pretended to be a good father figure to Elizabeth, was friendly with her, and talked flowerily about her with Bethena. Elizabeth enjoyed his company because of his humorous nature, stayed at home with Elizabeth, and the domestic staff whenever Bethena was out of town. On a faithful weekday when Bethena was out of town, he made passes to Elizabeth, and she rebuffed him. He raped her that night and threatened to tell her mother that she was not a virgin.

She was sad because it was not consensual and could not tell her mother because of her secret and his threat. She feared the blackmail. When he raped her again, she reported it to her mother. Bethena did not believe her daughter. He believed Brandon's word over Elizabeth's and claimed that Elizabeth wanted him out of the relationship with her mother and lied against him. Bethena had caught Elizabeth in lies in the past, and that had eroded her trust in her. She had stolen from her and lied that Brandon stole it. She hated Bethena's relationship with him and wanted him out. His attitude after the incident changed. He became a bone in Bethena's neck, but she did not want Brandon to leave as she had become fond of him; besides, it would be her third relationship to crumble and did not want people to judge her.

Bethena blamed Elizabeth for lying, pacified, and bought her way through gifts and extra pocket money. Elizabeth was unhappy and detested her mother for taking sides with her lover and not believing her. She became rebellious and did her own thing unabated. With a stalemate with Brandon, Elizabeth had the freedom to do whatever she liked especially when her mother was away. She was no longer on speaking terms with Brandon. They avoided each other. The only domestic staff remaining no longer lived in the house though she had no control over Elizabeth.

Bethena apologized to Elizabeth for not believing her. Her distrust was contingent on the lies she told in the past as well as her rebellious attitude and headiness. She exited the relationship when it became toxic and physical. He started talking over her loudly, shoving, pushing, and eventually hitting her. She endured it on occasions and hid her bruises from Elizabeth and her colleagues. She became afraid when he tried to choke her on the day she went to get Elizabeth out of the juvenile center. The acceptance and apology made Elizabeth feel better. Bethena also felt better knowing she had done the right thing by coming clean and apologizing. A part of her believed he assaulted Elizabeth while a larger part was in disbelief. She had harbored the guilt for so long and felt relieved that she had revealed the truth to her daughter. She confessed to Elizabeth that Brandon gave her an infection, and the symptoms were the same as Elizabeth's.

Elizabeth was ashamed, winced, looked down with regret and remorse, confessed the disease she had, and apologized to her mother for the trouble she had caused with her waywardness. Working together in unity of purpose and agreement of minds was the decision they made on their first official outing in a long time. Her mother agreed to scale back on her workload in the company and concentrate more on the home front.

"What about Jason, your new live-in lover, and his baggages?"

Bethena laughed aloud, hugged Elizabeth, and whispered into her ears, “Let us leave that for another outing. We must do more of this, don’t you think? Remember, we agreed to work together. Our next outing would be on Jason. In the meantime, be nice to him!” They giggled and left the restaurant happy.

C H A P T E R 3

Rude Awakening

Gina called Elizabeth severally while she was having lunch with her mother. She was too preoccupied with her mother's life story and not willing to miss any of the juicy gists. She called her as soon as she got home. She was upset with her. Gina had a strong hold on her friends. It was her way or the highway. Gina hung up on her before she could explain herself. She held the four aces in their relationship and believed she was better than Ella and Elizabeth, richer, more beautiful, more fashionable, and outspoken; and she inscribed it into their thick skull that she was the best relationship they could ever have. They needed her and not the other way round.

Elizabeth could not be bothered. She had just returned from the doctor's visit, not fully recuperated. She still felt indisposed. Her body needed rest, and her prognosis was not fully under control. Her laboratory report indicated that she was not all right. She needed some "me" time—better life is better than no life. She had some illicit drugs in her room that would last some time, so Gina should wait! She watched a movie in her room, took her evening medications, and went to bed. Ella called and left a message. Ella was the first to call her the following morning. She inquired about her health and how she was fearing.

She wanted to visit her that morning, but Elizabeth told her she would see her over the weekend. She needed time to ponder over some salient points she could deduce from the discussion with her mother. Bethena was a hardworking, quiet, fast-paced, intelligent, unassuming, well-grounded, and strong-willed woman. She climbed the professional ladder with ease, at her age, and as a woman. She had accomplished so much. She was too busy to keep friends. She had no friends but lots of acquaintances just like her deceased parents.

According to Bethena, her mother always warned her about friends. She once told her, "Friends can make, unmake, and destroy you. Choose your friends wisely. Your success or failure in life depends on the friends you choose. Good friends are difficult to find. A problem or trial would indicate who your devoted friends are. Your true friends are the ones who would give you good advice and stand with you through thick and thin. When you find a good friend, hold fast to her. Don't lose such a friend. Fair-weather friends would disappear at the first inkling of a problem. Do not surround yourself with people of no or low integrity. Mingle with people with integrity and uprightness. Integrity is the key to success and accomplishment in life, not money. People with sound integrity would love you for who you are and not for what you have. Be wise. It is better to have many acquaintances than to have one friend who is an enemy in disguise."

Elizabeth pondered over Bethena's issues. She enjoyed what she does not because of the fat renumeration. Her success was due to her great passion for her job. If it were for money, she inherited a fortune from her parents. Money was not her driving factor. Integrity, passion, productivity, dedication, and determination equals success, and she had all the qualities in abundance. She was successful, highly respected in the community, the banking world, and by all and sundry but had gone through so much in the hands of men. Her acumen and accolades never translated to success in keeping a man in the home. She brought in another lover, another leach with his children, waiting to suck her dry, her number four for that matter! What was the problem with her? Whatever the problem was, it needed an urgent solution. What was it with handsome, tall, and cute guys? They had the same qualities. Were the qualities her hindsight?

She pondered over it for a long time just rolling on her bed. Her mother knocked, came in, and distorted her thoughts. Jason made breakfast, and Bethena wanted Elizabeth to come to the table.

"Jason is a wonderful cook. You must eat so you could use your medications," she announced.

"I am not hungry and do not want to eat the food he prepared," she snapped.

Her mother smiled and responded, "You would like him. He is a good man, and I love him. Remember the discussion at the restaurant? I promise to tell you everything about him."

"Did you just say love? Tall, handsome, cute? Just like the other ones. Another one, Mum? Can't you see? They are all using you. Won't you learn? Won't you just stay off these men and concentrate on me and your job?"

Her mother smiled again, turned it into a joke, and said, "I sense some jealousy in your tone. You want me all to yourself, no competition. I get it, but come to the table."

Elizabeth smiled at her mother's response but would not go to the table. Her mum promised to fix a plate for her and bring it to her room.

"I love you," she said and left the room, laughing.

Elizabeth could not help but smile. She returned a few minutes later with two slices of toast bread, a sizable portion of scrambled eggs, bacon, some sliced strawberries, mango, kiwi, oranges, and a cup of cold orange juice. She smiled as she entered and enjoined Elizabeth to eat and take her medications, planted a kiss on her forehead, and exited the room. She said nothing as her mother left. The aroma of the scrambled eggs filled the room. She looked at it. It smelled good and appealed to her eyes. She had never tasted a breakfast so delicious. The eggs were perfectly made. She finished the food and wanted more. She was, however, ashamed to go for another filling, ashamed of herself for eating the food prepared by the person she detested so much.

*****

Gina did not call to check on Elizabeth as expected of a good friend. She was always so full of herself and expected them to bow to her wishes, whims, and caprices. Elizabeth also did not call as she was still recuperating. When Ella did not see Elizabeth over the weekend as she promised, she drove to her house and felt bad that she was not available on time to nurse her partner in crime to good health. Elizabeth recounted the last escapade that landed her the health scare. Ella was no show and for no reason, so the two remaining crime seekers decided to hit the club, party wild, and do drugs. They had no money and depended on the men to foot the bills and fix them up. They embarked on the destructive behavior that led her to become indisposed for more than two weeks. She had gone through hell. More tests are needed to ascertain the level of damage to her health. She had a little crack cocaine left in the house. They shared, got high, and stayed indoors for a long time to evade suspicion from her mother and Jason who were downstairs in the living room.

Ella left late at night after the lovebirds had left for the bedroom. Ella called Gina to tell her about Elizabeth's illness. Gina had missed their company and feigned compassion. She later went to Elizabeth's place to see her. She saw Jason reading the newspaper on the porch and said a shy hello on her way inside. She knew Jason saw her as a bad influence on Elizabeth from her encounter with him the last time. She cared less. While inside, her focus was on hitting the road and painting the town red. Elizabeth explained what she had gone through in the last week. Gina dismissed it as nothing. She had treated herself on many occasions, needed no one to know her health issues, and took care of herself without the knowledge of her mother. She chastised Elizabeth like a kid for involving her mother. She should discuss it with her next time, and she would get her covered. She asked if Elizabeth had any leftover heroin or drug in the house. She said no. The doctor had advised her against sharing needles. Gina got angry.

"Why would you involve your doctor in your private life? Are you not an adult?" she exclaimed. Elizabeth explained to her that the doctor saw the needle marks on her body and asked questions. Gina had a way of bossing over her friends. They felt subdued by her presence. Luckily, her mother was not in the consultation room with her and neither around to hear the conversation. Jason, however, heard everything because Gina was loud and domineering.

Jason knew about addiction, the stages of addiction, and the stages of treatment. His late wife was a therapist and a clinician. She had a PhD in psychology. He knew that Elizabeth needed help fast. She was treading on a journey of no return. She needed immediate intervention and dedicated professional help. His property was ready and would be moving in the next two weeks. He wanted it furnished with everything new. Bethena was the interior decorator, designing the house. Jason wanted to engage a professional, but Bethena wanted to decorate and fix it to her taste. They planned to marry in the next few months, and Bethena had planned to move in with him into the new house.

He loved Bethena so much and gave her the nickname Goodness. He called the nickname with pride and love. According to him, Bethena was the good woman God had sent to replace his late wife and be the mother to his children. In fact, his children wanted him to marry Bethena. They fell in love with her the first time they met her at a social gathering where an acquaintance introduced her to Jason.

Gina had the temerity to command Elizabeth to get out of bed and follow her to the club. When she reported that she was not strong enough and that her doctor recommended another week of bed rest for her, she became livid. The unhinged Gina was not ready to buy the idea. She insulted Elizabeth, promised to boycott, and deal with her as well as make Ella sever relationship with her. Jason was furious. His soon-to-be stepdaughter was in a toxic relationship. How did she get herself entangled in this unhealthy relationship? He wanted to go inside and ask Gina to leave, but he was not sure how Elizabeth would react. He was not in Elizabeth's good books and do not want any insult from either of them. He was an upright man who respected himself. Gina stomped out of the house in great annoyance and bumped into Jason who was already coming to march her out of the house. She did not even apologize to Jason for almost pushing him down. She drove off with screeching tires that left marks on the driveway. Jason looked at the car as it sped off. He wondered where she got such confidence, attitude, and boldness from. She was not good company for Elizabeth. He must support Bethena to rehabilitate Elizabeth.

*****

Francine returned to school and was already in her third year at the university. She was studying biomedical sciences with a minor in psychology. She had grown into a beautiful young lady, the toast of young guys. She had no time for relationships. To her, it was a distraction. She needed to concentrate on her studies and proceed to the college of medicine or law school. Her brilliance shone so much that her professors allowed her to tutor those in the first year. She also tutored her classmates and whoever sought assistance from her. She was a rear gem. She loved to do good. She offered help as much as she could to people of all races and believed we would pass this earth but once. Kindness flowed in her veins. She never discriminated or showed hatred toward anybody. Her parents visited her every month to give her whatever she needed and above all offer moral support. The support from her parents was a big encouragement to her. They were only out of pocket for her personal needs since she had a full-ride scholarship for her undergraduate studies and had already secured two scholarships to study medicine or law, torn between what to study. She loved to study medicine so she could help humanity, but a Law professor once advised her to go to law school. He told her she would be a brilliant law student and lawyer.

*****

Gina was now on a total path to destruction. When she left Elizabeth's house in total rage, she drove to Ella's house to pick her up for a night out at the club. Unfortunately, Ella's grandmother was sick in the hospital and Ella was with her. With no friends available, she went alone. It was a night of disaster waiting to happen. She overindulged in drugs and alcohol out of annoyance and boredom. She sat all by herself in a corner, did not dance, ignored, and snubbed everyone that came her way. She drank herself to a stupor. By three in the morning, she got up to leave, and her legs buckled. She collapsed back to her seat and continued using. She became totally inebriated and disoriented. She was told to leave when the club was about to close. She struggled, tumbled, got to her car, and slept off.

By five in the morning, she decided to leave but could not find the ignition. She tried and tried without success. She slept off again, holding the car key in her hand in the parking lot. The workers at the nightclub closed and left through the back door, unaware that Gina had slept off in her car in the front parking lot alone and vulnerable. Anything could have happened to her. A police officer on patrol sighted a lone car with its door ajar. He drove to the car and saw Gina fast asleep. He tried to wake her up. She was belligerent. He called for backup and an ambulance to ascertain that she was not in any danger of overdosing. The paramedics checked and cleared her. She was transported to the police station to sober up with her car towed away. When she eventually became fully alert (over nine hours), she was released. The police chief had a heart-to-heart discussion with her before she left. He pointedly told her she needed professional help urgently, that addiction would eventually kill her if care was not taken. He gave her examples of those who had died from drug and alcohol poisoning and overdose. He knew her parents as responsible people in the community. Her continued abuse would show her that the law is not a respecter of persons. Her parents' position and clout would one day fail her.

Gina's attitude became an issue for her parents. Drugs, alcohol, and lackadaisical attitude toward life became a big cause of concern to them. All avenues to support and rehabilitate her had failed. They could only watch and not talk. If they dared talk, she would respond rudely, curse them out, and forcefully take whatever she needed or asked for. She became a dilemma to them and constantly caused quarrels between them. They started apportioning blame to one another for why Gina became the monster she became. The happy relationship between her parents had gone sour because of Gina. They could never agree on the best parenting skill when she was growing up.

Gina saw the inconsistencies in their parenting skills, chanced, and used them against one another and to her advantage. Now a full-grown woman, control was no longer possible and out of the picture. Gina got back home and seemed remorseful for the first time. She stayed at home all day, and likewise the following day, her partners in crime were all missing in action. She was tired, restless, and craving for drugs. She needed her fix after two days of forced sobriety. As she was about to leave that night, she heard her parents arguing at the top of their voices. She knew the argument must be about her. What else would they argue about if not her? They were a lovely couple in society and held in high esteem. They never argued, fought, or quarreled. They loved each other dearly. Gina's character and addiction had erected a wedge between them and had turned their affection for each other into a nightmare. Gina waited for a little while as if to pacify and quell the argument, but she could not be bothered.

She left the house and did not return that night. She spent the night with a stranger she met at the club because she did not want to be part of her parents' quarrel. When she got back home the following day, both her parents were gone. She was happy, good riddance, she thought. They were not of any significance or importance to her. Her conscience had been seared by her addictive brain. All they meant to her was to supply money, abundant money for her to enjoy and lavish, turned them into her personal ATM; in fact, they needed to exit this world and let her enjoy what they acquired all their lives, her inheritance. Anytime her addictive brain kicked in, nothing and nobody was of value or important to her.

*****

Ella's grandmother had a health scare. She woke up on a Tuesday morning and felt seriously unwell. She struggled to get out of bed and called for Ella's attention. Ella tried to make her comfortable. She made her a hot cup of tea and a slice of toast bread. Ella was not a good cook. She never cooked or learn how to cook and knew nothing about the kitchen. The stove in the house was dormant since the last housekeeper left over a decade ago. They ordered food or ate out. Grandma was too sociable and psychedelic to bother with kitchen or household chores. A cleaner came once a week to clean and do laundry. Grandma started going in and out of consciousness, and Ella called the ambulance. She was scared to see her in such a state. She was a healthy woman who took her health and annual physicals seriously. The doctor ran a series of tests and kept her for observation for a day. Her test results were inconclusive, and more tests were ordered. The doctor wanted to be certain of the situation before he gave the prognosis. Her situation seemed dire and scary. A group of consultant doctors met with her and had discussions upon discussion. As far as Ella was concerned, nothing must happen to Grandma. She was the only relative she had besides Carol who had been incarcerated for years. She had not been a good granddaughter, and she had not been there for her too. They were like strangers living together. Her mother was still serving her term and had some years more to finish. If Grandma dies, she will have nobody. Ella did not want to inform her mother. There was nothing she could do from behind bars. All her attention was on Grandma. All other things had become secondary, drugs and her friends inclusive.

*****

Francine called Ella to know how she was doing with her sobriety. She told her about her grandmother's situation. Francine encouraged her to stay strong and that her grandma would be okay. As they were discussing, Elizabeth came in. She was upset that Ella was talking so freely to their mutual *enemy*. Ella no longer viewed Francine as her enemy. She had been nice to her and had encouraged her to work not only on herself but also on her addiction. Ella never told Elizabeth or Gina about her encounter with Francine. Elizabeth called Ella a backstabber and left the hospital in annoyance. Elizabeth called Gina and told her of the "frenemy" (friend enemy) between Ella and Francine. They promised to deal with Ella. They would ostracize her from the group and make her life miserable.

Grandma spent three weeks in the hospital and was diagnosed with cervical cancer found at an early stage. It was stage 2, treatable and manageable according to the consultants. They started chemotherapy immediately. The chemo was torturous for her. She looked pale and sick after the first two bouts. All her beautiful blond hair fell off. She became bald suddenly. Ella bought beautiful wigs for her to cover her bald head. She was too sick to put the wigs on. She was discharged after the last chemo and was to be on bed rest with an initial weekly visit recommended.

Ella was preoccupied with her grandmother's health. She lived virtually in the hospital beside her for three weeks. Drugs or alcohol use became secondary. However, she used minimally because she was really stressed out but smoked a lot of cigarettes. She was a chain-smoker like her mother and grandma. She tried to keep her head clear from drugs to assist Grandma and avoid the prying eyes of the doctors and nurses. She prayed and prayed as little as she could. People remember God when they had problem. She promised to turn a new leaf if Grandma recovered. She would become clean and serve God more.

Her notorious friends had not called since the day Elizabeth visited her and Grandma at the hospital. Ella was ashamed of the way some of the nurses and visitors looked at her when Elizabeth left. Her appearance showed signs of an addict. She wore a skimpy dress, unkempt and reeked of alcohol. She wore an expensive dress, but her appearance did not do justice to the price of the dress. Her grandmother saw Elizabeth's appearance but was too weak to comment. She was indecently dressed for a hospital environment. She seemed high on something. Her eyes were glassy and thinned out. She was, however, happy when she stormed out and never visited again. Ella renewed her vow to work on her addiction and choice of friends. GINA AND ELIZABETH HAD TO GO! She had gone down the drain enough with them. Time to redeem herself had arrived. She had managed to use drugs minimally and controlled her cravings for three weeks—a good starting point! Her life needed a new meaning and upliftment. She could do it; she must do it. She must break the hold of addiction, unhealthy lifestyle, and crime. She promised to be better than her mother. The lane she had towed with Gina and Elizabeth would lead her to where her mother was. She needed not to end up like her. She had not hit rock bottom but would work on it. Whoever and whatever stood in her way, she promised to uproot.

Ella reported all that happened in the last three weeks to her mother when she could no longer hide the truth from her. She was distraught and cried bitterly. She felt terribly sad that she was not able to offer support to her mother due to her incarceration. It was the first time her mother would fall sick and be admitted to the hospital. She enjoyed good health all her life. She regretted her life and all she had done that got her where she was. She sobbed and sobbed. Ella consoled her. She was inconsolable. It touched Ella's heart. She felt sad and distressed. Her mother had become a new person, a better, understanding, and responsible person in recent times. She worked on her diploma and learned different arts in prison. She learned hairdressing, flower arrangements, and fashion designing, and excelled in all.

She begged Ella to keep a good eye on Grandma. She was all they got, the matriarch of the family. Ella promised to do her best. Her mother called on call collect severally every day to check on Grandma and Ella. She was happy and thankful that the cancer was in the early stage and getting better by the day. Her calls became a source of inspiration to Ella and Grandma. Carol apologized profusely to Ella and her mother for her absence, what she had put all of them through over the years, promised a better and responsible person when out of prison, and would never put them to shame or bungle her second chance. Everyone deserved a second chance. A first chance could be negative, unproductive, and dissatisfying, but with determination, motivation, and strong will, a second chance could be a life changer.

She had hurt the people she loved the most in great measures. She would make amends and make them proud of her. On one of Carol's calls, Ella came clean on her issues with addiction, criminal involvement, and wayward lifestyle. She narrated amid tears all her escapades with drugs and alcohol, excessive clubbing, criminality, inability to excel in school due to bad friends, unhealthy lifestyle, and many more. Her mother was dismayed and could not believe her ears. She created and birthed a true replica of herself, she thought! She thought Ella coped academically and was well-behaved as exhibited during the visits to the prison.

Before Carol could respond, Ella apologized and begged her mother for forgiveness amid sobs. She had realized her folly and ready to make amends, determined to change her ways. Carol could not utter a word. She sobbed bitterly at the other end. All she could think of was that her mother failed again as she failed her, and there was nothing she could do. When she stopped sobbing, she encouraged Ella not to hate her grandmother but focus on turning her life around. She was the only person that can effect a positive change for her own good. A mother is not someone you choose; nature and creation chose you for your mother. You accept through inception the vessel to bring you to the world. She made up her mind there and then that she would do her best to support Ella fight her addiction and become a better person even from behind bars.

She told Ella that she had the opportunity to use drugs even behind bars but choose not to because she wanted to break the destructive cycle that had caged her in a cubicle for years. She promised herself to be a better, refined individual in and outside of the prison. She, however, found it difficult to believe that her daughter involved herself so much in all the atrocities she discussed and committed, and her beloved mother kept it a secret and never informed her. There was not much she could do, but all hopes were not lost. She must get her only child reformed and rehabilitated, and the journey starts *now*.

Carol gave her mother time to get better before discussing Ella's issues. In the meantime, she instructed Ella to immediately register at an outpatient recovery facility for counseling sessions. She checked on Ella frequently and asked questions about her recovery process. Ella enrolled herself for counseling sessions in an outpatient rehabilitation center in town and started therapy sessions in earnest without even informing her grandmother. She did not want to bother her with her personal issues because she was recuperating. She paid out of pocket to the facility. Her therapist had a two-hour session with her to get her history and psychosocial analysis. She was impressed that she came willingly, ready to pay out of pocket for her sessions. It showed her level of determination and readiness for change. Her zeal pointed to the fact that she had accepted that she had a problem and was powerless over her addictive and behavioral tendencies—a positive sign that she was ready to work on her issues.

Ella gave her history as much as she could (thanks to the prison visit where her mother opened up the truth about her birth and mother's history). The first session was a two-hour of sobbing, tearing up, and sharing. The therapist was attentive and allowed her to cry when she needed to. She never offered her a napkin because it would disrupt her flow of verbalization. She allowed her to verbalize freely. Ella's story was pathetic. She shared her family secrets. At the end of the session of verbalization, she felt better. She felt as if a five-hundred-pound weight got lifted off her shoulders. The therapist asked her several questions as well as questions about her mental health status.

Her responses showed that she had a co-occurring disorder. She had a lot of stressors, depression, severe anger bouts, cravings, and sleeplessness. She was prone to taking decisions without thinking and at the spur of the moment. She had used drugs and alcohol to mask her feelings and disorder unknowingly. She needed help with her addiction as well as her mental health. The therapist recommended individual and group therapy sessions daily during the week. Attendance at AA (Alcoholics Anonymous) and NA (Narcotics Anonymous) meetings in the area as permitted. Ella was also referred to a psychiatrist for evaluation. Her report showed that she needed urgent treatment with psychotropic medications. She was reluctant initially and did not want the stigma of the prognosis. It would shame her in the community that she had psychiatric issues. People would call her crazy and mad, she thought. The stigma of a mad lady would be too deep to erase.

Ella agreed with the counsel of her therapist and psychiatrist that it was better to treat both prognoses at the same time and follow the treatment regimen for the desired result she sought. Ella became well informed that a mental diagnosis was not a stigma. Mental illness is an issue with the brain's function that needed treatment just like any other illness such as cancer, diabetes, or any other ailment. A disease is a disease irrespective of the area of treatment. Drug addiction is a disease—a fatal one for that matter. It is a disease with a negative, dangerous progression with each use. She did not believe it until both the therapist and psychiatrist confirmed it. Addiction is a disease that deals with the composition of the brain's chemistry. It alters the brain's effectiveness and functions. She eventually came to terms with her prognosis and embraced them. She dedicated/devotedly worked on them, with utmost thanks to Francine's advice. The encounter at the library made the dispensation and desire possible. Francine was a great encourager. She called her often to lend her support. No matter how busy her schedule was, she made it a point of duty to call twice a week to offer her well wishes without any strings attached.

Francine was the angel God had sent to set her on the right part. Their meeting was an accident, an accident that was remolding her life for good. Things happen for a reason, and the reason could sometimes be good. All things work together for good if we believe, she thought. She remembered Francine humming the song "I shall pass through this earth but once, any…" Francine had shown her goodness and kindness, thought about their encounter, and smiled. All thanks to Francine for being her eye-opener. She sang the song severally all day. One day, she would be able to extend the healing process to Gina and Elizabeth, but for the moment, her recovery was paramount and personal. You can only give what you have not what you do not have.

Her therapy sessions began smoothly and followed religiously her medication regimen. She felt different, alert, slept better, and focused. She stayed at home, except for periods of therapy, attendance at AA and NA meetings, and appointment with her psychiatrist. She felt an improvement even in her health and eating pattern. She was happy with her new self. She avoided Gina and Elizabeth and made sure their paths never crossed. She knew all their daily routes. She was once the third wheel. She did not call or pick up their calls. She avoided them like a plague or incurable disease. They left nasty and threatening messages for her. She never responded.

Her therapist had discussed the term "people, places, and things" with her at the inception of her therapy sessions, she counseled her that to succeed in her desired recovery and attain freedom from addiction, she had to stay away from certain friends, places, and things that could derail and cause her to relapse, she must strive to shun them at all costs. Incidentally, Francine also discussed the same term with her. Was she studying psychology or what? She had no idea of her major and knew she was a sapiosexual. She related with everyone but mostly highly intelligent people. Her knowledge of issues seemed infinite. She would excel in whatever course she did.

Ella became more depressed, lonely, and fighting the battle of withdrawal symptoms that were plaguing her daily, an unseen war, a battle she was fighting alone. She had no friends anymore, and her grandma was battling cancer. At this point, she had hit rock bottom. She must cold turkey it by "fire by force." She understood better the signs and symptoms of depression and mental health, thanks to her therapist and psychiatrist. She became a caregiver and nurse overnight. It was a stressful job, but she was happy to do it for Grandma. To make matters worse, her grandmother was not the regular patient that listened. She was noncompliant with the instructions of her oncologist and had started smoking and drinking little quantities of vodka and her favorite red wine. She tried to hide her actions from Ella who was a pro in such areas.

Ella was at her tipping point. She sat Grandma down and told her they needed to help each other. Drinking alcohol and smoking would derail her recovery process as well as make Grandma's health situation worse. They agreed to discard all the alcohol in the house and throw away the cigarettes. They encouraged each other daily, and the recovery process got well on track. Ella attended daily individual and group therapy sessions and attended AA and NA meetings. When possible, she had to drive long distances to avoid her friend's routes, avoid areas where she bought drugs, bars, and clubs they patronized. She threw away all her drug paraphernalia. She felt happy, relieved, and accomplished. She was tired at the end of every day and even woke up in the middle of the night to help Grandma.

She suddenly had her cups filled to overflowing with activities. She was unfamiliar with waiting on people. She had to wait to see the therapist, be in groups with people she would under no condition mingle with, and then meet with other sets of people at the AA and NA meetings. It was loads of responsibilities but was happy to do them. Francine called early the following day because she would be busy later in the day. Ella was tired and still in bed. Francine recognized immediately from her voice that she was tired and depressed. Ella explained everything to her new friend. She was now her confidant. Francine encouraged her to discuss the issues with her therapist and psychiatrist and, in the meantime, cut down her daily therapy sessions to three times a week but had to discuss them with the professionals first.

Ella was uncomfortable with such a rigorous schedule where she had to be on time or work with schedules. She was not an on-time person on any occasion, never had structure, and was her own boss besides the almighty Gina. With regards to her grandmother, Francine encouraged her that she needed a nurse or a nurse assistant to cater to her needs. They could afford it anyway. She needed to act fast before the pressure would lead to a relapse. The truth was, she was so stressed and on the verge of a relapse. Francine was once again her redeeming grace. Ella met with the therapist and discussed her situation and schedule. They agreed to a change in her individual sessions. It was just as Francine proffered.

A registered nurse and two nurse assistants were employed to relieve Ella of the stress in the home. She was not used to such rigorous activities and man-made sleeplessness. She was happy to support her grandmother, but it was telling on her health and recovery process.

C H A P T E R 4

Threaded Needle

There is the saying that a needle with a thread attached to it would always be visible. The thread would show where to locate it. As difficult as threading a needle seemed, the moment it becomes threaded, looking for it becomes a simple task. Threading a needle could indicate one's upbringing, character, and personal disposition to things. A threaded needle becomes personified; a person could identify who owns the needle with the thread's color. The trio had well-known parents and guardian in the community. Everybody knew to whom they belonged. They bear the names of their families, and whatever atrocities they committed became a stain on their families.

Gina and Elizabeth were still fully in their game. They excluded Ella but not totally. They were angry with her uncalled association with Francine who they saw as their "supposed enemy," were monitoring all her movements, and waiting for the best time to strike. Ella seldom leaves the house unless on scheduled visits to the therapist, psychiatrist, AA, and NA meetings. She got a sponsor at the AA and NA meetings who looked after her well-being in terms of situations that could lead to a relapse. A sponsor is a person who is also in recovery but had been in the program before the newcomer. You can discuss anything with your sponsor. Call them even in the middle of the night if needed. All discussions with a sponsor are confidential just as with the therapist and psychiatrist.

Ella was not out of the woods yet. She was still struggling with cravings, withdrawals, loneliness, acute stress, and depression. The stakes were still high for her. A little mistake could rubbish all she had achieved in the last few weeks. Carol knew she had not been there for Ella; motherly intuition was her hope. She knew Ella loved her to death despite being away for so long. Ella cherished her mother and was grateful that Grandma was there to keep a roof over her head. Though Grandma was not a home-based person with a laid-down family structure, she, however, supplied all she needed and kept her comfortable. Money was never an issue for Ella. Carol was willing to support her daughter's recovery from behind bars. She was never there to thread the needle for Ella, never experienced motherhood or nursed her as a baby, but it was never too late.

She had been clean and sober for years, walked the lane previously, and had a firsthand experience when she was young. She knew it would be difficult and understood how addiction and recovery worked. She called Ella daily on call collect to encourage her. She used her experience and story to counsel other inmates. She had become a pillar of encouragement to other inmates. She had a 360-degree behavioral and value turnaround for the better. She was ready to make up for all the years she had lost and was fortunate that her mother was there to pick up and clean up her mess. Though she never measured up to her expectations, she was still grateful. Carol knew that Ella's drug use could be a result of her brain being accustomed to drugs from her womb. A little introduction to drugs could activate the dormant effect of drugs in her brain. Ella's use was precipitated by pressure and influence from friends. A onetime experiment catapulted into a full-blown addiction over time. Carol had expended almost twenty years out of her twenty-five-year incarceration and was in line for an early release due to good behavior and prison calendar.

Grandma was getting better by the day. Her support staff had been incredible. Carol had a heart-to-heart discussion with her mother on her health, lifestyle change, disposition toward life, and most especially Ella's issue. Grandma never knew the situation with Ella was precarious. She never knew she had become addicted to alcohol, drugs, and other vices. She was dazed that such a level of addiction happened right under her care. She knew she had friends and partied hard. She thought it was just youthful exuberance. She was disappointed in herself for not being vigilant and knew she was an absentee grandmother who left Ella to raise herself. She apologized profusely and begged Carol not to hate her for letting her and her only granddaughter down again. She promised to lend her support. No wonder Ella had a talk with her on her noncompliance, alcohol, and cigarette smoking.

Amelia believed that money could solve all problems. Money is good. We all need money, but money cannot buy love, raise children, instill discipline, or lay structure and foundation. All of Grandma's so-called friends and rich women's associations disappeared since she became indisposed. They went on with their lives as if her living or death meant nothing to them. It was only Ella that was there for her. Grandma vowed to care for her family devotedly with sincerity of heart from henceforth. Friends are good. They are visible only when things are good and smooth. The moment life turns the negative lane, they disappear. There are friends that stick better than family. Such friends are rare. Whenever you find such a dependable and loyal friend, do everything to keep the flame of friendship burning. Discard the bad ones in a jiffy and never look back. Do not hate them. Just keep them at bay. All said, it is always good to keep your circle of close friends at two, a maximum of three. When you are rich, you have friends. Everyone aspires to be close to you or related to you. Let your friends value you genuinely, not value your wealth.

*****

Gina and Elizabeth had no threaded needles, lost, living on the fast lane as the days rolled by. Gina and Elizabeth's parents were addicted to work while their children had drug addiction and other vices. They failed woefully at home but had great success in the eyes of the corporate world. Both parents lacked time, access, and intimate moments with their children but delivered abundance of cash to them. Gina and Elizabeth had abundant access to money, to comfort, and all good things of life. Having and spending money is good. It has its value and relevance. It gives stability and confidence, but money does not raise children and does not supervise or help with homework. The value of money can only be seen outwardly on a child while home training lived inside. When home training becomes absent, money that was supposed to be on the outside would fill the inside with vices, such as drugs, alcohol, criminal activities, and obscure character. Their character had brought so much shame to the parents on many occasions. They felt the shame for the moment and off they returned to their flowery world of the who is who in the community. A child who lacks home training and proper structure would eventually sell cheaply houses built with hard work, sweat, and great resources. They have no value for money. They never worked to accumulate resources. It meant nothing to them. They got it cheap and would treat it as such.

When Bethena returned home from work, Elizabeth had gone out. She was supposed to be on bed rest as advised by the doctor. She had missed two doses of her prescribed medication. She left home before noon, the same time with Jason who had gone to supervise his house. Elizabeth and Gina left without any acknowledgment of Jason who was on the front porch ready to leave too. He did not acknowledge their presence anyway. His focus was on the love of his life, starting a family, Elizabeth inclusive. Bethena drove in at the same time with Jason who informed her that she left with Gina. Bethena was disappointed that her daughter would jeopardize her health for an outing with Gina. Elizabeth returned around midnight, wasted and inebriated, wasted to the extent that it was a waste of time talking to her. She was in a different world that night.

Jason supported Bethena to get Elizabeth into bed. Bethena took the following day off to accompany Elizabeth to her doctor's visit for the result of her laboratory tests and hoped they would have lunch like the last time and do some catch-ups. She was disappointed with Elizabeth's drunken malady and drug use. Gina was a bad influence and vowed to sever Gina's unhealthy relationship with her daughter. Elizabeth's behavior turned for worse when she became friends with Gina. Bethena went into her bedroom and cried on Jason's shoulder. What has she done wrong to deserve these acts from her only child?

Jason empathized, consoled, and told her that the foremost duty of parents was to be there for their children, lead them with dignity and integrity, inculcate home training in them, and lead them by example. They must be included in the parent's daily agenda and activities. Children learn by example from parents and mirror them. He encouraged her that it was never too late to rehabilitate her. He used himself as an example and how he created time to bring his children up after the death of their mother. He learned to balance making money with being present in their lives. If a parent is absent in a child's life, the street would occupy the space created by the absence. He did not blame Bethena but admonished her on the way forward. She could not deal with the past but could work on going forward.

Elizabeth made bad choices. She must face the consequences because actions have consequences. Their major concern now was how to support her to embrace the recovery process. Jason told her to brace up and buckle up because the road ahead was about to get bumpier. She should also be ready to act fast to safeguard her reputation, which Elizabeth's behavior was about to pull down into disrepute. Bethena agreed she was at fault one hundred percent. Her job became her priority the moment she got on the corporate ladder. Higher heights became her focus. She never looked back. She became class conscious and aimed at the top echelon in society, country, and the world.

She rubbed shoulders with heads of states, presidents, ministers, governors, mayors, CEOs (chief executive officers) of big corporations, and more. Her position opened doors for her around the world. She was always on the news, made headlines in newspapers, and graced the front pages of magazines. She made money and inherited money. With money and position, her equation became balanced, and the home front was not on her horizon. Elizabeth got left behind. Nannies took care of her and later left her to fend and care for herself. One thing led to another when she became Gina's friend. She turned into a new creature, almost unrecognizable, and the rest was now history.

*****

Gina also got home totally drunk and high on drugs. Her eyes were glassy. Only God knew how she made it home. She could have killed herself or someone. The worst thing for anyone drunk and high on illicit drugs was to get behind the wheels. She could have gone to jail if the police had pulled her over for driving under the influence. When she entered the house, her father was in his study, preparing for a high-profile case that had featured him on the news during the week. He was a well-known attorney who defended the rich and mighty in society. He had made a name for himself and his law firm, employed many attorneys in his firm, had made money, and still making money. His firm advertised on television and radio daily with his picture as the focus.

Even without advertisement in the media, he had satisfied clients to advertise his competence. The cases he had worn were enough advertisements for him. He had name and face recognition. If the police had stopped Gina, it would have been bad for his high-profile case. Gina staggered inside, and he shook his head. Why was he unfortunate to be a father to this nuisance? Gina's mother strolled in from the kitchen with a smile and two cups of red wine in both hands. They drank socially on occasions. They were having a chat, gossiping. It was a makeup for their last quarrel over Gina. She saw Gina's state of drunkenness, and her countenance fell. She placed the cups on her husband's table. They looked at each other in dismay.

Her husband took the wine back to the kitchen, threw it away, and returned to his study. Gina's mother knew their chat was over and had to leave before another quarrel erupted. Gina's mother was a company executive who had also made a good name for herself. She had refused all entreaties from her husband to be a stay-at-home wife and mother. Her husband promised to pay her salary to stay at home, but she refused, enjoyed being the boss at work, ordered people around, earned six-figure salaries and emoluments, and met important personalities daily. She enjoyed the position and the class her job had placed and offered her. She mingled only with people of means. If you are not rich or in a prominent position, you are a nobody and not welcomed in her world. Madeline and her husband had a social problem of belongingness. They associated only with people in their socioeconomic class. They treated people of little means rudely, treated them shabbily, and enjoyed making certain people feel inferior. Gina saw their behavior, took after them, and copied them perfectly. They were her mirror. She was a privileged kid with rich parents and behaved like them. Children see their parents as role model, look up to them, and copy what they do. Classism, high class, and position in the society they exhibited birthed the negative result Gina turned out to become, had brought ruin to them. They discriminated and treated people differently with prejudice. Gina mastered it all; in fact, she surpassed and overmastered them.

Madeline was ashamed of herself over Gina's conduct. The look on her husband's face was that of "Have you seen what your refusal caused? Have you seen what your daughter turned into?" Benjamin said nothing, but his countenance spoke a thousand words. Madeline turned to a statue for a moment and could not move. It was as if something glued her to the floor. She was frozen and short of words. She unfroze herself and walked dejectedly to her room, her heart pounding heavily and rapidly. She feared her marriage was about to hit the rocks, scared and humiliated.

If her husband filed for a divorce, the shame would be too much for her to bear. Being an executive and married to a well-recognized attorney had added to her status in society. She was not ready to lose her status and clout. She knew her husband too well. He had gotten to his wit's end and was upset. He placated and begged Madeline for many years to concentrate on the home front in the bid to reform Gina and cut off Gina's allowance to reform and bring her to her right senses, but Madeline doubled her allowance, bought her undeserved, expensive, ostentatious gifts, and made money available to her without any form of hesitation or question. Madeline negated all the actions Benjamin took to cut Gina to size, made Gina hate her father, and saw him as wicked while she saw her mother as her best friend and greatest supporter. She used her parents against each other to get whatever she wanted, and the manipulations had worked in her favor while wedging a gap between her parents.

Madeline went to bed brokenhearted. She tossed and tossed, had murdered sleep, her eyes wide open counting the ceiling, and her blood pressure shot up; she almost died of a heart attack but for the quick intervention of her husband. When her husband got into the bedroom and saw her, he called the ambulance. She was admitted into the hospital that night while Gina was fast asleep, unaware of what she had caused. The siren of the ambulance that took her mother to the emergency room did not wake her up. She was totally wasted. Benjamin stayed with Madeline all night. She was stabilized but would be on observation for a day or two. Benjamin left in the morning to freshen up and go to court. He had a high-profile case to represent. His presence was very important. It would add credence to the case. If he had stayed a little longer in the study or slept on the couch because he was angry, the story would be different. His mind was in disarray. His concentration marred, thanks to Gina and his wife for ruining his ability to prepare effectively for his day in court.

Classism and egoistic high position in society ruin lives. Gina and her friends saw themselves as classy and above others because of the elevated positions of their parents and wealth. Position would fade when the position terminates. No one stayed in a position forever no matter the position. A day would come when "ex" would be added as a prefix to the position. A rich man today might become a poor man tomorrow while a poor man today could be the rich man tomorrow. No position is permanent in life. The earlier one realizes that positions change, the better. Nothing lasts forever. Position, money, and class are all vanities. Vanity upon vanity, all is vanity. Character, integrity, and a good name are the only legacies that would last forever. A good name is better than all the riches of this world. Money answered all things but cannot buy you happiness or peace of mind. Your character identifies you and speaks volumes about you. What you show and depict to people is who you are.

When Benjamin left the court, he rushed to the hospital to see his wife. He called Gina severally, but she did not pick up. When he returned home, Gina was gone. She did not return home that night. She refused to pick up her calls and never knew her mother was on admission at the hospital. When she returned in the morning, her father had gone to court. She listened to her messages and learned that her mother was on admission. She couldn't be bothered. She erased the messages and tucked herself into bed; in fact, she was too tired to bother. She spent last night abusing drugs and alcohol. She eventually went home with a stranger instead of going to the hospital. She slept off. She was very tired. She overused drugs.

Benjamin had scattered thoughts all day and all night. How did his only child get to this level? He had worked hard all his life to get to where he was. He started from a humble beginning with his poverty-stricken parents who immigrated to the United States and were uneducated. They did menial jobs to feed the family of eight. He lived as a second-rated, pitiable person. His parents had six children because they knew nothing about family planning. His mother worked as a maid in the home of a wealthy family and sometimes took him with her to work. He sometimes played with their child, but they mostly looked down on him. They saw how eager and brilliant he was to acquire an education and gave him scholarship to the university level.

He was very brilliant, so they sponsored his education until he became a lawyer. He got his first big client through them, and the rest was history. He mingled with the rich, got more clients and retainerships of big companies through his benefactors, and later, Madeline, when he became rich, his outlook toward life changed. He became saucy, arrogant, and full of himself. He looked down on the poor and downtrodden and forgot his humble beginnings. He amassed so much wealth. His wealth, position, and opportunities overshadowed his sense of rational reasoning to the extent that he forgot about his family members and left them in abject penury while he enjoyed his wealth alone. His parents died poor, and he had no inkling of where his siblings were. They were too poor to be associated with, never cared, never bothered.

*****

Ella called Francine to check on her. She was excited to share her recovery experience and her efforts to remain clean and sober. She also told her that her grandmother was much better and supported her recovery process. Francine was happy with her ability to grab the bull by the horn, forging ahead without looking back. Francine encouraged her to visit her dorm at the university anytime she wanted. Ella had been very dedicated to her treatment and recovery process. She had self-determination and plan to make her mother proud. Grandma had cut down on smoking and drinking. She did it for two reasons. The first was because of her health, and the second was to support Ella in her recovery process.

She used them only when Ella was away because it was difficult for her to cold-turkey her addiction; she had not hit rock bottom. As a functional addict, she cut down gradually until she became fully sober. She knew she could trigger Ella's craving and relapse if she saw her smoking or drinking. She had been a bad role model. She disappointed her daughter and now Ella. Two generations were destroyed by no one else but her. She needed to be the adult in the room and must redeem her image with the right example. She gave her life a good and long soul searching and thought of ways to become the real matriarch of her family who needed to set the right boundaries. The lonely situation she found herself in when her husband traveled the world in search of money precipitated her behavior. Situational factors affected her. She mingled with the wrong people that influenced her to do the wrong things instead of being a devoted wife and mother.

Ella visited Francine at the university. It was her first time in a university environment. She was captivated by what she saw. Many people in her age bracket going in and out of lecture rooms. She was moved to tears on how she messed up and wanted to be like one of the students who held folders on their left chest. Her mother would be proud to see her in college at her release. She added admission to college to her to-do list. Her SAT test score was low. She would attend community college for two years and transfer to the university. Francine was happy to have her. She showed Ella around the university and encouraged her to further her education, willing to coach her on the SAT examination if she wanted. Ella was not willing to study for the examination. It was too rigorous for her when she was in high school. She would attend the community college and use it as her stepping stone to the university. In the meantime, her recovery takes precedence. Francine was thrilled with Ella's plan and willing to support her plans.

*****

Elizabeth slept all night and woke up around noon the following day. Her doctor's appointment was at two o'clock. Her mother told her to hurry. They left home around one o'clock. Jason left early and did not see Elizabeth. He called Bethena to know how she was doing. Elizabeth was still sleeping when he called. Bethena called to tell him when she was up. They got to the clinic on time. Her urinalysis showed drugs in her system. The doctor was not happy with her despite his advice on her previous visit. Her STD had not totally responded to treatment because she had it for so long before committing to treatment. She would not have treated herself if her mother had not brought her in. Her HIV (human immunodeficiency virus) test came back negative, that could however change in the future because the virus could be in its window of incubation. The doctor advised her to use her medications as prescribed. Improper treatment could render her infertile and rob her of having a child in the future.

She was also advised on safe sex practices. He gave her new prescriptions till the next visit. They left the clinic and headed to their favorite restaurant. She did not discuss her test result with her mother and kept her in the dark. Secret was a usual weapon of drug addicts. When her mother asked, she glided over the topic, she asked again, and she lied. Lying was another major characteristic and behavior of drug users. Even when caught red-handed, they would lie to cover their tracks. All untrue and half-truth statements are lies. She painted a good picture to her mother and made her believe all was well when it was not. They sat in their usual spot and ordered food and drinks. The doctor's visit opened the discussion, then to Jason. Bethena asked if she had been able to assess Jason and what she thought about him. She was nonchalant, evasive, and later told her point-blank that she wanted him out of their lives for good.

She reiterated that her mother was fine without a man. Why did she need one? She jealously told her she was not ready to share her mother with anyone, not with Jason or his children, and discussed that Jason was after her wealth and position and would leave after he laid his hand on her money and leave like all the others. Jason was well-dressed and articulate, drove nice cars probably leased or bought by her mother. His children looked well-catered for like children born with silver spoons in their mouths. She then went ahead and threatened that her mother had to send him away, or she would send him away her own way. Bethena smiled, put her right hand on Elizabeth's right hand, and rubbed it gently and lovingly.

She looked intently into her eyes and smiled again as the waiter delivered their drinks. Elizabeth had worked herself up and now visibly angry. She pushed away her drink. Her mother gently pushed it back to her. Her mother chose her words carefully as she started. She knew she was already angry and might walk out on her if she made her angry the more. She might disgrace her in public. She had severe anger issues. Her countenance reeked of anger, and she could throw a tantrum at the slightest opportunity. Her mother was always afraid of her angry bouts. Bethena looked at her straight in the eyes again and told her how much she loved and would do anything to make her happy. She massaged her ego by telling her how much she loved her and how she had been there for her through thick and thin, picking up after her, providing lavishly all she needed, promising to always be there for her no matter the situation.

A small ring of smile registered on her face. She quickly dissolved it and gave a bigger frown. Bethena sipped her drink and encouraged her to do the same. She did. The server brought their food. The aroma filled the air. Bethena kept quiet, and they ate in peace. Bethena discussed other issues, bordering on shopping and a particular bag in Vogue, an expensive bag for the high and mighty. Elizabeth loved it and had always wanted one. Bethena told her she already ordered two. She was happy and smiled broadly. Without saying thank you, she picked her phone to let Gina know about the bag. Her mother gently pulled her hand down and continued with Jason's issue.

Bethena professed her love for Jason to her daughter. Elizabeth looked at her in amazement. *What's wrong with my mum*? she thought. *What has the love for Jason got to do with her*? She had finished her food and got up in annoyance. Her mother pulled her hand and gently pulled her down to her seat. She sipped her drink and told her mother rudely she'd heard enough of Jason's issue. Her mother told her she needed to hear more to be able to make an informed decision.

She blurted out, "What decision? You already made your decision by moving them into the house. What decision?" She repeated, "I was never in the picture or informed that anyone was moving in. Why tell me now?"

Bethena kept quiet for a minute. She responded that Jason was not there to live permanently. He was only in transit while supervising the renovation of the house he just bought in the area. She encouraged him to stay with them instead of staying in the hotel. His children had returned to the boarding school out of town. Elizabeth did not even know the children had left and thought they were avoiding her because of her mean disposition toward them. Elizabeth's face lightened up. Bethena could sense her relief. She smiled wryly, not knowing that the bombshell was on the way. Elizabeth was not prepared for the next statement and was shocked to the marrow when her mother blurted it out that she planned to marry Jason very soon. She needed stability in her life, ready to settle down with the true love she had found in Jason. She had always wanted a settled home but had been unlucky with men. Jason was different and treated her with love, respect, and care.

Elizabeth's face turned red and looked like she was about to have a panic attack. She looked at her mother sternly and blurted.

"Stability, love, care, respect my foot!" she screamed.

She got up hastily, called for a taxi, and left in anger. Her mother was dazed. Her daughter just shamed her in public. Patrons at the restaurant saw what happened. She sat rooted to her seat. She feared her daughter's anger bouts once again; she had not seen her this angry in a long time. Before she left, she appealed to her to ride home with her, but she refused. Her prescriptions were on the table. Her mother picked them up, drove to the pharmacy, and got them filled. When she got home, Elizabeth was in her room with her door locked. She refused to open the door. Bethena dropped her medications by the door, asked her to pick them, and take her evening dose.

Bethena was sad that the outing and discussion did not yield the expected result. She knew her child and knew it would be an uphill task but thought she would be a bit receptive. She was too optimistic or unrealistic to expect her to agree on the first attempt. She planned it to be a meeting of the minds, but it failed woefully; in fact, it failed worse than she ever thought. She took the day off to discuss Jason with her daughter after the doctor's visit. She told Jason what happened. He told her she should have expected the response. Jason was a nice, well-calculated, and articulate man who knew that Elizabeth was not a "nut you can crack" in one attempt. He encouraged Bethena to wait for another opportunity to discuss the issue.

Bethena finished the interior decoration of the house. It was breathtaking. Jason spared no expense and gave Bethena more than enough money to decorate the house to her taste. She was good at decorating; her house had all the details of a rich home. Jason wanted her to replicate it in the new house. She did above expectations. The furniture delivered, placed where they belonged, tastefully decorated, perfect, and looked every inch like a model home. Bethena learned the skill of interior decorating from her mother who knew how to put colors together to bring out the beauty. She chose the colors she loved, colors that best suit the mansion and its worth. The combination brought out the beauty of the mansion as well as Bethena's inner beauty. Her mansion was a masterpiece in terms of the interior decor. She loved every inch of her home and the home where she grew up. It was a superlative, surplus replica of the homes she previously lived.

Jason loved what Bethena did and complimented her for her skill, elegance, and ambience. The house had eight bedrooms, ten bathrooms, with a two-bedroom mother-in-law suite, complete with a kitchenette adjoining the house on the side, built on an expanse of land overlooking a big lake. The view was heavenly. It had a private gate that led to the main building. Access was by remote with a breathtaking entrance. No way anyone would drive past the property and not look twice. It had a hotel-sized swimming pool, an Olympic-sized gym, a tennis court, a basketball court, and a garden with an array of colorful plants, flowers, roses of assorted colors, and a well-manicured lawn.

The inside boasted of three massive chandeliers, three living rooms, a big formal dining area, a study, winery filled with exotic, imported, and expensive array of wines in beautiful shapes, sizes, and colors. Jason was a social drinker. He drank only on occasions or when he had important visitors and never drank more than half a cup of wine at any given time. The expansive kitchen had a state-of-the-art design and marble countertops with a big kitchen island in the middle. The kitchen had a big section for a dining table and was fitted with a seventy-two-inch TV.

Jason was different from all the men Bethena had married, lived with, or dated in the past. He was a perfect gentleman who had never taken advantage of her like the others. His children were the most well-mannered kids Bethena had ever met. They were well-behaved, homely, warm, cleaned up after themselves, made their own beds, did laundry, cook, studious, did their homework on time, never distracted their father when busy or on a business call, were soft-spoken, and never raised their voices at each other. He did a marvelous job on his kids. Bethena envied him in a good way for that and knew he would be a wonderful stepfather to Elizabeth. She always thought of how lucky she was to be introduced to him and for him to choose her. He had not taken a dime from her; instead, he gave her sufficient money to fix and decorate the house, took care of her, took her to the best restaurants, showered her with gifts, had been brutally truthful when asked for advice, and never sugarcoated anything or situation to make her feel good. He was blunt but kind. She was ready to have him keep her heart forever.

Elizabeth's peeve did not deter her from calling Gina to tell her about the bag her mother ordered. Gina wanted one also. "I will tell my mother to order one for me immediately" was her response. Gina hated it when anyone got such a luxury item before her. She had to dictate the pace for others to follow. The two of them agreed to meet later at the club. She had more gists for Gina. It would be sweeter if discussed face-to-face, she blurted.

Jason drove in as Elizabeth was leaving. She refused to make eye contact or wave. Jason was not bothered. He smiled and waved, but she discountenanced him. He smiled again and thought in his mind that he would eventually become her best friend. It must happen, but when? He did not know, but it must happen. Elizabeth shared her mother's discussion on Jason with Gina. She poisoned her mind the more. They devised ways to run Jason out of the house and out of Bethena's life, would lie against him that he made passes at her or better still at Gina, would paint him as a cheater and gold digger, and they thought of different scenarios to achieve their devilish act. As an adult, she needed no babysitter or someone monitoring her movements and behavior in her house. If she was able to care for herself when she was much younger, she could do it now. Besides, he came with three baggages (kids) who were being sponsored in a boarding school by her mother. How dare him? What effrontery?

She needed no stepsisters or brother. Her life was perfect the way it was. Her mother was using part of her inheritance to train the kids, she blurted. Maybe it was time for her to ask for her inheritance like the prodigal son. She was willing to become a prodigal daughter, take her inheritance, and spend it as she wished instead of her mother using it to train strangers and gold diggers. They, however, got distracted when their drug suppliers and male friends arrived. The night went by fast. They danced, used drugs, drank, and gossiped about the ladies at the club. They hated most of them, and they hated them too. They had run-ins with some of them. The club was not filled. Most usuals were absent. Ella was still missing in action. She would be dealt with at an appointed time. Her punishment would be so severe that she would cry and beg for mercy. Nobody would dare them and go scot-free.

CHAPTER 5

The Cyclone

Madeline was discharged from the hospital; her doctor recommended bed rest, to stay at home for two weeks, and the doctor sent an excused duty note to her office. Her office staff could not believe it. She had never absented herself from work. She got to work earlier than everybody and was always the last to leave. She was a diligent worker who loved her job and the attention that came with it. Gina did not bother to visit her throughout her stay at the hospital. When she got home and saw her mother, the first thing she told her was to order the luxurious bag for her. Her mother shook her head. She could not wrap her head around the fact that her only daughter did not bother about her health or visited her. She cried softly into her pillow and regretted not listening to the pleas of her husband for more children. He was a good husband and father and spared nothing in taking care of them.

Her addiction to work, position, and socioeconomic status had robbed her of enjoying motherhood and her daughter. Benjamin had gone to court when Gina returned in the morning. The clubhouse and homes of various strangers she met at the club were her new home. When her mother did not respond, she took her glassy eyes to her pillow. Benjamin went straight to the house to be with his wife after the court proceedings and news conference with the press. Gina had caused so many problems between them over the years. Despite that, he loved his wife. They had come a long way together. As he walked inside his house, the news conference he had after the court proceeding was airing on television. He paused and watched it, then went to the room to see his wife. Gina was sleeping when he arrived, made sure Madeline was fine, and went to his study.

When Gina woke up, she went to inquire if her mother had ordered the bag. The fact was, she slept off due to the sedative medications. When she said no, hell was let loose. Gina threw a big tantrum and ready to battle with her mother. When her father heard the commotion, he ran to the room. Gina was not ready to listen. She needed the bag ordered immediately. Her father was mad at her and tried to attend to Madeline who was already crying. He mistakenly shoved Gina who was all over the place. Hell fell instantly on her parents. The wrath of a spoiled brat. She ran to her room, returned with a gun, pointed it at her parents.

"Order it now or I'd shoot both of you. I would blow your brains out!" she yelled. "Elizabeth's bag was on the way, had been ordered, and why should she get the bag before me? Her mother was not as rich as you. Do it right now, or I would kill you!" she screamed.

Her mother slumped into the arms of Benjamin. She fainted or had another heart attack. Benjamin grabbed the phone and dialed 911. Gina left the house with her mother's unconscious body on the bed. The ambulance arrived in earnest, got Madeline stabilized, and took her back to be readmitted to the hospital. She was discharged just the night before. Gina knew she would be arrested by the police for pointing a gun at her parents. To make matters worse, she had no license to carry a gun. She stole the gun from the house of a stranger a few weeks ago, so she ran. She was planning to scare or hurt Ella and possibly Francine with the gun. The baron whom she stole the gun from had been searching for Gina. He was a notorious drug dealer and would have killed her if he found her.

Madeline was stabilized before being transported to the emergency room by the paramedics. Gina's father could not tell them what happened. He tried to cover up for his daughter. If he did not, it would be breaking news on all media outlets and on the front pages of newspapers. The newspapers would sell like hot cakes. The story could jeopardize his high-profile case and might ruin his career. He was downcast. Where did this monster of a daughter come from? He thought for a moment. He needed a DNA on Gina. He loved his wife and trusted her. Was she swapped at birth at the hospital? Unanswered questions fill his mind.

The doctor was surprised to see her again because her prognosis was good before she was discharged. He questioned Benjamin on what triggered the heart attack again. He was a very experienced cardiologist, and his reputation was also at stake. He knew Madeline was all right as of the time she was discharged. All she needed was bed rest, so what went wrong within hours? He called Benjamin aside and asked a series of questions in the presence of the other consultants. Benjamin was on a hot seat with the medical team who suspected foul play. Probably they had marital issues that aggravated her whenever she was alone with him, or domestic violence kept a secret because of their worldly positions. They seemed a perfect couple, but people sometimes fake positive portrayals of their personal lives outside and live a different one behind closed doors, making people see the good side of them when in public to earn public respect. Could they be among the statistics of fakers?

People fake lovey-dovey outside and become firebrands (fire versus fire) at home. Benjamin responded to the contrary. Madeline could not talk. She had another heart attack; the doctor and her medical team feared that she could get a massive attack that she might not survive. The hospital ran a series of tests all over. Gina did not return to the house for two days. Benjamin was about to file a missing person's report when she returned. She went straight into her room like nothing happened and did not say a word to her father or inquired about her mother's health. She looked unkempt, worn out, and had no change of clothes since she stormed out of the house. She seemed high on drugs and locked herself up in her room. Benjamin could tell but said nothing. The thought that she might not be his daughter crept into his mind again.

Could it be someone else's daughter he had been raising? She was surely a torn in his flesh, a bone in his neck. Benjamin had gone through so much in the hands of his daughter. She was one too many. She had been a troublesome child right from infancy. She was an example of a crying baby when born. She would cry all day and night for no reason. The doctors ran tests on her. All came back normal. Madeline on her part was not a woman cut out for motherhood. Her daughter's cries never moved or bothered her. She would toss her to a nanny nearby and move on to something else. Benjamin talked to her about her noncommittal attitude toward Gina. She was a mistake God sent to torment and torture her, severally disgraced her with two heart attacks in succession.

The nine months of pregnancy were torture. She was sick throughout and regretted putting herself through the experience. She never liked children, never wanted one, never cared, and never created time for a child. She never wanted anything that would bug or hold her down. She wanted to be a career woman with no strings attached, no dependents, just herself and her husband. She refused to have more babies despite Benjamin's pleas for at least one more. When Gina was five, Benjamin asked her for another child. She refused again. A young, beautiful, and intelligent single attorney got pregnant at a law firm close to Benjamin's. He heard from office gossip that she wanted the baby adopted. Benjamin discussed adopting the baby boy with Madeline. She refused any addition to the family. Benjamin gave up on the issue. Maybe one was enough, he thought. In retrospect, maybe he should have insisted. Adoption was not a bad idea; he probably would have found solace in the child during this turbulent period.

Madeline left the care of Gina in the hands of nannies. They raised her from her first day. She never bonded with her. She refused to breastfeed her for fears that her boobs would sag. She was on baby formula. Gina would hit, bite, throw stuff at them, throw tantrums, pull them down, and destroy their properties and belongings. Replacement of nannies was high because they could not cope with her incessant tantrums. Her parents, most especially her father, spent money on toys, dolls, books, and games to divert her attention to better things. She destroyed and turned them into tartars in no time. The doctor diagnosed her with ADHD (attention deficit hyperactivity disorder). She struggled to focus or pay attention to anything for long. Her attention span was almost zero. When she focused on anything, she was destroying it.

The doctor placed her on medications, which made her situation worse and turned her into zombie-like or outrightly allergic to them. Gina grew like she had a demon resident in her, had impulse, attention, hyperactivity problems, and was not interested in concentrating on any issue. Gina went to private boarding schools, was expelled, and changed school often. She hit and fought other students and teachers everywhere she went. She had issues in all elementary and middle schools and changed schools like clothes, fought both males and females, and made more enemies than friends. No private boarding school agreed to enroll her in high school despite her parents financial standing and name recognition.

Public school was her only option; she was enrolled with strict instructions for best behavior. The only school where she schooled for four years was in high school and was very eventful. Benjamin looked dejected, lost in thoughts, ruminating questions filled his brain. A reputable lawyer with high standing in the society was brought to his knees by his own daughter, his own blood—maybe not. Madeline was fighting for her life, she was unresponsive, in a coma, and a side of her body was weak. The doctors believed she would pull through, they worked round the clock on her recovery, she would be on admission for a while and thereafter a rigorous physical therapy session. Benjamin was joggling between work and visits to his wife at the hospital. He was no longer his usual bubbly self, lost confidence in himself, and lacked concentration at work. Sleeplessness became his companion, and his blood pressure had gone up tremendously.

Gina had become a terror to her parents. She had turned their lives upside down. Gina went in and out as she pleased. She was unperturbed by her mother's illness and refused to visit her. She had her mother's credit and debit cards in her possession and spent money as if it was going out of fashion. She ordered the expensive bag she wanted that caused all the furor and more items. She took the cards from her mother's bag without permission. She became a spend drift at the malls, clubs, bars, purchased drugs, and narcotics and became a carefree giver to everyone that sang her praise. A week after her spending spree began, the credit card companies and banks placed embargoes on the accounts. She had no money to throw around anymore. She began pawning her expensive items to support her lifestyle and addiction. The expensive handbag that put her mother in almost a vegetative state was the first item she pawned.

*****

Francine and Ella were more often in touch after Ella visited her at the university. Ella's zeal for school became paramount. On course in her recovery program, her sponsor had been tremendous and helpful. Anna, her sponsor, had a university degree. Her drug use started through peer influence; she fell in love with a no-good guy in the community, a school dropout who roamed the streets. They were classmates in high school before he dropped out. They started dating in the ninth grade. The lovebirds loved each other intently. He was underperforming in school and into petty crimes. Anna loved him all the same. He started beating her since the ninth grade. She would hide her wounds and scars. He would leave her for other girls and beat her if she dared complain. Anna would fight to get him back and made enemies because of him.

Her parents saw that the relationship was toxic and advised Anna to leave him, but she refused blatantly. It was Luke or no one else. On an occasion after Anna's graduation from high school, Luke beat her to a stupor for getting a cheese he did not like on his burger. On another occasion, he almost killed her for greeting someone at the store. She needed permission before talking to anyone when he was present. On both occasions, Anna refused to press charges. She went against her parents' wishes to drop the charges. Her parents knew he was a drug dealer and addict. They warned and begged her to leave him, but she refused. When she was in the university, he would visit, beat her for talking to even her coursemates, maimed her severally, would beat and nurse her, and beg her after each beating with the promise never to do it again but would immediately renege on his promise. He spoiled her with proceeds from his illegal trade. Beatings and putting her down became a normal occurrence. She ignored the domestic violence despite her education and exposure. She knew all the signs of domestic violence but did nothing to save herself from the horror she was going through.

She believed that she deserved what Luke did every time he beat her and would change with time. Her parents, uncles, aunties, and friends were not able to bring Anna to her senses. After graduation, she got an excellent job in the city and moved away from the prying eyes of her family. Luke moved in with her and collected her paycheck every two weeks with the excuse that he would invest it in more drug sales. He began to curtail her movements. She must return home immediately after work. If she branched anywhere, even to the store, a good beating awaited her. He gradually introduced her to drugs and alcohol and became an addict through him when they became live-in lovers. She was forced and would beat her if she refused, an abusive relationship with severe violence from the onset, but she was head over heels in love with him irrespective of the abuse.

Her parents, friends, and family saw all the markers of drugs and domestic violence. Anna saw the markers, but love overshadowed her sense of reasoning. Her drug use became excessive when she lost both parents in a ghastly accident and had post-traumatic stress disorder (PTSD) that she treated with drugs instead of seeking grief counseling. After the burial, Luke took all she inherited by force, the insurance payout inclusive. She lost her job when she failed random drug tests her job required on two occasions. Drug use, beatings, and maimings were her reward for loving Luke, who eventually eloped with another lady when there was no money left.

She picked herself up, and with the support of loyal friends and family, she returned to her parents' house and was rehabilitated. She got grief and domestic abuse counseling, dusted her degree certificate, and got another job. Her uncles, aunties, and friends whom she refused their initial advice, counsel, and warnings became her redeemers. They organized an intervention session immediately after an overdose that almost claimed her life. She attempted suicide when Luke left with all her savings and ran away with another woman. The scars of the abuse were visible. She could not bear any child in her life. He kicked babies out of her womb at will, her womb had to be removed to save her life.

Luke's drug and domestic violence had ruined her life, but thanks to the intervention of her family, friends, and therapist. The intervention was a session of love, tough love, and a truth-telling. She was made to hear the truth and nothing but the truth about her situation and what could happen if she returned to drug use. Reality dawned on her. She realized life was more important than drugs, and whatever she had lost, she saw reason with them. They cried together and reasoned together. At the end of the session, she saw clearly that she had people who loved her unconditionally and wanted her alive, well, and prosperous both in health and wealth. She could have died from the drug overdose, beatings, and domestic violence she endured. She encouraged Ella with her life story, the importance of going back to school, the need to rebuild her life, and the importance of loving herself. The first person to love in this world is "you." No love for anyone else should be greater than one's love for oneself.

Ella's grandmother was getting better by the day. She kept a low profile, had not called, or visited her so-called rich friends, and they never called or visited. Solitary was an understatement for what her life had become. Her love for her granddaughter had quadrupled. She became the most treasured individual in her life. She had never been there for Ella who devotedly took care and stood by her during her sickness and convalescence. Her recuperation had taken longer than expected because of age and periodic deviation from the doctor's prescription and advice. She feared dying. Her recent health scare made her rethink the way forward. Her new disposition toward life was the readiness to focus on her granddaughter's welfare. The discussion with Carol over Ella's issues was a watershed for her. She messed up on two generations: first was her daughter and now her granddaughter.

She called Ella and apologized to her and promised to be more involved in her daily activities and welfare, that her recovery had become her number one priority. Ella thanked her but made her realize that she was an adult. All she needed was support, not supervision, but would always listen to her words of advice. She forgave her wholeheartedly. Grandma became Ella's number one support in her recovery process. She kept an eye on her movements without Ella's knowledge. She was happy with her progress and determination to succeed. She made gradual progress daily. Her grandmother encouraged her not to despise the time of small beginnings.

*****

Elizabeth and Gina had not seen Ella for a while and were poised to deal with her whenever their path crossed. They saw her at the mall on a faithful Saturday and were ready to strike, ready to deal with her for backstabbing, abandoning them, and comingling with a perceived enemy. Ella left the pharmacy where she picked up Grandma's medications and branched at the mall to pick up another wig for her psychedelic grandma who lost all her hair. Gina spotted her, pinched Elizabeth, and pointed Ella's direction to her. They followed her into the wig store and accosted her. She told them off without mincing words that she was no longer interested in associating with them. They giggled and told her they shared plenty of secrets as a group and would spill the beans on her. She bluffed them, told them to go ahead and spill whatever they wanted. She bought the wig, stepped out, and they followed her, pulled her blouse, and tore it. She pulled herself away and pulled her torn blouse together by pulling both sides together to cover her chest.

She walked away and doubled her steps to avoid further embarrassment. They followed her to the parking lot where she rushed into her car. They were ready for a fight. Gina pulled out a gun. Ella and Elizabeth never knew Gina had a gun; they froze as she pointed it at Ella. Gina, who was cognizant of the environment, noticed a police car on patrol approaching. She spotted it from afar and quickly put the gun back into her purse. It was a miraculous escape for Ella who quickly started her car and drove off in fear, leaving Gina and Elizabeth rooted to the spot. The police officer in the patrol car noticed nothing. Gina ran to her car with Elizabeth trailing behind her in a bid to follow Ella and harm her.

Ella raced home, shaking. She told her grandma what happened. She wanted to call the police, but Ella insisted she should not. She feared the secrets she shared with Elizabeth and Gina. She bluffed when she told Gina to disclose any information she liked. Elizabeth was dazed, never knew Gina had a gun. When she inquired how Gina got a gun without her knowledge, she shouted at her and told her off. Elizabeth was afraid of what could have happened if Gina had shot Ella to death or harmed her. The relationship with Gina had taken a new dimension—a scary one for Elizabeth. Her mother would die of shame if she was caught in anything related to a shooting, manslaughter, or murder. She was not happy that Ella exited the group, but killing or shooting her was the last thing on her mind. All she wanted was to punish her, maybe two or three slaps, and then embrace her back into the group. She would find it difficult to trust Gina with a gun. She was too ill-tempered to be trusted with a gun.

Gina dropped Elizabeth on the side of the road. They had a heated argument on the gun issue. It was a scary argument for Elizabeth. She had never seen Gina that angry and knew her life and safety were in danger. She took the gun out of her purse again and hit her twice with the butt, roared like a lion for her to exit the car, Gina threatened to shoot her if she stayed a minute longer. Elizabeth was scared and jumped out of the car as soon as Gina parked. She zoomed off before she could close the door. Elizabeth got a ride home from a neighbor who saw her by the side of the road, unable to talk about her near experience with death. Her mother was in the kitchen when she entered. She knew there would be a barrage of questions if she stayed to even say hello. She went straight to her room, locked the door, thanked her stars for saving her life. She could not believe what just happened at the mall and what Gina could have done if she had refused to get off the car. Her mother followed her and wanted to talk. She would have gone with Jason to spend the first night together in the new house. He moved to the new house earlier in the day. Bethena knocked on her daughter's door for a long time. She refused to open the door. Bethena appealed to Elizabeth to open the door. After a while, she told her that she was going to spend the night at Jason's new house.

Elizabeth could not believe her ears. Jason moved to his house? When? Where? She still refused to open the door, and Bethena left for Jason's. Elizabeth waited for her mother's car to exit the driveway before opening her door. She went straight to her mother's bedroom to see if Jason was truly gone. She was happy that none of his belongings remained in her mother's room. She went all around the house. Everything that belonged to him was gone. "Gone for good!" she exclaimed.

She heaved a sigh of relief, happy that her mother would soon get off his hooks. Elizabeth suddenly became bored. What was she going to do this Saturday night? She was scared to go out and had to avoid Gina at all costs. She knew Gina would be at any of the clubs or bars. She was not willing to run into her. She needed drugs to calm her nerves down. She planned to buy drugs at the club that night. What would she do now? Cravings had resurrected in her, but fear disallowed her to go out. She got her phone with her hands shaking like leaves blown by the wind and searched the number of a drug dealer, dialed his number, and he picked at the first ring.

"Hello," he roared with a deep baritone voice.

She responded with a shaky voice and asked for her usual.

With her mother gone, she gave him directions to her house; he was there within minutes. When he arrived, he was astonished by what he saw—a big mansion, well-lit in an expensive high-end subdivision. He could not believe that the girl who frolicked with all manner of people, who he knew over the years lived in such posh, expensive area. She quickly paid for her supply, and as he was ready to leave, she invited him inside but refused with the excuse that he had to get to the club to sell his drugs. Elizabeth told him she would pay for all his drugs if he agreed to stay the night. He could not believe his ears. He calculated, doubled the price, and Elizabeth paid cash in a hurry. Luck smiled at him. He was happy with the sale and the free offer that came with it, received double for his drugs, use free drugs, and spend the night in a mansion. He left around five o'clock in the morning to avoid the prying eyes of neighbors. Elizabeth was stoned, fast asleep when he left. He ransacked the house, most especially Bethena's bedroom, picked pricy items, antique heirlooms, expensive jewelries, and almost half of the drugs Elizabeth bought and vanished into thin air. In his stupidity, he forgot about security cameras in rich neighborhoods.

Bethena spent the weekend with Jason, oblivious of what Elizabeth had done and the valuables she had lost. She was in a good mood in the company of Jason who was freer in his house, no longer under Elizabeth's prying eyes and mannerlessness. He loved Bethena so much and tried not to let Elizabeth's behavior get under his skin. He still loved Elizabeth despite her bad behavior. Change was what she needed, and change she would get. With patience, he would turn her around. They had fun in their new home. Jason loved how the interior decor looked and complimented Bethena repeatedly. She was happy he loved it. The decor looked exceptionally beautiful, befitting of the edifice.

Jason bought one of the most beautiful and expensive mansions on the block. He did it for Bethena and his kids, including Elizabeth. Jason made a sumptuous breakfast in the morning. They ate, rested, and went to the swimming pool around noon. He invited friends over, and when they arrived, they had lunch and drinks by the pool area. He planned to propose and confided in his invited guests. Bethena could not believe her eyes when Jason got on one knee and proposed. She was ecstatic and said, "Yes, yes, yes!" It was a beautiful event attended by a handful of Jason's friends, family, and colleagues, settling down again was long overdue for Jason.

The proposal was recorded on video, and pictures were taken. Bethena had no friends in attendance. Actually, she had no friends, only acquaintances. Her daughter would have been invited but for her horrible behavior and character. Bethena was on cloud nine. She was more than happy, on top of the moon, to say the least. She knew Elizabeth would not be happy, but she must hear it directly from her, from the horse's mouth. She did not want her to read the news on the internet. She rushed home as soon as she could. The news broke on the internet. Elizabeth did not know about the news until she woke up in the evening. By then, her mother had returned, counting her losses, and her joy had suddenly turned to sadness. She waited for Elizabeth to wake up before calling the police to report the burglary. As soon as she woke up, she checked her phone and saw so many congratulatory messages on her mother's Facebook page. Holy anger welled up inside of her. *What is this*? She thundered. She had to break them up as soon as possible. She got out of her room with the belief that she was home alone. As she stepped out, her mother demanded if she brought anyone home for the night.

Lying is one of the major characteristics of drug users. Half truth is no truth. Truth is truth. A lie is a lie if the truth is not total. A lie would always lead to another lie. To keep up with a lie, you must remember the last lie and build on it. A lie is always an uphill task that eventually would crash. Addicted persons master the act of deception, untrue statements, cheating, and stealing. Drug use depends solely on falsehood to themselves and others. A lie repeated often becomes truth to the liar. The ravaged/damaged brain cells of an addicted person become the permanent abode for lies. An addicted person's life depends on the availability of substances and would do anything to get it. Lying becomes the first instinct that comes to the mind of the user. Even when the user has money, he would use lies to get more than he paid for. A survival instinct built intuitively by addiction. Lying, stealing, gossiping, backstabbing, killing, bitterness, and hatred go hand in hand.

Elizabeth looked at her mother, asked her why she was ranting, ready to walk away, and asked if her ploy were to deflect from getting engaged to a mere jerk.

"It will not work I promise you!" she yelled. "You want to marry a gold gigger? Not while I am still alive."

Bethena pulled her back and asked questions back to back, "Did you bring somebody into the house? What happened in my room? Who took my prized possessions? Did you scatter my room? Did you take this and that heirloom? Did you forget to lock the door? Did you sleep at home last night?"

The questions were on and on. Elizabeth said only one emphatic "no" to all her questions and looked at Bethena as if she was a lunatic, and went into the kitchen to get a glass of water. She was having a hangover from last night's excessive drug and alcohol intake. Bethena followed her to the kitchen and started the questions all over again. Elizabeth said nothing, was not able to think, and her brain fogged with drugs. Bethena went back to her room to play the security camera. She saw that a car came into the driveway. The guy met with Elizabeth. The car left around five o'clock in the morning with the guy carrying things into his car. The guy made trips back and forth before driving off. Elizabeth was not with him when he left. She copied it on a disk, ready to hand it over to the police. Bethena came back. Elizabeth was still in the kitchen about to eat. Her mother questioned her again and showed her information she copied from the security camera. To her dismay, Elizabeth, with a bold face, told her she was not the person in the security footage.

Bethena looked dumbfounded. "How dare you lie when the truth was so glaring?" she yelled.

"I do not know what you are talking about" was Elizabeth's response.

Bethena started crying, she had lost so many of her most prized possessions on the day that was supposed to be her happiest. She called Jason and told him what had happened. Jason arrived at Bethena's house minutes later. Bethena was sobbing profusely while Elizabeth was in her room doing God knows what. She had her drawer filled with assorted illicit drugs. Jason tried to comfort her. Bethena was sobbing profusely. He asked if she had called the police to report the burglary. Bethena was torn on what decision to make and was inconsolable. Her daughter might get in trouble with the law, she thought in her mind, without telling Jason. She was scared for her daughter, for what the police would do. Jason watched the security footage. The guy in the footage was not very visible. He was a drug dealer who knew how to cover his tracks. He tactically covered his face and wore all black clothing. He was a hundred percent security conscious. He drove a rickety car with a not-too-visible plate number that was fake.

The person in the video was Elizabeth. *Why would she deny it?* Jason thought. *What game was she playing? Was she selling her mother's possessions and why? Had she been selling her mother's valuables without her knowledge until recently?* Jason was confused. He turned from watching the video and held Bethena in his arms as Elizabeth walked inside the kitchen. She looked at them with contempt, looked at Jason, and told him pointedly that she would never allow her mother to marry him if she lived. Jason did not utter a word. He kept tending to his fiancée. Bethena threatened to call the police. Elizabeth insisted she was not the person in the video, that she knew nothing about the burglary. She did not sleep at home, went to the club, and returned in the morning. Bethena made good her threat and called the police. Elizabeth was unmoved and unperturbed. She, however, could not believe her eyes when the police arrived. She never believed her mother would call the police on her no matter the situation. Elizabeth immediately turned the table on Jason. Her lying skill kicked in. She reported to the officers that Jason was the gold digger who recently came into their lives to steal and destroy the good relationship between her and her mother. They never had a burglary before and had lived on the property for a long time.

She reported that Jason had intentionally lured her mother out of the property with a fake weekend treat to perform his nefarious activity, that she saw Jason's car pull up into the driveway when she was leaving for the club. She then dropped the bombshell that Jason had made passes at her. She had ignored all his actions. He moved when he knew she would tell her mother about his antics and cheating tendencies. When Jason was not able to lay his filthy hands on her, he robbed the house. He lived with them, moved that day, and had an incident the same day—what a coincidence! It was glaring that Jason was the thief. Only he knew the house inside out. Only a person with insider knowledge could burgle a house. The things stolen were in the bedroom he shared with her mother. Jason was the thief. Jason and Bethena were dazed, shocked, and dumbfounded at the same time, to say the least. What was she talking about? Bethena knew instantly that she lied. She was with Jason all night. Jason did not come back to the house as reported by Elizabeth. With regards to Jason's passes, another big, fat lie; in fact, the biggest lie of the century. Jason was not that kind of person and would never be. Bethena rubbed Jason's hand to reassure him that she trusted him. She knew Elizabeth lied and had always been a liar. Jason was cool and calculated. He knew he would be exonerated. He had a solid alibi to back himself. He was, however, disappointed with Elizabeth's conduct and lies.

The officers waited for her to finish her rantings, asked her a series of questions on her whereabouts, the clubs she went to, the exact time she left the house, the time she returned, the vehicle Jason drove when he came to the residence, and what time he got there and more. A good liar that she was, she responded in a brilliant fashion. Only an intelligent person could lie so effectively. She had negative intelligence and perfected it. Elizabeth was not only an intelligent liar but a slanderer. She tried to destroy Jason's reputation. The officers knew who Jason was. The rich billionaire with vast businesses all around the world. They recognized him immediately they entered the house, but they were there on professional grounds. They exchanged pleasantries and were not respecters of persons but to investigate a burglary. Elizabeth tried to cast negative aspersions on Jason.

He kept his cool and said nothing. He knew her lies would catch up with her. They went to Bethena's room, toured all the areas where valuables were taken, and returned to the kitchen table. They watched the disk and started grilling Elizabeth again. She insisted she was away, not the person in the footage. The officers took her to her room, and the story changed as soon as they entered. The clothes she wore in the security footage were the first things the officers noticed on the floor. Empty bottles of alcohol littered the floor. There were residues of drugs all over. Used needles of heroin were on her dressing mirror. The wristwatch of the perpetrator was on her nightstand. It was a man's wristwatch. The dealer forgot it when he was rushing out. A necklace was later found in the driveway by the officers. The chain got entangled with one of the stolen items and broke. He did not know. He would have picked it up because he was careful and made sure everything that would point to him was taken care of.

A search of her nightstand revealed so much about Elizabeth. She had a stash of various illicit drugs. It would have been more. The dealer stole some of what she bought on his way out. The officers picked the empty bottles for fingerprints and took all the drugs, the clothes she wore in the footage, the used and unused needles, the wristwatch, and necklace. Elizabeth looked stupid but undeterred. She stuck to her lies. She insisted she was not the person and had nobody over. Stupidity and ignorance at the highest order and peak. Jason was interrogated; he had an alibi in Bethena, but that was not enough for the police. They needed more evidence. He mentioned the upscale restaurant where they had dinner. They got to the restaurant around eight o'clock and left for his house around midnight. They were in the company of friends and executives. One of the officers called the restaurant. They confirmed Jason's reservation, the time he arrived, and when he left with his guests. Jason, Bethena, and friends were at the restaurant at the time he claimed. He also informed the officers that the security cameras in his house could testify to his movements. The officers told him they would call him for more questioning when needed. The police handcuffed Elizabeth and took her to the station for booking. She looked sober and unhappy when she sat at the back of the police car. Her mother knew the time to show tough love had arrived on a platter of gold. She loved her daughter, but she needed to face the consequences of her actions. The officers took the disk and exhibits with them, promised to find the culprit, and took Elizabeth away.

*****

After Gina dropped Elizabeth on the side of the road out of annoyance, she zoomed off erratically. Anger had taken a total hold of her. She had missed torturing Ella. She had no intention of killing her. She only wanted to scare the daylight out of her to affirm her superiority. She was angry that she got away without any punishment. To make matters worse, Elizabeth had the audacity and effrontery to challenge and question her on why and how she got a gun. She vowed to teach them the lesson of their lives. She was speeding, doing seventy-five miles per hour at a thirty-five-miles-per-hour zone. She was supposed to slow down at the sign of a four-way stop. She did not slow down and did not stop. She was enveloped by anger and T-boned a car driven by an old woman who moved after her legitimate stop.

Gina picked the gun on her seat, waved it at the old woman, and sped off at high speed. She lost control at the corner; her car rolled over before landing on its side. The old woman, shaken by the ordeal, called 911 to come to her aid and Gina's. The paramedics had to cut the car to get Gina out. She was hurt but conscious. The police searched her car and found the gun, drugs, and an open container of vodka. An ambulance took her to the hospital for a checkup with a pending arrest awaiting her discharge. The old woman was treated for severe anxiety, nervous by the experience of a gun being waved at her. She was taken to the hospital and observed overnight because her blood pressure went sky high. Her children were furious at Gina. They vowed to sue Gina.

Benjamin was notified of her admission to the hospital and the impending arrest as soon as she was discharged. He almost fainted on hearing the news. He instructed the nurses to put off the television in his wife's hospital room so she would not hear the incident on the news. Her health could be at risk again. Ironically, Gina, who had refused to visit her mother in the hospital, was now in the same hospital. The old woman was on observation for one day. Her blood pressure was still high, but her children promised to care for her at home. They notified the insurance company of the accident. Gina was on her parents' auto insurance, so her parents were liable.

Benjamin took Madeline home the following day after her discharge. She was not aware that Gina was on admission at the hospital she just left. Benjamin went to see Gina. She refused to talk to him nor asked after her mother. She was heavily monitored by the police and nurses. She tried to escape on an occasion but was caught and arrested when discharged. She was booked for several offenses: driving under the influence, running a Stop sign, leaving the scene of an accident, illegal possession of firearms, waving a gun, elder abuse, possession of illegal drugs, possession of an open container, and planning to escape a police arrest. Gina had her plate full this time. She was interrogated by the police, most especially on the gun issue.

Gina lied that the gun was hers but could no longer find the receipt of purchase, then lied that she got it from a nameless male friend and later lied that the gun belonged to Elizabeth. She was only keeping it for her. She went from one lie to another. All the lies crumbled at her feet. The officers knew she lied and interrogated her more. The gun found on her was linked to six murders. She was in serious trouble. She could not figure out or remember who she stole the gun from and had no name or address of the owner. It was a stranger at the club who took her to his house that she stole it from and could not even identify him in a lineup. She was in a hot soup. Incidentally, the guy was also frantically searching for her, but each time narrowly missed each other. He probably would have killed her because killing people was nothing to him. She would be one of his many victims. Missing one another kept Gina alive.

*****

Elizabeth was on interrogation for the burglary that occurred in her house when an officer relayed that she was needed for interrogation on a gun issue. She could not believe her eyes to see Gina in the same police station. Gina held a bold face and accused Elizabeth as the owner of the gun. She claimed that Elizabeth gave her the gun to keep. Elizabeth could not believe what she just heard. She became dumb and could not speak. When she gathered her composure, a shouting match ensued between them. They were separated by the officers. Elizabeth told the officers she knew nothing about the gun. Her first sight of the gun was on Saturday at the mall when Gina pulled the gun on Ella, their third wheel who had pulled out of the group. She explained that Gina wanted revenge so bad and was willing to hurt Ella. She was shocked when Gina pulled out a gun. She never knew she had a gun or learned how to operate it. It was her first time seeing a gun with Gina. She did not own a gun, never held one, and had never learned to use a gun. She explained that Gina was trying to implicate her because of the quarrel they had the previous day. Elizabeth described the anger exhibited by Gina that afternoon, that she looked and barked like a demon in a cage frantically struggling to escape. Her eyes doubled in their sockets, ready to bust out. She was scared for her life. She was happy when she kicked her out of her car. The neighbor who gave her a ride from the side of the road could attest to it. The officers believed Elizabeth and allowed her to leave. They would call her if they needed more information. She wondered why Gina would fabricate such a lie that could land her behind bars for a long time against her.

The officers did a thorough investigation of the incident at Elizabeth's house. She eventually confessed that she invited a dealer to the house who stayed overnight. She gave step-by-step information about the scenario. She had no information about the dealer. She only had his phone number from a previous encounter at the club. She had no name or his address, only his nickname. She bought all his drugs so he could spend the night with her. She was lonely and needed company after Gina kicked her out of her car. She was too scared to run into Gina at the club. She threatened her with a gun and feared she could come to the house to harm or kill her, so she convinced the dealer to stay with her and keep her safe in her home because Gina might come for her.

She knew the dealer had a gun and would scare Gina away. She exonerated Jason and confessed that she lied on him to break up his relationship with her mother. She would be charged for the possession of the large number of drugs found in her room. Her mother might also be liable because the drugs were found in her house. Bethena was very crossed. She refused to bail her daughter and made her stay at the station with no one to bail her. Jason begged her, but she refused. She explained to Jason that it was not about the stolen items but that she needed to take responsibility for her action, and there are consequences for bad actions. She needed to be taught a lesson, needed tough love, and tough love she must get.

Jason persuaded her until she agreed that Jason could bail her if he wanted but on the condition that she must go straight to a rehabilitation facility for the treatment of her drug addiction. Elizabeth stayed at the police station for one week before Jason bailed her with the condition that she would go straight to a rehab facility for treatment. She had time to think and rethink her life in general. She could not believe that Gina tried to set her up for prison, close to the prison, closer to death at their last encounter. She thought they were cool, cool friends but now knew better that there are no friends. "You," only you, are your best friend and no one else.

Elizabeth went straight from the police station to the rehabilitation program. It was a residential facility. She had to live there during the period of her therapy and treatment. Jason picked the facility, an extremely comfortable facility with seasoned therapists on staff. She was drug-screened on admission; a cocktail of drugs was in the system. Her psycho-social analysis was incomplete because she was not forthcoming with answers to the questions asked. The preparation of her treatment plan was not comprehensive, but the therapist was willing to give her time to settle and ask more questions to complete her chart, and she was not ready to commit to treatment.

Jason was minimally briefed on what they noted and could not divulge anything personally because of confidentiality issues. He discussed it with Bethena, and they agreed to have a family intervention with her and the therapists. Bethena was her only family. She could not do it alone, and she might resist Jason's presence who paid for all the services and more. She was happy she agreed to go into therapy in the first instance. She had no choice anyway. It was the condition under which she was bailed. She was her only biological child, though she would soon become the mom to two more girls and a boy, Jason's children. She was eagerly looking forward to it and knew she could do it with the support of a wonderful man like Jason.

C H A P T E R 6

Depraved Minds

Francine heard what happened to Gina and Elizabeth on the news. She felt bad for them and wished she could reach out to lend her support. They had gone far into criminal activities and needed rehabilitation; their cases were gradually getting out of hand, into a state of no return. She was happy that Ella was doing well and making progress daily. She called Ella every other day, inquired about her progress, and encouraged her to keep up the good work. Ella was very forthright with Francine, and never hide anything from her. Having someone who genuinely cared about her made her happy. She had visited the community college and collected the admission form. Francine was happy for her. They met at the library and filled the form together. They had never visited each other's home. Francine saw her as a platonic friend. She was willingly supporting her out of a free will and outright volition.

Carol was extraordinarily happy when Ella told her she got admission into the community college. She was proud of Ella's seriousness and determination to excel and her zeal to do the right thing for herself. Carol underestimated Ella's ability to change so drastically. It was like an unseen spirit was propelling her, making her race to catch up with all she had lost. Carol came from the same high lane that Ella was on, the evil high lane that landed her behind bars for twenty-five years. She saw the determination Ella exhibited as miraculous. Could it be because she opened and told her the truth about her life story? Could it be because she found a good mentor in Francine? Whatever the "because," she was grateful and would forever be grateful to Francine for helping to remold her daughter's life.

*****

Benjamin underestimated the havoc, pain, and shame his only daughter could bring to him and his wife. In a spate of two weeks, they had gone from respectable, honorable, executives to objects of ridicule. His wife's health was failing at a fast rate. Their only daughter was in police custody with numerous offenses hanging over her neck—some that could send her to prison for a long time. All thanks to their only daughter! Madeline had been asking for Gina's whereabouts. Her husband could not tell her the truth. Her motherly instincts were at full blast, and she sensed something was amiss. Benjamin purposely disconnected the television in their bedroom, took away her phone, and told her she needed full rest as advised by her doctors. He made sure that Madeline used her medications on time. One prescription made her sleep for hours every day. Journalists besieged Benjamin's law firm in search of information on the allegations leveled against his daughter. He never believed that Gina could pull them down to this lowest ebb. Benjamin would not put all the blame on Madeline. He was also at fault. He blamed himself for not being assertive and firm enough. He condoned her offensive and morally wrong behavior from the beginning and believed that she would grow out of it with age. Unfortunately, as she matured in age, her behavior and character grew worse. Instead of curtailing her excesses, they pampered her tantrums with expensive gifts and money. She had so much money at her disposal from an early age. They thought supplying all she needed would reform and change her. The more money they gave, the more Gina got worse. Gina had been in custody for days. The gun found in her possession made the investigation difficult. The investigating officers through surveillance cameras from some stores where the bodies were found had zeroed on a male suspect, but Gina had to explain how the gun got to be in her possession. There was the likelihood that she might have also used the gun. The officers were not willing to rule anything out.

Benjamin was shuttling between the police station, home, and office. His doctor had doubled the milligram of his blood pressure medication again. He was not sleeping or eating well, had lost his appetite, and nothing mattered to him now. He could no longer focus on the high-profile cases he was overseeing. He left them for the other attorneys in his law firm. His firm had also taken a hit from the negative press. The investigating officers came to the house armed with a warrant to search Gina's room for more evidence on the gun. The search revealed more drugs, paraphernalia, and used needles, and they interviewed Benjamin if he ever knew his daughter had a gun. Benjamin was torn between lying to the law enforcement officers or covering up for his daughter. He could lose his license to practice law or go to jail. He was not aware if Gina already disclosed that she pulled the gun on them once. He had no choice but to tell the truth. The officers informed Benjamin of Gina's fraudulent use of her mother's debit and credit cards while she was on admission. She would also be charged for bank and credit card fraud as well as pulling a gun on her parents. Benjamin persuaded the officers not to question his wife because of her failing health. She was not aware that Gina was in jail. The information could kill her. Fortunately, Madeline was fast asleep when they came. They agreed not to wake her up. When Madeline's medical team learned of the fact that Gina pulled a gun on her parents, they were disappointed that Benjamin lied to them and jeopardized his wife's health. They held him in high esteem. He proved that he was not a man of integrity. They knew something triggered her second heart attack. Hiding the information was not in Madeline's interest.

*****

Bethena and Jason thought all was well with Elizabeth at the rehab facility. They hoped to receive a new Elizabeth in weeks. Jason paid an exorbitant amount to get her the best treatment. Elizabeth became uncooperative with the staff and therapists a day after admission into the treatment center. She was not ready for treatment and had not accepted that she had a problem. Acceptance is a key factor in treatment. Without an acknowledgment by Elizabeth that she had an addiction and needed help, dedication and determination would be a fallacy. Elizabeth believed that she was forced to the facility by coercion to give room and space for the love affair between Jason and her mother to flourish. She was a hindrance to their love life.

What was the total value of the stolen items that they had to confine her to a facility? After all, the stolen items were also part of her inheritance from her grandparents. Why keep her under lock and key? She refused to follow instructions and tried to escape. She already had altercations with both residents and staff. The facility informed Jason because he was the person that brought her and paid for her stay and treatment. Jason knew immediately that he underestimated what Elizabeth could do and knew it was her addictive brain that was at play. Bethena called the facility and instructed them that she must remain there. Her bail was contingent upon going into treatment, and they scheduled to have an intervention session the following day. The intervention occurred as planned but was not productive. Elizabeth insisted she was leaving the facility. There was no reason for her to receive any treatment because she was not an addict. Addicts are on the street corners, dirty, unkempt, and crazy. She had been functioning effectively all her life and knew what she was doing at any point in time. Her brain was intact and perfect. Why confine her to treatment against her will?

All counsel by Bethena and the therapist went on deaf ears. Jason sat at the reception, confused, thinking of what next to do in case she refused. She was an addict with subtle signs of mental illness. What would the next line of action be? Her mother tried to convince her of the repercussions of what an untreated addiction could lead to. She borrowed Elizabeth's words that she could one day be like those on the street corners, unkempt, dirty, and crazy, that they would not be at the street corners if they had loved ones to support them like they are doing, encouraged her to accept treatment for her own benefit and for her mother, but majorly for her own sake. It was a golden opportunity she was extending to her to avoid her becoming like one of the addicts on the street corners. Elizabeth flared up, cursed her mother out, and accused her of the intention to share her inheritance with a no-good gold digger of a man she was cohabitating with.

She became wild and combative, charged toward her mother, pulled her hair, and knocked her to the ground. The staff called for help and pulled her away from her mother who already had a concussion from hitting her head on the floor. Bethena felt violated. Her only daughter knocked her down and gave her a concussion. She was in total disbelief. She heard stories that some children beat up their parents. She never believed it could happen to her. Elizabeth would have beaten her up if not for the intervention of the people around. She probably would beat her to a pulp. She knew about domestic violence. Violence from her daughter was a no-no, and in the presence of staff at a rehabilitation facility, she had never raised her hand on Elizabeth despite her atrocities. She cried bitterly. What offense could have precipitated such an abomination? She was a good child to her parents, never disrespected, nor raised her voice or hands at them. The facility called the police, and Elizabeth was immediately Baker Act by the licensed social worker on duty. The therapist wrote an incident report as required by law, the facility, and for documentation. She would be at the facility until the Baker Act was over. After that, she would return to the jail and rebooked. Jason got medical attention for Bethena; he was thankful she was not seriously hurt. She assured Bethena he would give her all the support she needed to reform Elizabeth. Bethena looked at Jason and thanked him amid sobs, for loving her unconditionally. What would she have done with no support? Elizabeth was her only relative alive. She was thankful that God sent Jason into her life at this precarious time, thankful that he was godsent.

The psychiatrist assessed Elizabeth. She was not cooperative. He diagnosed her with dual diagnosis, substance addiction, and mental health disorder. She was a functional addict who had masked her mental issues with alcohol and several illicit drugs over the years. She developed tolerance to drugs over the years and could do several drugs at the same time. Every drug on this planet Earth had been tried by Elizabeth.

Drug use had always been a form of competition between the trio. It made them develop a strong tolerance to several drugs. Elizabeth's mental diagnosis was a surprise to her. She knew she felt depressed, angry, and extremely anxious but never thought it bothered on mental issues. Would she become crazy like the addicts roaming the street corners? Would she become homeless like them? No way. She was not crazy! *Not me*, she thought.

The psychiatrist must be out of his mind. She had no mental issue. When Bethena learned about Elizabeth's dual diagnosis, she cried bitterly. She was scared that her daughter could become a crazy person roaming the streets. She once had a dream, she seldom dreamed, but the dream looked real. In the dream, she saw a lady that looked like Elizabeth at a street corner picking food from a dumpster. She looked unkempt, dirty, and like a lunatic talking to herself. When she woke up, she was scared. She sweated, and her sheets were soaking wet. She was afraid. Could that be her daughter? God forbid! She shared the dream with Jason. He assured her it was a figment of her imagination. Her subconscious mind from the encounter at the facility the other day was playing tricks on her mind. She blamed herself for being an absentee mother. Her executive position was her priority. She had learned her lesson the hard way and was ready to change moving forward. Jason advised her to take an early retirement to focus on the home front. It could never be too late to fix an unpleasant situation. Elizabeth was already an adult, but reforming was possible. Without being a professional, she knew her daughter had a dual diagnosis. Years of drug use impacted her mental health negatively. She knew mental health disorder was not a death sentence or a stigma. Ignorance was the major reason for stigmatizing and why sufferers reject mental health diagnoses and medications to treat them. A mental health diagnosis does not deter anyone from achieving the highest potential.

Elizabeth's Baker Act took another turn the day after the inconclusive and unproductive intervention. She refused to take the prescribed medications by the psychiatrist, began to severely withdraw from drugs, and was craving for drugs to make the symptoms dissipate. Her system was yearning for drugs, and she was shaking profusely, pulling her hair, and itching all over. Unfortunately, there was no way to get a "fix" at the facility. She was immediately transferred to the detoxification center to be detoxed. Jason and her mother were notified. They were happy because it was a step in the right direction. They decided not to visit her in order not to cause any distraction. It was not the first time she would go through the detoxification process. She was once ordered to detox a few years ago. The detox worked, but she returned to drug use. Peer influence was the major reason for her relapse. She was peer-influenced and a peer influencer. The combination of friends she had influenced one another.

She spent five days at the detoxification center and discharged to the police station because the treatment facility rejected her. The facility notified Jason and Bethena of her transfer back to the police station. Jason and Bethena ignored Elizabeth at the station. They did not visit or made plans for an attorney to visit or perfect her bail when it was set. They wanted to teach her a lesson the hard way. She must personally ask to be bailed and would bail her only on the condition that she would return to treatment. Treating her addiction would make her a better person. She learned bad habits. She needed to unlearn them, and treatment would impact the skills to unlearn them. Unpleasant habits are formed over time and had their progression. Breaking them would also take time. Bethena had decided that changing her lifestyle for the better would be the only condition for her to will her hard-earned income to Elizabeth or receive the inheritance from her grandparents. Tough love at the highest order!

*****

Francine enjoyed favor in the eyes of all her lecturers and the school authority. She was recognized for good behavior, intellect, brilliance, and honorable deeds. She stood tall among her mates, participated in all charitable programs on campus, active in most organizations, tutored students free of charge, read their assignments, and corrected them for free. Her lecturers allowed her to become a student-lecturer who assisted them on occasions. The students loved her. They wondered how she was able to support them and have time for her own studies. Despite her support that was time-consuming, she still excelled in all her courses. Her time management and ability to prioritize her day and schedules were great and marvelous. Francine's motto was "Do good, and it would come back to you a million-fold." She supported several students, and her name had become a household name on campus, a force to be reckoned with.

Most of the students called Francine "Lady Do Good" or with the initial "GF," which stood for Good Francine. Francine did not discuss Gina and Elizabeth's recent issues with Ella. She was not a gossiper and would never glory in other people's downfall. She had no time for gossip and used her time for productive things, not wallow in idleness. She once told her classmates that idle people are those who use their time to gossip and discuss other individuals. People gossip mostly when they are bitter about the wonderful things in other people's lives; if you have no bitterness toward them and nothing of value was happening in their lives, why discuss them? To mock or praise them? People gossip primarily when good things are happening in the lives of others, and they are myopically envious. She loved them despite their personal hatred for her. Ella was her focus. Her recovery was paramount in her heart. Discussing their issues with Ella would amount to distraction for her. Francine followed up with Ella and her courses at the community college. She was making satisfactory progress on both recovery and academic pursuit. Francine was in her third year in the university, still flying with high colors.

*****

Gina had been in police custody for a while. Benjamin had decided not to bail her even if bail was set. He planned not to bail her for the sake of his wife who was still battling with her health. Gina's presence would continue to aggravate and set her back. He feared losing his wife. He would be lost without her. They complemented each other perfectly well. They had known each other for years before getting married. They were childhood friends who had each other's back even when they were not lovers. They later fell in love and knew it would lead to "I do." Gina had withdrawal symptoms in custody and was able to subdue them. She had cravings that made her bust out with great anger and fight both officers and other inmates. She needed serious anger management classes. Benjamin refused to visit her and only gave instructions to his attorneys to follow up. When one of the attorneys visited her, she refused to talk to her and blurted that she would deal mercilessly with her parents when released. She was a terror to everyone she was in contact with and was nicknamed "Lady Lucifer" by the other inmates. A psychiatrist was scheduled to assess her. She refused to give her audience.

*****

Jason thought about how Elizabeth tried to ruin his reputation by lying that he made passes at her. It hurt him deeply. What if Bethena did not trust him? His choice of Bethena was known only to him. She possessed qualities a man wanted in a woman, except for home management. She was hardworking, independent, jovial, kind, never pretentious, spoke her mind truthfully on issues, objective, not an eye server, dutiful, beautiful, rich, humble, and not proud of her achievements or wealth. She was helpful and highly principled. He would encourage her to cut down on work to manage the home front or take early retirement.

He was rich enough to make her a stay-at-home mom and fly around the world with him. His wealth was enough for her and their four children, Elizabeth inclusive. She was not a woman that would depend on any man's wealth, but he was willing to share all his wealth with her, and a partner in his businesses. Jason was wealthy, rich in money and businesses. When he spoke, money listened and obeyed. He was cute with sexy looks, beautiful gray eye color, nice kissing lips, powerful dresser, wore the best perfumes, and his perfume would linger for minutes after his exit. He was amazingly honest and blunt. He was not perfect because nobody is perfect. We are all working toward perfection. He was easygoing, never provoked, personable, never flaunted his wealth, never raised his voice, and a fine gentleman to the core. He was irresistible to women that met him, but he never disappointed himself by falling for their flirtatious plans to bring him down or crawl under his skin or duvet. He was sometimes lonely, very lonely but was not willing to lose his integrity for a few minutes of pleasure.

He made his business empire and children his focus and never deviated from them. During summer, Thanksgiving, and Christmas holidays, his three children were his focus. He had a live-in sitter watch them only when he was out of town, which was not often, only when necessary. He personally cooked their meals with his children watching. They learned from him how to cook and do house chores. He taught them the value of money. He had lots of money but did not spoil them with money. He taught them good manners worthy of emulation. He was a wonderful father and could receive the father of the year award every year. Bethena marveled at their mannerisms, the well-groomed manners his children exhibited the first time she visited his house. She immediately thought of Elizabeth, realizing how woefully she had failed in properly raising her. If Jason could raise three children effectively as a single father, she had failed as a single mother with only one child. Her zeal for executive accolades had robbed her of impacting sound home training in her daughter. She felt ashamed of herself. She needed to learn good parenting skills. Bethena discussed her issues with Elizabeth with Jason after a few dates with him. He sensed the disappointment and shame in her voice and the desire to make amends fast. He promised to support her in turning Elizabeth around. He was a people person and knew how to effectively change people's attitudes for the better. He had done it severally with some of his staff and family members over the years.

Jason was a big catch for Bethena, and vice versa for Jason who never had a serious relationship since the death of his wife. He was a ladies' man, the toast of any occasion. Ladies gravitated naturally to him, seeking his attention, love, and money. They threw themselves at him shamelessly sometimes. He purposely distanced himself, avoided their cupid arrows and darts, and he would go celibate for two to three years at a time just to avoid their drama. He concentrated on his children and business empire. He knew what he wanted in a woman. He had faith and believed that God who took his late wife would produce a perfect replacement at His appointed time. He knew his awaited wife was Bethena the moment he set his eyes on her. It was not his first encounter with her, but his instincts were strong at this encounter.

During their first encounter, which was extremely brief, there was no connection. She was on her way out when they met and were introduced. The second encounter was totally different. He could not take his eyes off her. A friend introduced them to each other again, and the rest was history. Bethena was not looking for love. She was not seeking or searching. She had been hurt deeply and had decided never to try the institution called marriage again, never! But this introduction was different. The few relationships Jason had after the death of his late wife were extremely brief. He was able to read their ulterior motives and dropped them fast like a bag full of worms. Some people loved to reap where they had not sown, and some loved to reap a different fruit from the one they sowed. A particular lady wanted his children gone all the time and needed them to stay permanently in the boarding school or ultimately disappear from the face of the planet. She wanted a relationship with Jason only, no strings attached. Anytime she came around, she wanted them to stay in their rooms.

On an occasion, she scolded them for no just reason, made them cry, and confined them to their rooms all day. Jason was mad when he returned. She narrated what happened and could not even fathom how at fault she was. Jason politely asked her to leave and never return. He was a man of few words. The lady was full of drama. She cursed Jason and his children out with profanity-laden statements, unhinged, not kind with words. Jason's philosophy in life was "Do to others as you want others to do to you." If, eventually, he wanted a wife, she had to be a person passionate with kindness and compassion. He knew what he wanted in a woman; his late wife had a tall standard difficult to match by the women that came his way. Bethena was the lucky woman. Favor shone on her at last, to wipe away her tears, sorrows, and frustrations she had suffered in the hands of the men she fell in love with. Jason chose her when she was not looking or seeking.

To get out of jail, Elizabeth had to play "eye service." She called her mother and appealed to her to bail her out. Her mother knew she was tired of being incarcerated and appealed to her conscience as a mother. She told her emphatically that Jason would be the one to bail her out with the same condition as before. She agreed and played a nice girl card on Jason who was too intelligent for her game. *Once bitten, twice shy*, he thought. He did not treat her with kid's gloves this time. He was firm and told her that he would have the lawyer revoke the bail if she played pranks with her mother again. He advised her to take her treatment seriously. Elizabeth moved to another rehabilitation facility. She was highly pretentious with everybody, the rehab staff, therapist, psychiatrist, Bethena, and Jason inclusive. Her lying skills and habits kicked in. For the first time, her mother cut off her pocket money. She could not believe it. She wanted her to imbibe the importance and value of money. She needed no money at the facility, and every need had been paid for. Elizabeth secretly contacted a dealer and used smartly in between drug tests. Her therapist had days for drug tests. She mastered the days to circumvent the tests. Everyone at the center loved her, not knowing she was faking it. She said what they wanted to hear, pretended she was following instructions, and doing the right thing. She became friends with a guy from a rich family too. They used drugs together and kept it low-key. Unfortunately for Elizabeth, she was pulled for a random drug screen and tested positive for cocaine she abused two days prior. Her therapist was very disappointed that she had been lying and deceiving them. She was transferred to a secured facility immediately. When Bethena and Jason heard of her transfer to a secured facility, their worst fears were confirmed. They knew she must have violated her contract, fought with someone, or done something horrible. They were however happy about the transfer; it might have a positive effect on her. Elizabeth had no exposure to drugs at the new facility. It was a twenty-four-hour surveillance facility, and she could not go out or have visitors.

Bethena and Jason came to see her because they had important news to break and were permitted by the facility. They were ready to get married, and she needed to know about the upcoming wedding, Jason's children would be part of the wedding. Jason sat at the reception while Bethena broke the good news to Elizabeth. Not that she needed her permission, she deserved to know, and there was nothing Elizabeth could do about it. Her present predicament had humbled her a bit. She uttered no word. She just looked at her mother with disgust, as if she were a loose woman. Bethena had always been a disciplined woman but unfortunate with her choice and the men she fell in love with. Jason came inside when Bethena beckoned to him. He discussed with Elizabeth like a father, told her that he loved her mother, was not a gold digger as insinuated by her on occasions, reiterated that he meant well for her and Bethena, and promised to be a good father (not stepfather) to her. He told Elizabeth a little about himself, his late wife, his children, and how he had refused to remarry long after the death of his wife.

He purposely left out everything to do with his finances, businesses, and status in the community, country, and around the world. He kept Elizabeth in the dark about his vast wealth for two reasons: first, he wanted her to accept him for who he was and not for his financial standing; second, he was not a person that would flaunt his social or financial status. He was a humble man to the core. Elizabeth pretended and wished them well with her maniacal laugh followed by a wry smile. He bailed her out of jail on two occasions when her biological mother refused. She hated Jason with passion and had great disdain for him despite that he bailed her out. He did not pay for her treatment. Her mother did. Bethena lied to boost her likeness and gratefulness to him. He a was manipulator, who had brainwashed her mother, who had never been firm, adamant, nor heartless toward her.

He must be the one instigating her mum against her. She found love in a stranger who was out to milk her dry to her daughter's detriment, must be a good con artist or a romance scheme scammer who had come to defraud and destroy their lives, most especially hers. He looked smooth like butter and honey blended, rich, well-dressed, walked with an aura of confidence, and carried himself with grace to deceive her mother. Why would her mother not see how things had changed in their lives since Jason came into the picture? She would deal mercilessly with the two of them as soon as she was out of the rehab facility. If only she could get a gun like Gina, she would scare him out of their lives forever and ever. Her mother would be scared and would never date any man again. Her thoughts ceased when Jason informed her that they planned to have a small wedding with a few families and friends in two weeks. Two weeks? She should ask the facility for permission to attend the ceremony. She was silent for a while. When she got her composure back from the shock, she wished them well with no congratulations. Ask for permission to attend her mother's wedding? What effrontery? They did not wholeheartedly carry her along or involved her in any way, why would they treat her like an outsider? They got her under lock to plan their wedding. She would teach them a lesson, a lesson they would not forget in a hurry. She would take permission and make sure the wedding did not hold. Jason and Bethena refused to take her cold composure toward them to heart. They told her they loved her irrespective of her response.

Elizabeth's peeve with Jason and Bethena knew no bounds. She, however, pretended to the staff and other patients at the facility that she was overjoyed with her mother and Jason's visit. She feigned happiness; they were all happy for her when she relayed to them her mother's impending wedding to Jason. She suddenly became nice to everybody. The staff noticed her change in behavior and were happy for her. They saw it as good progress in her recovery, but she had an ulterior motive—ruminated on the best plan to sabotage the wedding. Elizabeth planned all sorts of devilish propositions. She went from one evil plan to another. When alone, she would make maniacal laughter. Her mental health diagnosis was in full play. She became helpful at the facility and tried to do things that would make the staff notice and commend her.

She was able to fool most of them, except the psychiatric nurse. He noticed she was exceptionally happy when around the staff. His instincts and professional training made him focus more on her whenever she came to take her medications. He knew she planned to go home for her mother's wedding and knew she hated her mother and Jason. How could she change so fast? He kept monitoring her. Elizabeth did not know she was on the radar of the nurse. She asked for permission to go home for the wedding, had her revenge and plan to sabotage the wedding all planned out, and had all the planned evil written out step-by-step in her secret journal. One week before the wedding, she was in line for her medication at the nurse's station, exhibited her faked happiness, was jovial with the person in front of her, distracted her, and stylishly took medication from the person. It was pain medication, a narcotic. The nurse saw her, kept quiet, and served her. She pretended she had swallowed her medications but instead dropped them in her pocket.

The male nurse called on a female nurse to search her. She refused. When searched, her medications and a narcotic belonging to the other client were in her pocket. She had intentionally distracted the nurse and client to steal the medication. A search of her room revealed more medications she was supposed to have consumed and a journal with a well-planned activity to sabotage the wedding. Her request to attend her mother's wedding was denied. Elizabeth exhibited the greatest anger any of the staff had ever witnessed. Her anger went from zero to a thousand in seconds. She charged toward the team of clinical professionals that deliberated on her case. They ran for their lives while the male nurse tried to restrain her. She flipped the tables and chairs upside down, hit some with the chairs and fists, and banged her head and fists on the wall.

Her forehead became swollen. Her right hand bled. She was eventually restrained and transferred to the psychiatric hospital for further assessment. It became evident that she had mental and anger issues that needed urgent attention. Her psychotropic medications were resumed and enforced.

She previously kept or threw them away instead of consuming them, and she needed anger management classes also. Jason and Bethena were happy that she was in treatment at the psychiatric ward. Hopefully, the drugs administered to her at the hospital would help with the mental diagnosis she refused to acknowledge. The psychiatrist diagnosed her co-occurring disorder a while ago. She had refused to commit to the treatment of her disorders.

CHAPTER 7

Rehabilitation

Ella was doing well in her recovery progress. She never joked with her individual and group therapy sessions, AA, and NA meetings, and she had not missed an appointment with her psychiatrist also. Francine had been of great support. Ella had severed all relationships with Gina and Elizabeth; in fact, she deleted all their numbers from her phone and unfollowed them on Facebook, Instagram, and Twitter. She focused squarely on her recovery process. Her new acquaintances were her AA/NA sponsor and Francine. Her therapist was immensely proud of her progress. She participated well in therapy sessions, and her drug screens had all been negative. Ella owed all her progress to Francine and others, saw Francine as her hero, and wanted to be every inch like her. They met for lunch twice and would end their outings with the song "I shall pass through this earth but once…" Francine encouraged her to never shy away from helping and doing good to others and encouraged her to start by doing good to others at her rehab facility.

Ella started mentoring a single mother who was in her therapy program (a mentee now a mentor). She advised her to avoid drugs so she would not end up like her mother who had been in jail for many years, explained to her that she was raised by her grandma from when she was less than one-month-old. Helping others made her happy. She felt fulfilled and had an inner peace that had eluded her for many years. Helping and doing good made her more determined to succeed in her recovery process. Ella had been clean for many months. She became a pillar of support to her grandmother. She nursed her back to good health with the assistance of the nurses. The nurses are gone. She was now in full control. They could afford the nurses, but time together without outsiders was paramount to them.

They had become best of friends, appreciated each other, and enjoyed quality time together. The health scare worked positively for her family. It was a horrible experience that birthed a positive response and a valuable experience. In the end, it rekindled family togetherness and became a blessing in disguise. Grandma was grateful to Ella for her unflinching, unreserved, and unconditional support. Ella did her utmost best in nursing Grandma to good health. If it were the era of drugs and clubbing with Gina and Elizabeth, Grandma's story would be a different one. She would not have bothered or had time for Grandma. Grandma's health scare simmered her down and made her rethink her life. She realized that money was not everything and that power was transient. It was a big wake-up call, a watershed experience. None of her rich friends cared for her. They moved on as if she never existed. She no longer gallivanted all over the community with the rich and mighty. Some even leached and took advantage of her despite their riches. They perceived her as the stupid fool with the slang "money-miss-road."

Grandma became domesticated. Her endearment to her family became foremost. She started cooking meals instead of ordering food deliveries and went to places with Ella instead of her friends who deserted her. She realized that blood would always be thicker than water. In her time of trial and adversity, it was only Ella that was present. Family always take precedence over friends, though there are friends who stick better than family in rare situations, friends that are like family members. Amelia and Ella bonded together and shared experiences, stories, and words of encouragement. It was the best time for Ella. She heard more stories about her mother and most especially her late grandfather and enjoyed the company of her grandmother.

Ella was a well-liked student by her lecturers and coursemates. Her attitude, behavior, and disposition toward life and people had changed for good. She was no longer the rich, proud, pompous lady. She humbled herself, never hid the fact that she was in recovery. Being ashamed of one's recovery could spell doom and lead to a relapse. Never shy of asking for help when necessary. Incidentally, she was coping extremely well on all fronts. Francine advised her to limit her courses in her first semester in college to assess how capable she could cope and juggle all she had on her plate. She surprised Francine, Carol, and her grandmother, not to mention her therapist and her sponsor. She showed total determination and pushed herself as if she were in competition with herself.

Her grandma, who had always seen her as not too prone to academic performance, was joyous with her skill and ability. She was higher and greater than her ineptitude. Carol was the happiest, though behind bars. She shared her daughter's recovery progress and admission into college with those who cared to listen. Her life story had been pathetic, not worthy of emulation, but had vowed to support her daughter through guidance not to turn up the same way she did. She made bad choices; the consequences had been enormous and paid dearly for it. The choices a person makes in life can define what the person becomes, not only in terms of character but also in how far they would go in life. Our choices mold our destiny and brings our destiny to fruition. It is a person's right to choose what's best for the individual. A choice could hinder one's progress for a long time if it is not the right choice. A person's destiny could have hiccups or become stagnant along the way if it is not the right choice. The right choice plus determination as the watchword would become the liberator needed to excel.

One would surely arrive at one's destination; you could run late but will eventually get there. Your destination is determined by your choices. It could be at the top, middle, or the bottom, ending under, or below is a no-no. Guide against going under, it is never a positive word. Regret is the ultimate of under. Life gives chances and embraces positive changes. Choosing those we relate with are some of the choices we make in life. Either in the form of friends, enemies, and acquaintances, they can make or unmake us. Not everyone should be your friend or your enemy. They come our way at a time or the other during our lifetime. Choose the people in your life wisely. Tap the benefits in other people; in fact, in everyone, a person perceived as unworthy or enemy could one day be beneficial to you or become your saving grace. Look up to people. Don't look down on them.

In her first semester, Ella got one A and two Bs in the three classes she took. She could not believe she did so well. She was studious, turned in her assignments on time, stayed up late at the library, and asked both lecturers and coursemates for help when needed. She had additional support from Francine and got emotional support from Grandma, Carol, and her sponsor. She did not shy away from asking for support. Francine congratulated her on the performance and encouraged her more. Ella decided to enroll in more courses in the second semester. Her performance superseded that of the first semester. Ella cut down on her therapy sessions because of her schooling but visited the rehab as often as possible to encourage other recovering addicts. Her therapist was always proud of her change of attitude and sobriety. She encouraged others with her story and her mother's. She became a motivational speaker both at school and at the rehab facility and became a great encourager who emphasized the importance of support in the recovery process.

The ease of her progress was the support she enjoyed from the people who wanted her to excel. Ella learned of what Gina was going through, the effect on her family, most especially her mother. She felt sorry for them, but she was too fragile in her recovery to meddle in Gina's situation. Gina was far gone in terms of addiction and criminal activities; she rather not be involved to avoid being sucked in. Her therapist had counseled her on the need to avoid people that would cause her to crave or relapse.

Carol was to be released soon. She had become a new person, a new creature, totally reborn. She had turned her life around in a good way and had become an inspirator and influencer to many behind bars. She was poised to regain all the years she had lost behind bars. Her hopes, yearnings, and aspirations were high. She planned to become an entrepreneur, a motivational speaker to make people see that change could truly occur in a person's life. Second chances are always available after blowing the first. Everybody is open to second chances; our first chance could be negative while the second could become a life changer. Making a second chance positive depends on one's motivation, dedication, and determination.

Our lives are like a bed of roses. Roses are beautiful with an array of eye-catching colors. Everyone loves the beauty and fragrance of roses and the aroma it emits, but roses have thorns and spikes. If you think of the spikes and thorns, you would miss the beauty of roses in your flower vase or garden as well as the fragrance. When you pick your roses wisely and gently, you would avoid the prickly thorns. We all need to pick our roses of life the proper way to avoid the pains. Roses bring beauty and fragrance to life, and so are our actions. If you make your bed the right way by eliminating the rumples, you will avoid bedsores. Carol had learned to pick her roses correctly and was willing to lay her bed right. She learned different trades while incarcerated. She would pick one of them or two and inscribe in her heart that only a person can change the trajectory of one's life. Grandma and Ella were eager to have Carol back home. They had started planning for her arrival, which was a few months away. Ella would have her biological mother living under the same roof with her for the first time in her life. She knew the reunion would be sweet, a game, and life changer. Carol recently had been her rock from behind bars. Having her physically present would be an experience she would treasure and cherish for life.

*****

Gina's attitude became worse with her stay in jail. She fought and quarreled with everyone that crossed her path. Her father had refused to accept her call collect from jail, and she had been on edge with anger bouts at the least provocation toward officers, staff, and inmates. The investigating officers had not arrested the owner of the gun found in her possession, she cannot be off the hook because of the murders and the charges she had. Gina was proud and arrogant even in jail, she saw herself as better than everybody, even the staff. Her criminal tendencies had risen due to frustration, loneliness, and inability to get drugs and alcohol. She, from time to time, displaced her anger and frustrations on people around her.

Madeline was not doing well at all. Her health had gone from fair to worse. She took time off work to care for her health. The same job that dispossessed and took her away from her from training her daughter was running smoothly without her. Employees must keep it in mind that the life span of a company is longer than the life span of an employee irrespective of position. The moment you are unavailable, someone else would step into the position. No position would be left vacant for you even if you are the best qualified for the seat. No one on earth is indispensable. She missed her daughter; Benjamin had not disclosed her whereabouts despite inquiries from him. Even Benjamin had become a shell of himself. He feared ending up like his wife now confined to only their bedroom. Benjamin's doctor switched around his medications because his blood pressure kept rising.

The old woman Gina hit in the car accident had sued her and her parents. She sued Gina for driving under the influence and harassment with a gun. She claimed the occurrence had caused her severe anxiety, fear, inability to operate her vehicle, sleeplessness, and untold body pains. She asked for $50 million in the lawsuit. Benjamin knew Gina was culpable, and they were liable because Gina was on their insurance. Gina brought the menace on the family and instructed a staff to take a copy to Gina in jail. When the attorney told Gina her mission, she laughed her to scorn, let out her evil maniacal laugh, and told her without mincing words to get lost. Her parents should pay the old woman from the inheritance she would receive at their demise. The attorney could not believe her ears. Her eyes could not even fathom the unrepentant attitude she displayed. Gina refused the copy. The report of the visit broke Benjamin's heart.

Gina did the unthinkable right after the attorney left. She went to dinner and sat at a table all by herself. The inmates knew of her anger bouts and avoided her; nobody neared her table. A new inmate who knew nothing about Gina sat on the table since she was alone. Gina gave her an evil look, eyeballed her, but she did not understand. She was not a criminal. She was arrested for a minor offense and put in jail while her bail was being perfected. Gina roared for her to leave. She was scared, and while scampering to get her tray to leave, Gina grabbed her knife and stabbed her. There was commotion all around. The officers arrested Gina and transported the girl to the hospital. Luckily, it was not a life-threatening stab. Gina added attempted manslaughter to her charges. The news was all over the television stations.

Madeline heard the news about Gina. She never knew she was in jail. Benjamin mistakenly left the remote control close to Madeline, and she put on the television. She cried her eyes out before Benjamin returned. She had a stroke overnight. Her left side became paralyzed. Benjamin blamed himself for his mistake. He only left for less than thirty minutes to pick her medications at the pharmacy. He cried like a baby. There was nobody to console the two of them. Madeline's health had turned from worse to worst. Benjamin could no longer take care of her alone. The doctor recommended an assisted living facility, but Benjamin said no. He would rather employ nurses to care for her on a twenty-four-hour basis in the comfort of her home.

The authorities moved Gina to twenty-four-hour confinement with surveillance and had only one hour per day for exercise. She was adamant, angry, and refused to accept responsibility for her action. She was not remorseful; her mental health crises were about to explode with her inability to move around. She would moan, bark, and scream at the top of her voice. She had refused to accept her dual diagnosis and all medications. Gina's last act made her father break down emotionally and psychologically. He could no longer concentrate on his cases. Thank God he had able hands, but his absence and negative publicity had scared big clients away. Madeline's health was draining him financially. The case of the old woman was pending. His competitors in the profession were happy to have their pound of flesh. His law firm had dominated over them for years, happy everything was in disarray for them and got some of their big clients. Unfortunately, Gina was not helping matters. His team at the law firm advised him to seek an amicable settlement with the old woman. They had a series of talks with her lawyer who insisted on $25 million. After deliberations, they agreed to take $5 million with a signed nondisclosure agreement to avert media scrutiny.

Gina's case went to court with all odds against her. Her father's law firm represented her and did their best to let her off the hook. It was not possible. The offenses were too many. Besides, she had no report of good behavior. She recently knifed a fellow inmate while in jail. As a well-celebrated case, all media stations were agog, newspapers flew off the shelves, and those who could not get a paper visited the library to read the news. Her attorneys argued brilliantly while the prosecuting attorneys were also up to the task.

Gina looked overconfident and believed that she would be set free or bailed. Her father was a well-known celebrity attorney who never lost a case. Her disposition and composure in court showed she was proud, ill-mannered, and not properly brought up. She had no regard or respect for constituted institutions or the law. Her utterances to her attorneys were uncouth and uncultured. She had no regard for them. They were her father's employees, must bow to her, and do her bidding. Despite her behavior and attitude, they argued brilliantly for her. They were professionals and did their best despite her demeanor and attitude. The case was adjourned for another three months.

Gina was to remain behind bars. Her charges included attempted manslaughter, driving under the influence, illegal possession of firearms, leaving the scene of an accident, adult abuse, and probably murders. The bank fraud charges were dropped because her family lied that she had permission to use the debit and credit cards. For the first time in Gina's life, she looked subdued. She looked around, as if to beckon to her parents to pick her out of the courtroom. It was too late. She could not believe she would stay an extra day in jail and planned to return home that night with plans to hit the club immediately. Her attorneys applied for bail; the judge denied the application because she was a flight risk. She felt betrayed by her parents, and her mother was not in court. Why? Why would they allow her to go through all the stress when they were supposed to be the toast of society? Her mother was lying almost motionless at home. Even if she knew, she would not care. As far as Gina was concerned, they should die so she could inherit their wealth. Gina was selfish. It was all about her and no one else. She abandoned her mother, left her when she needed her most, caused her to have multiple heart attacks, caused her paralysis, and got her heart broken. As for her father, she had caused losses to his business, finance, health, and psychological well-being. To make matters worse, the family of the woman she knifed in jail had sued her family, demanding an exorbitant amount.

*****

Jason and Bethena visited Elizabeth at the psychiatrist's hospital. They could not stay with her for more than five minutes because she was sleeping and restrained to her bed. Her mother rubbed her hands and told her she loved her. She opened her eyes but seemed to be in a trance. She looked at them and slept off again. The nurse asked them to let her rest and escorted them out. Bethena sobbed softly, and Jason comforted her. It was a difficult sight to see her daughter restrained. She knew Elizabeth needed the desired treatment for her diagnosis. The medications in the hospital were what she needed to begin a journey in the recovery process. The staff was not able to disclose her prognosis to them because of HIPPA (Health Insurance Portability and Accountability Act) laws. Elizabeth had to give consent for the release of her prognosis, and she would never do it. They met with the psychiatrist who reassured them she would be fine; he could not disclose anything. They gave their telephone numbers for contact if needed. They left unhappy but happy that she was in the right place.

Bethena put in a letter for early retirement. Her staff were sad. She had been an excellent leader and boss, always a shoulder to lean on. They loved her, but her happiness and family were uppermost, most especially Elizabeth's rehabilitation. They were all aware of what she had gone through in the hands of her daughter. She had brought shame, disgrace, ridicule, disdain, and pain to her. They also knew what she had gone through in the hands of men and how she became celibate and disinterested in men. Her job had been her succor, a hiding and sacred place to soothe her pain; unfortunately, she did not do justice to work and home balance, used work addition to cover lapses in her life. She loved her job, totally committed to it, and the company had rewarded her in great measures. Her staff was happy for her when she started dating Jason. Her spirit became uplifted. Happiness became her companion. It radiated through her.

Her staff and acquaintances knew she would be fine with Jason. He loved her wholeheartedly. It was visible to everyone. The company and staff celebrated her with a lavish send forth party. It was well organized. Everyone in attendance said good things about her, and the accolades were great. Jason was by her side; his three children flew home to attend the party; Elizabeth was conspicuously absent. Jason's eldest daughter gave a moving, rousing speech about her mother-to-be and told everyone that Bethena perfectly stepped into her late mother's shoes effortlessly. She was happy to call her mother and not stepmother. She testified on the encounters with Bethena that had made permanent, positive prints in her heart and the hearts of her siblings. Everyone applauded her speech. Bethena could not be prouder of her new daughter. Tears of joy welled up in her eyes, and Jason rubbed her shoulder lovingly. Jason spoke glowingly of Bethena. He reported that he was the one who found Bethena and was grateful that God sent a wonderful woman to replace his late wife and be the mother of his children. He had to convince her to give marriage another chance. He was happy that she accepted after so much persuasion.

Bethena responded, "I thank everybody present. I acknowledge that I am human and not perfect. I did my best with 'truth' as my guardian angel. Integrity had been my watchword. I dedicated my totality to my job and neglected vital issues along the way. My early retirement would enable me to retrace my steps and make amends where possible as fast as I could. I made mistakes. Nobody is above mistakes. I truly regret my mistakes and take full responsibility for them. Living on regrets and the past would not solve the problems I caused. I would use my time in retirement to right the wrongs. To this company, I say a big thank you for the opportunities given to me. I appreciate the experiences and would cherish them forever. This company made me who I am today. It molded me and never looked at any of my flaws, allowing me to grow. I thank my staff. You made my job easy. What could I have achieved without all of you? My personal assistants over the years, my secretaries, you have all been wonderful. I appreciate you sincerely and deeply. Like I said at the beginning, I am human and not perfect.

"If I have offended anyone in my journey with you, I apologize. Please forgive me. To my children, I could not ask for more. You are godsent to me. You are my inspiration, my heartbeat. I love you more than life itself. Elizabeth is not here today to be part of this glory. The four of you will be what to live for. I will cherish you for the rest of my life." She turned to Jason, looked at him lovingly, and touched his shoulder. "Thank you for believing in me even when I no longer believed in myself. You told me I could do it, gave me all the support and encouragement, looked away from the flaws of my family, and never for once took it to heart.

"You gave me a shoulder to lean and cry upon, wiped away my tears, covered my nakedness and inabilities. You are dependable, kind, loving, and true to your words. You are my rock. You stood solidly behind me through thick and thin. Since you came into my life, you have salvaged me from shame, ridicule, and ruin. You came into my life when I least expected it. You made me realize that money and position are transient and made me focus on the right things of life.

Thank you." She paused for a moment and then said another emphatic "Thank you." "I love you and will be yours forever."

Everyone got up and applauded her with a standing ovation for over five minutes. The toast was made by the CEO (chief executive officer) of the company, and she got nice parting gifts. It was a glorious day for Bethena.

Jason and Bethena had a beautiful small wedding attended by close friends and family members at Jason's new mansion. Jason's three children were in attendance and looked extremely happy for their father and Bethena, their new mother. They could afford a superlative, expensive wedding, but they did otherwise. Bethena and Jason looked every inch in love, happy, fulfilled, and accomplished. Bethena's dress was simple, expensive, and fitted perfectly. The food and cake complemented the event. The handful of guests had a wonderful time. It was a short occasion, lasted only two hours. The new couple and the children had different flights to catch that evening. The children were returning to school after a week of vacation while Jason and Bethena planned to honeymoon in Paris. Bethena was long overdue for a beautiful vacation, and the honeymoon came at the right time. She had been preoccupied with work all her life. The opportunity came on a platter of gold for her. They drove to the airport at the same time but in two different chauffeur-driven cars. Jason and Bethena waited for the children to take off before flying out in a private jet owned by Jason. It was a beautiful experience for Bethena. She had flown in private jets as a company executive but never in one owned by her. By virtue of marriage, whatever Jason owned now belonged to her. Bethena wanted a prenuptial agreement signed before their wedding. Jason understood why Bethena wanted one signed. She had bad experiences with previous relationships. They both agreed that it was just to safeguard each person's property. Jason told Bethena that all his properties belonged to both and their four children. They are both stinkingly rich anyway, though Jason was far richer than Bethena. Jason's riches were like the sky and Bethena's the earth.

The trip was long and sweet. They rested during the flight. Jason left no stone unturned for Bethena's pleasure and enjoyment. The hotel reserved the best suite for the lovebirds. It was beautiful, spacious, and tastefully furnished. It was like being at home on the moon, so beautiful and out of this world. Bethena loved every inch of the honeymoon suite, felt like being in paradise. Jason spoiled her rotten. He made life so sweet that Bethena forgot all her sorrows for the two weeks they were away. Jason took her to the most expensive and exclusive restaurants. They went shopping at the most expensive high-end shops. Jason spent money on Bethena and their four children lavishly. He spared no expense. They shopped and shopped.

Jason bought special ornaments and items to replace the stolen heirlooms. They needed not to think of excess luggage. They had a private jet to carry all the luggage. They visited two other countries before they returned home. The couple returned on a Sunday. They looked well-rested; the best honeymoon money could buy. It was two weeks of de-stress; it was like all her stress evaporated, never to return, and happiness radiated all over her. When they returned, Bethena went to her house to pick up personal items. She got inside and felt lonely. She went around the whole house, picked up the glazed pictures of Elizabeth, her parents, and looked at them intently for a while and placed them back at their special locations. The house was big, a big mansion that suited her executive position and wealth. Bethena went into her bedroom again, looked at her bed, the locations where her priceless family heirlooms were. She thought of what the investigative officers had been able to unravel. She missed the heirlooms. Her parents passed them to her. She intended to pass them on to her offspring too. She kept her expensive jewelry in her safe and wished she kept the stolen pieces of jewelry in the safe. She had them on her dresser from the last time she wore them. She was too tired to open the safe and place them back, more regrets, hissed, and shook her head. *Why worry*? she thought. Jason bought her more pieces of jewelry than she needed, more expensive than the ones stolen.

Bethena called the psychiatric hospital to know if Elizabeth was still there. She would like to visit her in the evening, and Jason would be at a crucial meeting that evening and would not be able to go with her. At the hospital, Elizabeth had stabilized. The medications had worked wonders. She looked healthier, well-rested, focused, and alert. She was receptive to her mother, who greeted her with a big bear hug. Bethena was happy but confused. She was short of words and didn't know how to present it to her that the wedding and honeymoon were over. She summoned courage and told her about the small but expensive wedding, the glamorous honeymoon in Paris, the other countries they visited, and all the things she bought for her four children.

Elizabeth was speechless. She looked lost and felt out of place. She had lost her mother and her inheritance. She got up, paced back and forth, turned, looked at her mother, and opened her mouth, words gushing out like water. When she started talking, there was no stopping.

"What becomes of me?" she questioned. Looking at her sternly, she blurted at the top of her voice, "I want out. I will never live with you guys. I want a place of my own when I leave this place. I will never return to that rehab facility. You are free to live your life as you wish. I am out of the picture. Give me my inheritance. Whatever I am worth, my entitlements, what my grandparents left for me, give it to me. I am a grown woman. I can take care of myself."

She paused and then continued, "I have always taken care of myself. You have been an absentee mother all your life. All your life, you were absent. Now you are a mother of four, how funny? You could not take care of only one. You want to take care of four to become the mother of the year I suppose? It was all about your work and men, all about you! Give me my share, and I will be gone from your lives forever."

Bethena sat dumbfounded. She knew her daughter and expected more bombshell than she did. She was in awe but patient and kept her cool. She expected her to react more than she did. She was cool, calm, and mute. With patience, she would find a way to penetrate her, win her over, and get on board. She moved closer, held her hands, pulled, and held her closely. Elizabeth was shaking with rage. The nurses heard her outburst and rushed to see what was happening. Bethena waved to them that she had it under control. When the nurses left, she reassured Elizabeth that she was her daughter and would always be her daughter irrespective of what had happened. She belonged to her and Jason now. The mention of Jason's name irked her. Bethena calmed her down.

Bethena appealed to Elizabeth that she would like her to give Jason a chance. There was no going back. They are officially married. She would be moving to Jason's place and would put her mansion up for sale as soon as possible. It would be economically unwise to lock up her house or rent it out. It was too big for rental. Elizabeth looked at her disgustfully. She asked Bethena to leave. She would call the nurses if she refused to leave immediately. Bethena appealed to her. Elizabeth walked out on her mother. Bethena sat in the visitor's room rooted to her seat, confused, sad, torn between her daughter and husband, and was confused about the next line of action.

She left after Elizabeth did not come back. When she got home, she relayed what happened at the hospital to Jason. As usual, he pacified her and reassured her that Elizabeth would eventually come around. It might not be immediately but would surely happen. Bethena believed him but wanted her daughter to come to her senses right away. Bethena called a realtor. She needed to put her mansion on the market and sell the property immediately. Elizabeth must move in with her and Jason, or she would rent an apartment for her. Her decision was final. She took full responsibility for being an absentee mother. That was now in the past. She got herself off the hook of work addiction and had turned a new leaf ready to be there for her children. As for the inheritance, her parents stipulated in their last will and testament a hurdle for her to jump before acquiring a cent. Elizabeth had only a high school diploma and was only twenty-three years old. She had no knowledge of what the testament contained.

Elizabeth became depressed and moody after her mother's visit. She displaced her anger and annoyance on the nurses and staff at the psyche hospital. She became uncooperative and refused dinner and all her medications. Elizabeth then became extremely recalcitrant. She flung all the items on her bedstand over the floor, and when the staff tried to peep into her room, she threw pillows at them. The nurses had to call the doctor on duty to intimate her with the development. The doctor responded immediately and came with the therapist to see her. Elizabeth was out of her senses, mind, and rational reasoning. They could not make her stop the rage, restrained, and sedated her.

Bethena was oblivious of what her visit had caused. She was hoping that Elizabeth would change her mind, call to apologize, and be happy for her. She wanted her to be part of her new family. She had so much to share, but Elizabeth gave no room for discussion, got angry, never willing to listen. Bethena took early retirement to make amends for the times lost. She was ready to become the mother she was supposed to be. It seemed late but never too late. She could do it; she must do it; she must turn her only daughter's life around for good. She would use love, more love, and tough love. When necessary, anyhow, anyway, she must do it. It had become a matter of must; she must show her that she was a good mother, support and walk her back to the right way.

She used her long hours and commitment to her job as a cover-up for her pains, loneliness, and inadequacies. She now has a good man willing to support and bring out her hidden potential to excel in home management and motherhood. Elizabeth had turned into an obstacle difficult to jump or surmount. She thought her recalcitrant, rebellious, and defiant posture would make her mother back off from the relationship with Jason; unfortunately, it was too late. Jason and Bethena are now Mr. and Mrs. Andrew. She would either be in or out. Bethena needed love, companionship, family, peace of mind, and a settled home to be precise. Jason was more than willing to give all and more. Elizabeth slept all day the following day. Her medications were administered intravenously and restrained all through. She would pull off the drip if not restrained. The doctor and therapist had a word with Jason and Bethena and canceled all visits till further notice.

CHAPTER 8

Phase of Dehumanization

Carol finished her term at last! Amelia and Ella were on hand to pick her up from the prison gate. Carol had become a changed person; the prison had simmered her down. She used her time in prison to better her life and turn it around for her own good. Criminality led her to a life of pain, loneliness, and castration. Initially, she was part of different gangs in her first and second prison locations. She was a terror to other prisoners. She personally refrained from the groups and realized her involvement would lead to more years added to her prison term or outright death. She called herself to order during a new prison rotation. The report that the prison relayed to the new placement was that she was notorious, evil, heartless, and highly insubordinate. They should keep an eye on her because she was devilish. To the dismay of the staff at the new location, she was well-behaved when she arrived. Carol used her time in transit between facilities to ponder on her life, took a stock of her life rolling out of control at a fast pace, and made the decision to change. She became an inspiration to others, an example to follow, and never participated in any form of fight or gangsterism at the new facility.

Her behavior earned her a good name in all the prisons she was transferred to afterward. Many inmates turned their lives around because of her influence and impact. Carol came out to the warm embrace of her loved ones. She knelt on her knees as soon as she got outside, kissed the ground, turned to look at the building, and vowed never to return to incarceration again in her life. She spoke to the building as if it were a human being that could hear. Hot tears rolling down her eyes, she told the building that nobody in her generation would go through its doors again.

The drive home was smooth, full of apologies to Amelia and Ella. She begged them to forgive her for all she did that sent her to prison, for her absence in their lives for two decades. She spent about twenty years in prison, arrested at sixteen. Her case took three years and was sentenced as an adult for an offense she committed when she was underaged. Life without her family had been difficult for her. Lack of freedom almost made her run mad. The visits by Amelia and Ella helped keep her sanity. She would have been in a psychiatric ward permanently for the rest of her life if not for their unflinching support. She took full responsibility for her actions and accepted her punishment as the consequence of doing the wrong thing. She apologized over and over. Amelia told her she was forgiven, had forgotten, and would want the past to remain in the past, revisiting, apologizing, and regretting would keep the wounds open and fresh.

Ella told her that she harbored no animosity against her and happy to have her back. Everywhere looked different, beautiful, and big. Many things had changed. Twenty years was a long time for situations to be stagnant. There were major developments all around. Big, tall high-rise buildings, cars, SUVs, and trucks on the roads in different colors, shapes, and sizes. The roads were wide, tarred, well-manicured, and maintained. She saw malls, big and small. She could not believe her eyes at the magnificent buildings all around. To her amazement, her daughter was on the wheels, driving. Carol was not able to learn to drive before her incarceration. She was happy to see her daughter driving. She had grown into a beautiful young woman. When they got home, her amazement knew no bounds. They lived in a beautiful house when she was young but not as beautiful as where they lived now. Her mother and Ella lived in a mansion, a mansion fit for royalty. The house boasted of the highest taste of furnishings only a rich king could afford. Cars littered the driveway, three cars and two SUVs. Wow, she had missed so much in life, all thanks to herself and no one else. She caused it for herself. Her waywardness robbed her of a good life and made her suffer untold hardship. Prison life was not the best for anybody. She lived in a small room with two small twin-size beds, shared space, a room with others, and shared bathroom.

Home sweet home. She returned to a life of luxury, a king-size bed with fluffy mattress and pillows, well-laid bed, dresser, nightstand, delicious meal, and more. She had a long hot bath as if washing off the prison. She slept in the same room with her mother and Ella. They could not be separated that night. They almost slept on one another. They had so many stories to tell and catch up on. The following day was spent at the spa by the three women. Amelia pampered Carol. She got all the best treatments money could buy: facial and body massage, hair treatment, skin treatment, body scrubbing, manicure, pedicure, and more.

When they left the spa, they went to register Carol at a driving school. She needed to learn how to drive. She started training that week. There were cars in their four-car garage mansion for her to drive around town. They visited the malls the following day. Carol had a day of shopping. She shopped till evening. They visited many stores, but she was not interested in ostentatious goods. She shopped reasonably. Her priorities in life had changed. Prison life had taught her that "vanity upon vanity all is vanity." Her priority after prison was to love her family dearly and reciprocate the support she got from them emotionally and psychologically. Her other interest was to support and help others to avoid a life of crime and addiction. She planned to start at least two businesses, employ youths and people in the community, and lastly begin an NGO to support individuals with co-occurring disorders and another one for victims of domestic violence/intimate partner abuse.

Service to humanity was her main goal. Amelia did not do any business or get involved in any business with anybody since the death of her husband, but with the advice from her rich friends and acquaintances, she invested in short- and long-term fixed deposits and treasury bills. She rolled the money over and over in the banks. It yielded interests in millions. She made money through stocks that she invested money. She also got lots of dividends in money and allotted stocks. Money does not sleep. It works 24-7 all around the world. Money not invested will become depleted and eventually run dry. Amelia invested her money well. It worked for her. She made money, had stock in big companies, and received high dividends yearly. Amelia had money. She was fully loaded.

She had no assets in properties. She was not interested in acquiring properties for rental. Rental issues were too much for her to deal with. She sold all the properties her late husband left and kept the money in the bank. The stress she went through with tenants and management companies was too much for her, so she sold all the properties out of frustration. The only property in her name was the mansion where they lived. Carol was happy to be home. It was not about the money, comfort, and luxury at her beckon and call. Her paramount priority and interest was family. She had missed them so much and had every reason to be. Her mother and Ella gave and showered her with so much love, all the love she could get. Besides her family, she had an abundant reservoir of love and kindness to extend to all and sundry.

Ella took time off from therapy. Her therapist knew she needed time to support and bask in the euphoria of having her mother back at home for the first time in her life; in fact, her mother's return was therapeutic. She spent more time with her mother and grandmother. It was a time she would not forget in a hurry. Carol went daily for her driving lessons while Ella juggled between school and therapy. Her mother and grandmother were proud of her. Ella got support from different angles. Support in therapy is important, and the support had been of tremendous advantage to her. Carol's return geared her to be more disciplined and enthusiastic in all her undertakings: schooling and therapy.

Carol hit the ground running. She was posed to conquer and take back all the years she had lost. It was as if she was in a relay race. She was ready to receive the baton from her mother and sprint forward. She started discussing business ideas she loved to embark upon with her mother. Amelia told her she had her backing on whatever she decided to do. Carol got her diploma in prison and learned other crafts. She learned designing and interior decoration and was excellent with flower arrangements. Putting colors together was an added skill. She planned to open a florist store with probably a spa and hair treatment center. She got her entrepreneurial teeth sharpened while in prison. She knew she would never get a job as a felon but had her inheritance to back her up.

She had learned how to be independent, focused, and stand firm on her belief. Carol went through a lot when arrested and eventually sentenced. She never believed she could end up in prison. One bad decision led to another and another. Her attitude and behavior kept rolling out of control until she got herself into the serious mess that got her years in prison. She had depression, mood swings, suicidal thoughts, cravings, and an untreated PTSD after her father's death. They played a large part in her attitude, behavior, and criminal involvement. All that was now in the past. Moving forward was the ace on the table at the moment.

*****

Gina got another day in court. As usual, she believed she would be bailed and allowed to return home pending the court proceedings. The case was adjourned again and bail denied. Gina cried bitterly, accused her attorneys of not working hard enough to get her released, and trashed them with her sharp tongue. She naturally had smart responses to situations that were borderline insult. When she returned to the jail, she became a terror to the other inmates, nasty as usual. Madeline's health got worse than her doctor thought but kept managing her. She began physical therapy three days a week. Benjamin returned to work but was absent-minded. He relied more on his attorneys for the running of his law firm. His days of glory faded. Respect in the eyes of people had dwindled, diminished. He had become a shadow of himself. Shame no longer allowed him to accept interviews on television as he used to. All said, he had his life to live and took full responsibility for not training his daughter well, but he comforted himself with the fact that there was little he could do for a child who decided to be rebellious and recalcitrant; after all, well-trained children sometimes depart from their home training too. All he could do as a parent would be to do his best and leave the rest. He cannot live someone else's life. If Gina must learn her lesson the hard way, so be it. As a father, he would do his best, and that would be it.

Madeline's health got a boost after weeks of physical therapy; her prognosis was much better. The parents of the inmate Gina knifed wanted a day in court. They sued Gina, her parents, and the jail facility. Benjamin hid the information from his wife. Her health was too fragile to withstand another problem that was associated with Gina. Benjamin told his legal team to work out a settlement. The negative publicity had become too damning. He needed the issue taken care of. His peace of mind was at stake, and he was going through too many things that were making his heart race and skip all the time. His doctor had advised him to slow down and take it easy. He could have a heart attack also. He dared not have one. Their lives would take a drastic turn if he did. He could not be like his wife who was almost bedridden.

The inmate's family agreed to settle out of court. Benjamin was low on cash, and he sold one of his choice commercial properties to raise proceeds for the settlement. His finances were steadily going down the drain, thanks to Gina who cared less. She was selfish, self-centered, and self-conceited. She believed that what her father parted with was a tip of the ice bag of his worth. Benjamin knew Gina would not stop her evil ways until he became ruined and penniless. Gina was the cross he had to bear. His attorney, as usual, had the family sign a nondisclosure, the second nondisclosure in one year. Benjamin parted with a chunk of his savings to save the face of his family, his future. He vowed in his heart that what he had paid out would be Gina's inheritance. He would write her off his will and testament. How would he cope if he had two or three children? Only one child had destroyed him socially, economically, emotionally, and psychologically. What if he had three? He pondered. He had lost so much money but had peace with the two lawsuits settled. The media would rest and leave him and his family alone. The media wanted information on the settlements, but the nondisclosures forbade the families from revealing the terms of the settlements to any media.

Francine was at the top of her game; her academic performance was at its best. She had distinctions in all her classes, checked on Ella from time to time, helped her with her courses, and supported her coursemates and juniors in the university. In the dorm, her room was always filled with people needing one thing or the other. Many people wondered how she was able to help others and still excel. She was seldom seen alone. Students were always milling around her to solve one problem or the other. She planned her daily routine well, had no time for idle chatter, and created time for rest also. Carol invited her to the house for dinner on a Saturday. She thanked her immensely for turning Ella's life around and for all her support. She shared her story and plans to open her business with Francine, and she gave input on areas where her business would thrive.

Carol saw how intelligent she was the moment she opened her mouth. She spoke with wisdom and had knowledge of issues, especially politics, economy, and medicine. Carol was happy that she influenced her daughter positively. Francine was rounding up her third year in the university and shared with Carol that she was torn between going to law or medical school. She was yet to decide. Carol marveled at her brilliance, beauty, intelligence, and charisma. Carol settled for a florist store. There was a store up for sale not too far from where they lived. She had the resources to purchase, and the asking price was great, but she wanted a business she would nurture from its onset. Francine offered to do a feasibility study for her. She sacrificed her weekends for Carol, and she appreciated every bit of it. She opened the florist store in an upscale area with residential homes and businesses. Her clientele were people from all spheres of life. She named it "New Beginning Florist." The business picked up from the day she opened. Orders poured in from day one, and the location was good for her kind of business. In real estate, agents talk about location, location, location, and the right location makes a business flourish. Francine found and chose the location, and Carol and her family agreed with her choice. It was the best for a florist store. Carol became busy from day one. Her mother, Ella, and two assistants all became great assets. Her mother was always with her at the store. Ella returned there after her daily activities. The store became their second home. People wondered who Carol was and where she came from. That was their headache. She needed no explanation to anybody.

*****

Francine's maternal grandmother became sick due to old age. Francine was the apple of her eyes, and she reciprocated more than a hundred percent. Her grandmother would cook her best food and send it to her every Saturday. Since she became sick, she could not do it anymore, and Francine missed the meals. She visited Grandma more often to make sure she was comfortable. She advised Grandma to sell her home and move into her parent's home, her parents had discussed it with Grandma before, but she disagreed, she wanted her privacy and independence. She fell on the stairs a few weeks ago and had to be hospitalized for a few days. Thank God she did not break her hip. The latest development was of great concern to Francisca and Francis.

With Francine's concern and fears, they all visited Mary, Francine's grandmother, and she agreed to move in with them. Francine offered Grandma her bedroom. It was big, spacious, and self-contained. She wanted her to be very comfortable, but she declined it. Francine convinced her to stay in her room. She was in school, and the room was vacant. There are two other rooms in the house. She would use any of them when around. The fact was, she seldom spent time at home except on holidays, which was rare. Besides, she would be attending law or medical school, which would be out of state. Grandma eventually agreed to her proposition. Mary's home sold in less than thirty days; it was a beautiful house with lots of upgrades. Her mortgage was fully paid. She made almost half a million gain on her house. She walked away with over a million dollars. Staying with her daughter and her husband meant she had no more bills. She offered to pay for staying with them, but they declined. She paid her dues raising her daughter years ago. It was payback to care for her. Besides, they were well-to-do, comfortable, and could afford their bills and more. Grandma kept her proceeds in the bank. Francine gave her ideas on investing in treasury bills. Grandma agreed. Her investment started yielding good interest, and she was smiling at the bank.

Francine began her final year in the university. Her popularity soared. Her coursemates held her in high esteem and loved her. She sat for the law and medical school admission examinations and passed both with distinctions. She was torn between what profession to choose. Ella began her second year in the community college. She had been clean for over one year. Her therapy sessions were long over. Her attendance at AA and NA meetings continued unabated. She became the sponsor of a single mother of three who was hooked on drugs and alcohol. She had gone through therapy sessions and attended the same meetings with Ella. She needed to work on her addiction and prove her sobriety to claim her children back from the department of children and families. She had her three children in the car when she had an accident. She was under the influence and highly intoxicated. When the police arrived, she was arrested for DUI and child endangerment. Her children were taken and placed in foster homes. She would lose them unless she cleaned up her act and became clean and sober. It was not the first time she got in trouble with the department. It was the second time her children were removed. Ella supported her in great measures and asked Carol to support her too. Carol employed Kimberly; she became one of her assistants at the florist store. Andy, her live-in boyfriend, was an absentee father. He abused Kimberly throughout the time they lived together, the children inclusive. She ran away to avoid his abusive tendencies, at a point, was a resident at a halfway house with her children for months and resorted to alcohol to mask her pain and anxiety. Ella became a good mentor to her. Kimberly was able to save money from her job at the New Beginning Florist, maintained her sobriety, rented an apartment with her savings, coupled with the support from Ella and Carol, and got her three children back. Ella and Carol were happy to see her settled with her children. She became one of the most loyal staff of Carol.

*****

Gina had been in jail for over one year. The judge kept adjourning her case. Her inherent disposition to drugs and criminality had kept her locked up. If she had been outside, she probably would have been killed by the owner of the gun she stole because he was frantically looking for her. He was still on the loose, evading arrest. Being behind bars was a blessing in disguise for her. She had gotten used to life behind bars, wreaking havoc on people around her. Her father's law firm was not doing well anymore. A sizable number of his attorneys resigned or moved to other law firms. Attorneys representing Gina also changed from time to time. Benjamin's business had gone down drastically, and revenue had dwindled considerably. He visited Gina in jail on occasions, but she snubbed him every time. Her mother's stroke had left her in a wheelchair. She took early retirement from her lucrative job, become reclusive at home, and mostly idle. She was high-handed at her job and was disliked by her staff. She was prideful to them, and they refused to reach out to her when she had her health issues. They believed that karma was at play.

Gina had become a hardened criminal in jail. She parleyed with the notorious inmates, was insubordinate, never followed instructions from the authority, failed drug tests while in jail. She refused to snitch on how she got the drugs. Benjamin became an unhappy father and husband. His relationship with his wife had turned sour. The love they shared for so long had turned to hatred. He could not file a divorce because of her state of health. Benjamin had the willful thought that maybe Madeline would ask for one. If she did, he would gladly oblige her. Their once beautiful lives had turned upside down. The respect accorded them had vanished, and they had become objects of ridicule in society. Benjamin's finances took a hit. He sold his choice properties. He was no longer able to pay his staff on time. He started lagging on bills. As things got tougher, his properties became targets, sold with great losses. The banks foreclosed on others. His fortune had become misfortune.

*****

Bethena placed her mansion on the market, a beautiful masterpiece with expensive upgrades. It sold within three weeks. The buyer paid cash because people were interested in purchasing the property, mouthwatering bids that could not be overlooked. It sold far above the appraised value and asking price. All furniture, personal items, decorations, and items inside the property were sold through a reputable estate sales company. It was a bazaar for the community, with beautiful items at higher-than-expected prices. Jason and Bethena moved all furniture and personal belonging in Elizabeth's room to the largest bedroom in Jason's mansion, awaiting her eventual return. Elizabeth was very upset when she learned that the house where she grew up had been sold. She inquired to know what Bethena did with her personal items and car. She called Bethena and scolded her for selling the property. She vowed never to move into their home as well as sever all relationships with her. Her thought process was that if her mother could buy a property for Jason, she should buy a property for her also, settle her. It was part of her money, her inheritance, and she needed her portion immediately. Bethena laughed. She told her that Jason bought his property with his hard-earned money. She contributed no dime to the purchase. Elizabeth laughed her mother to scorn, told her she was a liar, that she would deal with her. She remembered her partner in crime and tried to reach Gina. They have not heard from each other in a long time. Gina's phone was not reachable. Every time she called, she got the same message. She never knew that Gina was still being held in jail. As for

Ella, she was already out of the picture, she was a backstabber, an enemy in disguise. She already wrote her out of her mind. With no allies to back her up in the desire to deal with her mother and Jason, she decided she would do it alone.

Elizabeth left the psychiatric ward to the treatment center. Her family uprising had stressed her beyond her elastic limit, and she started using again, failed drug tests, and was discharged for noncompliance. The facility informed Jason and Bethena that her continued use was detrimental not only to her but to the treatment of the others who are diligently working on their abstinence. Elizabeth called Bethena that she was leaving the facility, was discharged, and needed her mother to bring or send her car, personal belongings, and money. Bethena told her it was impossible. She should take a taxi and return to the police station because she had violated the terms of her bail. She cursed her mother out, took a cab, and went straight to the club. With no money or credit card, she sold her expensive gold earrings and necklace to buy drugs. In the early hours of the following day, she left with one of the patrons at the club, an established drug dealer. They began a relationship as live-in lovers. She resumed her drug use in earnest and threw all caution and treatment to the wind. It was as if she wanted to use all she had missed in arrears, nearly overdosed again if not for the timely intervention of her live-in boyfriend. Jason and Bethena became perplexed. Bethena's joy of finding her soulmate had problems from the beginning by her only daughter who was supposed to be the happiest for her. She became stressed and depressed. Jason encouraged her to seek counseling, most especially to learn new skills that could help Elizabeth. Seeking and learning new skills are never too late. Learning and acquiring knowledge never terminates until death terminates breathe.

Elizabeth's whereabouts were unknown. Her parents reported to the police. Elizabeth's disappearance was a big blow to Jason and Bethena. Though she was a problem child, a missing child is a parents' worst nightmare. They needed to be sure she was not in any form of harm. Bethena missed her child. Though she was a criminal and drug addict, she was still her only child. She loved her unconditionally and would go to any length to find and rehabilitate her. The police combed all known areas she patronized, and within one week, her whereabouts were known, but she moved from place to place often because her partner was always on the move. She was an adult, free to do whatever she wished, so she was not a missing person in the eyes of the law.

As an adult, she had the right to be free and stay wherever she liked. Her mother and Jason wanted her to return home. It broke Bethena's heart. Elizabeth's live-in lover evicted her for fear of having his activities under a horoscope, harboring Elizabeth could keep him in the eye of the storm, and Elizabeth became homeless, moved from club to club for days before disappearing. Weeks passed without any news from Elizabeth. Her mother was worried sick. The police told her it was not a missing case when she contacted them about her disappearance again. No one had seen or heard from her in recent times. Bethena contacted Ella. She told her she had not seen her in a long time and explained to Bethena that she had severed ties with Elizabeth and Gina and that she was on her personal rehabilitation track. Bethena was happy for Ella. She was happy and at the same time sad, happy for Ella's desire for change, sad for her daughter's insistence to neglect change. The change was the antidote that her daughter needed. She would do anything to imbibe that change in her. Jason and Bethena decided to put their trust in God, hoping for the best.

*****

Carol's support for Ella knew no bounds. They have become best friends. Ella was almost through at the community college; she had applied to transfer her credit to the university and decided to study business administration and psychology as a minor. She initially wanted to become a social worker so as to help others with her life story but changed her mind. She had a story to tell the world, whoever was willing to listen. Whatever course she studied, she could still help others through her chosen course of study. She wanted to encourage as many people as possible to avoid the path of destruction she once embarked upon, be an inspiration to others, put her marks on the sand of time, to do good in general, and pay forward what Francine did for her. If not for the encounter with Francine, she might probably be dead from a drug overdose or serving a jail term. Carol was doing well in her business and on the home front. She was now in control of the whole family and glided effortlessly into the front seat. Amelia stepped back to let her run the affairs of the family. She saw how mature she had become, the change she had acquired while behind bars. She became focused, had no time for nonsense and trivialities, disciplined, amiable, kind, and truthful. Her customers loved to do business with her. Her probation officer was proud of her seamless integration back into society. Carol was very diligent in her business; she was lucky to have access to money, which enabled her to open her business in a big way. Her mother bought two delivery vehicles for deliveries to be done on time. Amelia was all thanks to God for what her daughter and grandchild had turned into. It was as if the demons inside of them melted, evaporated, disappeared into the sea abyss, or a bottomless pit never to resurrect. Amelia's health had improved tremendously. She glowed and was filled with vitality.

Carol named her NGO facility "Ariel's Turnaround Center." Her father was Nicholas Ariel, the biggest diamond seller of all time. The money to fund the NGO came from the inheritance he left for them. The turnaround was to signify a turnaround to a new beginning in her life, her family, and residents that would benefit from the services. Doing good for others was paramount in her heart. The years behind bars had taught her that vanity upon vanity is vanity. The Bible said it, and so did common sense. Money that does not speak into the lives of others in need is worth nothing. Money translates into happiness but cannot buy happiness. Loving money is the root of every form of evil imaginable. The wealth her father left for them had quadrupled, more than what the three of them could finish in their lifetime. She realized that life had so much to offer, so much good left to be tapped, harnessed, and shared. If she were to be behind bars for longer than she did, the money would have been useless to her. If Amelia had died due to her health scare, Ella would have died mismanaging the money.

Life had given her a second chance, a chance not only for her but also a second chance for her mother who was lucky to have her cancer detected early, and for Ella who had turned a new leaf through rehabilitation. Destiny had given them a new lease on life. Her thinking and value had changed, and the same for Ella and Amelia. Carol's business generated so much money in its first year. the florist store had become a household name in the community, well patronized. Carol's NGO had become a force to be reckoned with in the community. She bought a twenty-room property to house women in abusive relationships and people with dual diagnoses. Her probation officer was so impressed with her involvement and support for battered and abused women, as well as the provision of a halfway house for those with addiction and mental health diagnoses. He reported her contribution to society to his boss who in turn shared the efforts with the authority who highly commended her. She was abused when she was young, taken advantage of by those who were supposed to be her protectors. Those who were supposed to stand in the position of "father" for her, who knew better but introduced her to drugs at a very tender age, made her partake, toe the line of criminal activities, taught her lies and so much evil, encouraged, defiled, and gave her drugs that altered her brain chemistry. Her life was destroyed by those she was supposed to trust. She planned to liberate women from the shackles of abuse and destruction lurking its head all around. They were pedophiles, plain and simple.

*****

Francine finished at the top of her class. She was the doyen of all, the students, and lecturers alike. She was the valedictorian at the university's commencement ceremony. Her parents were the happiest, likewise her grandmother. Ella and her family graced the occasion in the company of many other important people in the community, the many acquaintances she made over the four years in the university, and many people she had been good, helpful, and kind to. They threw a graduation party for her. It was well attended. The news media gave it primetime coverage and gave her the honor she deserved. Francine got a full-ride scholarship to study medicine at the best university in the country, felt highly honored by the show of love, thanked all who attended for the love they showered on her, and told them she appreciated their labor of love but only did what made her happy: doing good, being helpful, and kind was her way of life. She encouraged all in attendance not to relent in doing good. Being good says a lot about an individual's identity and personality. When you do good, be happy. Do not expect a reward for your deed. A good deed puts a smile on the face of the beneficiary. That smile is the best reward/thank you on this planet Earth. A good deed that changes the life of another for the better is worth a million bucks. Do good and never regret it even when your good deeds are repaid with evil by the people you extended kindness to. Be aware that not all the people you help love you intently. Sharing kindness makes the world go around. There is no sense in keeping your talents, kindness, and acumen to yourself and yourself only.

*****

Gina had her day in court. As usual, her bail was refused. She was sent back to jail. Her spirit was downcast when she got back to the jail, poised to wreak more havoc on the other inmates and staff when she returned. Everyone stood out of her way. They knew she could do and undo. Her case was like the case of a leper who could not milk a cow but could throw away the milk others milked. She opined that her parents had not done enough to get her off the hook. Her father had a history of winning lawsuits. He had represented mafias, murderers, drug barons, and rich domestic abusers and got them off the hook. Why her? The only daughter of the almighty Wiggins? Even in jail, those who knew her family revered her. They knew her father was a prominent attorney in the society, rich, mighty, above life. Despite his connections, he left her to languish in jail? He had failed her as a father. For that singular reason, she would make him pay dearly.

As for her mother, she would get a full dose of her medicine, an overdose of her wrath would serve her better, and she would make her groin in pain for her abandonment. Her refusal to order the designer bag catapulted into the ripple effect that caused all she had gone through. She was accustomed to Madeline's acceptance of her entitlement mentality, satisfied with her unnecessary needs, and wants that expanded daily. She was not built up morally, wanted everything, and whenever she got turned down, there would be a problem. Her mother was a freewill giver, no questions asked. She would serve the revenge when it is cold, almost frozen. She would do it at a time she least expected. The owner of the gun found in Gina's car was still at large. The investigators and prosecutors wanted Gina held until the gun owner was found, and the mysteries behind the deaths had to be unraveled.

In the meantime, Benjamin and Madeline's relationship had broken down irrevocably. They no longer see eye to eye. They repulse each other daily. Madeline's health had remained stagnant, no improvements. The improvements she made a few months ago had retrogressed. Her state of health presently had turned into an eyesore. Her daily and incessant needs had become a burden to Benjamin who had to move her around in a wheelchair, bathe her, help her to the bathroom, and so on. The nurses were let go due to the bills that were surmounting. He had to cut down on his bills. At his law firm, the story was the same. He had only a handful of attorneys left. Gina had successfully destroyed her parents' union, their livelihoods, and the good standing they had in the community. The name recognition had become repulsive.

*****

Elizabeth started living with another guy she met at a club. She feared homelessness after being homeless for days. Her pride deprived her depraved mind of contacting her mother and Jason for support. She tagged on with the first guy that seemed willing to accommodate her. She needed an accomplice to support her in dealing with her mother and Jason. Elizabeth had the best enjoyment for weeks after which the evil in her live-in lover erupted. Nightclubbing took a massive leap. They clubbed, wined, and dined with the most notorious criminals and drug barons in the community. Initially, the barons were skeptical of Elizabeth's involvement and knowledge of their activities. Her lover persuaded them to give her a chance and planned to turn her into a mule, to courier his drugs to and from other communities.

To get her fully on board, he knew he had to dehumanize her, demean, humiliate, and bring her to her knees. She had nowhere to go and was allergic to the harsh life on the streets. She needed a roof over her head. She told him her story and plan to get an accomplice to take down her mother and new husband. He promised to support her though he had no plan to do anything for her. He had his well-planned ideas of turning her into what he wanted. Weeks into their relationship, she became comfortable around him and trusted him with her life. He had extended a good amount of largess to her. She felt loved and happy. She never knew that hell was about to let loose on her. On a faithful day, clubbing was particularly good. The sale of drugs went well and smoothly. She kept the drugs, kept proceeds from the sale, and she had gained his total trust and was happy. Ralph knew the time to strike and unleash terror on her had come. He took part of the money when she was high then accused her of stealing part of the proceeds. He gave her the beating of her life when they returned home. She was in disbelief. Nobody had slapped her talk less of beat her to a stupor. She could not explain how the money disappeared and accepted the beating and humiliation in good faith.

She justified in her mind and believed she deserved the beating for being careless. She had nowhere to go anyway. She nursed her wounds, begged Ralph to forgive her, promised never to be careless again. Within one week, she was beaten three times, and it gradually became the order of the day. Elizabeth became Ralph's daily punching bag. He would hit her for every flimsy reason, sometimes, for mere looking at him. He derived joy in his sadomasochistic behavior toward Elizabeth. Her smooth skin disfigured with bruises and scars. She dared not complain. She did all his biddings with uttermost servitude. She couriered drugs for him and kept all the drugs in her possession while he held nothing, a smart move. If Elizabeth was caught by law enforcement, he would walk free because no drugs would be found on him. He made Elizabeth drive a car while he followed her with another car. He played smart. Elizabeth had to account for all proceeds. No loss was tolerated. He supplied her with drugs for her personal use as a reward and made sure she was high all the time. She was no longer in control of her life, movement, food, people she mingled with, and more, she virtually lost her freedom. Her brain had no rest from drugs. She was always under the influence, which was exactly what Ralph wanted. He needed to be able to manipulate her to do his will.

CHAPTER 9

The Turnaround

Carol invested money into her NGO. Her mother and Ella gave her all the support. Helping others became a new meaning to their lives. The dividends realized yearly from the investments funded the projects. It was a sizable amount of money. She employed professionals to run the two projects and reserved the two biggest rooms as offices. The rooms served as offices for the staff. News of her NGO spread like wildfire in the community. The media wanted to interview her, but she declined, likewise her mother and Ella. There was no need to blow any trumpet; in fact, there was no trumpet to be blown. She was only giving back to society, wanted to remain a silent giver, and her zeal made other companies partner with her. They donated items, especially food, clothing, and other things to support the project. She made it clear that donations could be anything. No money was accepted.

Residents at the facility received treatment for various diagnoses; support for battered women and counseling for all others were available depending on the areas of need. Carol bought another piece of land and began building a bigger facility that would accommodate more women in dire need of rehabilitation and a safe abode for men and women fleeing domestic violence as well as a more comfortable place for women with children. She believed that the children had to be kept with the mothers. It would help the healing process considerably. Admission to the facility was kept confidential to keep residents safe from their perpetrators.

Carol did very well in her florist business in her first year. She bought another place downtown and opened another florist shop, a hairdressing salon on one side. Her clients were the high and mighty residing in the area. She encouraged those who could not pay but needed a cut or wash to get it done freely. She realized that the downtown had homeless people. She made hot meals available to them twice a week after she received permission from the county office. She was a busy bee. She had an abundance of energy to burn. It was as if she had excess energy bottled up that needed release. She did not get tired easily. Sundays were her rest days. She rested after church service. Church attendance became a norm in her family, and she reiterated the need to be close to a higher power.

Her mother was happy at the turn of events in her family. She became involved in church activities and encouraged Ella to do the same. Amelia had not been to church since she was ten years old. The pastor of the church incidentally remembered Amelia when she was young. He was a young guy in the same community where she grew up. He was just a little older than her. He was delighted to see her family at the church he pastored. He became their greatest encourager. Pastor and his wife became the first visitor to their home. They came for pastoral visitation. Amelia and her family entertained them nicely but were not interested in any form of interference in their family setting. They had learned great lessons, negative lessons from so-called friends and acquaintances.

Ella's first semester at the university went smoothly. She combined her schooling with attendance at the AA and NA meetings, support at the florist shop, and continuous visits to Carols NGO. She shared her story at will to encourage those with addiction and mental health diagnoses. She had walked in the shoes and knew where it pained and pinched. They were living a life of hurt and pain she once lived. She became a source of motivation and inspiration to the women. With the level of wealth that Carol's family controlled, one would think they would always deck up in diamonds and sparkles, but on the contrary, Carol's perception of money had changed totally. "Money is good, but the love of it is evil." She did not believe in ostentatious goods and did not buy high-end materials or brand names as they were called.

To her, money should be used for the benefit of the poor, the downtrodden; after all, if her father who worked and made the vast wealth had spent it on frivolities, they would not be the beneficiaries. He saved it for them, for humanity. She made her mother and Ella get on board with her reasoning, and they agreed with her views. They could afford the most expensive items/brands, but was it worth it? A soul saved from the destructive grip of a dual diagnosis prognosis, or a domestic partner saved from a premature death would be more appreciative than a brand owner who does not know you existed despite the million dollars spent at its store or on the brand. Carol allowed the residents at her NGO have unfettered access to her, her life story, the mistakes she made, the years behind the bar, and that what she gained behind bars far outweighed her regrets. She would be dead if not for her incarceration. She explained to them on occasions that "regrets" would retrogress a person. They should learn from their mistakes, make amends, and move on. Being stagnant would amount to a refusal to get up when you fall. When you fall, get up, dust yourself, and move on. Life is full of obstacles. You cannot climb your mountain if you stay at the bottom, afraid of the height. An unrefined past would serve as a hindrance to the present and future. Our destiny is for us to guard jealously, refined for our progress.

Ella finished her first semester with flying colors. she talked to Francine occasionally but not as often as before. Francine's first year in the medical school had been busier than expected. She, however, made room for Ella and called to check on her progress. They were age mates, but Ella revered her, especially for her outstanding love and good deeds toward her. She often thought of what Francine had done for her and wished she could help Elizabeth and Gina change their ways as well. She had not seen any of them for over two years going to three and wondered what they were up to. She severed all relationships with them the day Gina pulled a gun on her, deleted their numbers from her phone and heart, and avoided them like a contagious disease. She had no news of them and was not interested in them any longer.

She immersed herself in her education and rehabilitation process, had done so well for herself, and became an object of pride to her parents. Whenever the thought of her former friends crept into her mind, she suppressed it, but in the last few days, the thought had been so heavy on her mind. She left school early to run an errand for her grandmother at the mall. Lo and behold, she ran into Bethena at the mall. She was happy to see her and Jason, thinking of the coincidence of her thought and the encounter. She inquired about her friend, and Bethena burst into tears. Ella was surprised. She was totally embarrassed to see a VIP and VP cry in a public place in the presence of her husband and onlookers. Ella pulled her to a seat and wiped her tears off while hers were flowing down her cheeks.

Bethena took time to explain what she had gone through at the hands of Elizabeth. They were there for almost two hours. She went from one horrible experience to the other amid sobs. Jason allowed her to verbalize to Elizabeth's former partner in crime that had turned a new leaf. Maybe verbalizing to her would help her de-stress. She had been under a lot of stress in recent times. Jason had done all he could to support his wife, but all efforts to console her over the disappearance of her daughter had been in vain. All the luxuries at her beckon and call were of no significance. All she wanted was Elizabeth. Jason was hurting for Bethena. Her problem was his also. They had not had a moment of bliss since the wedding. It had been one problem or the other caused by Elizabeth. Ella was surprised by the burglary orchestrated by Elizabeth for drugs. Her violence against her mother, which was nothing short of domestic abuse, and, above all, her disappearance.

Ella was attentive and an incredibly good listener. Her psychology program had equipped her for the way she managed the encounter. She allowed Bethena to verbalize, cry, and empathized with her. She promised to be on the lookout for Elizabeth's whereabouts. They exchanged phone numbers and agreed to stay connected. Ella was touched to the core when Bethena shared that Elizabeth assaulted her verbally and physically. It is a great sin for a child to hit, beat, or talk back to a parent. Under no condition should a child raise his or her hands on a mother after nine months of pregnancy and eventual labor pains. Motherhood is a great job; children should be thankful instead of bashful. To say what Bethena shared was absurd seemed an understatement. Ella pondered over it day and night. She explained all that happened to Carol who was as amazed as Ella. Carol thanked Ella for being understanding toward her, showing her love instead of being repulsive toward her. She expected Ella to hate, curse, or even assault her as Elizabeth had done, but Ella had shown the opposite, and for the singular act, she was grateful. Ella shared what Bethena told her with Francine, not because she wanted to gossip but because she believed they could work together for the good of Elizabeth. Both ladies agreed to be on the lookout for Elizabeth. Francine visited Carol's facility during the end-of-year break. There would be no breaks after the first year. During the visit, she was extremely impressed with Carol's give-back effort. It was a great sacrifice on her part to invest so much in the lives of other people without any financial support from other sources.

What Elizabeth went through in the hands of Ralph was nothing but domestic violence in its highest order. She had lost weight, looked haggard, unkempt, and pale to say the least. Clubbing, booze, and drugs became a daily occurrence. She barely slept or ate well. Her eyes were sunken from lack of sleep with a puffed bag under her eyes, but she still had to keep a bold and happy face; if not, she would get the beating of her life. Ralph had her under his total control. She became a shadow of herself. Even her mother would look twice to be convinced it was her daughter. Ralph's days of showering her with gifts, shopping, and many more were long gone. She had been fortunate to evade the prying eyes of law enforcement officers. If she had been pulled over, the number of assortment of drugs in her possession at any point in time would send her to prison for a very long time. She had no say in whatever Ralph did or say. Her servitude to him had no end.

After a night of clubbing, Elizabeth got a generous beating of her life as usual from her man. One moment, he was loving; in an instant, he would be full of rage. They returned from the club happy for once in a long time. It was a pleasant night. The sale was impressive, the proceeds were intact, and for no reason, Ralph descended on her, almost killed her. She was bloodied and bruised all over. He was too drunk and under the influence to realize what he had done. It was the second time he would kick a pregnancy out of her womb. As soon as the beating was over, he slept off on the couch. Elizabeth had to nurse herself. She could not call the emergency service to the house because of their nefarious activities.

When he woke up the following day and saw what he had done, how maimed Elizabeth was, he apologized, gave her gifts, and shopped new clothes for her. Elizabeth knew he intentionally kicked out her pregnancy because he had instructed her never to get pregnant. Elizabeth thought she had lost the pregnancy. She had morning sickness days later. A urine test confirmed she was still pregnant. When she told Ralph, she got another severe beating that flushed out the pregnancy. Elizabeth had a wet blanket as her covering! Ralph was supposed to be the strong, thick, dry blanket that covered her, but the reverse was the case. He became her wet covering weeks into their relationship. He had ruined all the fun she thought came into her life when they met at the club. He had ruined her physically and emotionally, knew she had nowhere to go. She thought she had an ally to fight Bethena and Jason. She was homeless when he picked her. There was no love for Elizabeth in his heart. She was a means to an end as far as he was concerned. Elizabeth thought she was in love and forced herself to love him. They were both users, using one another for their selfish desires. She became depressed, dejected, and demoralized but dared not complain. She believed a pregnancy would change his behavior toward her and tie him down. It was the biggest mistake of her life.

Francine and Ella devised a plan to search for Elizabeth. The simplest search was to search the internet, Twitter, Facebook, Instagram, Messenger, WhatsApp, and so on. Social media was the order of the day for the youths of today. They searched all social media apps, but Elizabeth had not posted anything in a long time. All her postings had been deleted. She was nowhere to be found. Her phone was not going through, which was unusual. Francine and Ella were shocked. Something terrible was amiss. Why would she be totally off all social media platforms? Was she truly in hiding, jail, prison, or dead? The situation was dire. There was no time to waste. They contacted the jails, prisons, and hospitals—nothing. The onus was to search more. They started visiting the clubs. They would park afar and check on the patrons as they went in and out. They saw her on occasions but could not recognize her. She had changed drastically and dramatically. Weeks after, they had a break.

They saw a lady park the car and followed by another car that parked beside her. They went inside the club lurking hands together. She looked nothing like Elizabeth. They sat in the car and waited patiently. Francine's holiday would be over in a week. She had to return to school out of state. If Elizabeth was not found, Ella would be alone to keep searching for her. About an hour later, the lady came out alone to pick up something from the car. Francine immediately recognized her, called her name, and she looked up. They could not believe it. They rushed to her. She wanted to run back into the club out of shame, but they quickly surrounded her and prevented her from going inside. A quick look at her told the situation in a million words and phrases. They rushed her to Ella's car and pushed her inside in the nick of time of Ralph's exit. He was furious, screaming a name at the top of his voice. He had changed Elizabeth's name to Marina Aberdeen. He already got her a new identity card with the new name. He searched everywhere, furious, with a gun in his hand. He went all around the building. Ella, Francine, and Elizabeth were scared to death. They kept mute in the car. Thank God, the ignition was not on, and the car was parked in an obscure corner. He went into the club in annoyance, screaming her name, ready to pounce on his "Marina" again. Ella sped off as soon as he went back inside and gave Elizabeth a great escape!

Finding Elizabeth was a miracle. She looked nothing like the Elizabeth they knew. She had emaciated, frail, pale, and ugly to look at. She was visibly depressed; a doctor was not needed to diagnose that she was mentally unstable. She had gone through months of horror and terror. She had bruises all over her body. Her jaw looked dislocated from severe beatings. On an occasion, he threw her to the wall. She hit her jaw badly. It was swollen for days. She bled profusely from her mouth, the nose, and had a black eye that was covered with makeup. She needed to see a medical doctor for proper assessment immediately. She had one tooth chipped from the front of her mouth. She looked horrible and different. Francine and Ella cried their eyes out. She looked at them in disbelief sometimes, as if ruminating on why they were crying.

A while later, she would cry and smile simultaneously. She looked like an actress to whom a movie makeup artist had applied layers of makeup on her face. It was a ploy to cover her battered face. The new Marina needed a halfway house for domestic violence victims that would keep her and her identity safe. She needed treatment fast. They took her straight to Carol's NGO facility, got her admitted, and made her comfortable. Ella explained the saga with the dual identity to the admission personnel and promised to take her to the DMV (Department of Motor Vehicle) to obtain her true driver's license. Elizabeth begged Francine and Ella to keep her whereabouts confidential, not to discuss it with anyone, most especially her mother. They agreed but told her she would eventually be reunited with her family, and she agreed.

Francine had to return home, but Ella stayed the night with Elizabeth at the facility. They shared the same room and did not sleep all night. Elizabeth had horrific stories to tell. The horrors she had endured by sheer stupidity. Her stories were without correlation and disjointed. Ella listened and allowed her to tell her stories without interruption. Francine was happy that they found Elizabeth. It was her last weekend before returning to school. She was able to recognize her through the way she walked and not by her face. It was a miracle that came to them in a small package. They were lucky to get her into the car at the niche of time before Ralph came out. They were also lucky he did not come toward their car. He probably would have killed all of them. Drug dealers do not joke with their enterprise. They are madly money conscious. Elizabeth would also have been in serious trouble if he had spared them. Whatever the case, it was a night of miraculous breakthrough. The focus now would be to seek medical treatment and rehabilitation for Elizabeth.

Ella called Carol and explained the situation to her. She was happy that they found Elizabeth but scared that Ralph might have followed or trailed them. She called the facility and instructed them to be vigilant and security conscious. Domestic violence cases coupled with a drug enterprise is a delicate issue. Criminality could become a possibility. Ella thanked her mother for her support and understanding. It was her first night outside the comfort of her home, a big sacrifice for her former friend. Ella had to be careful of relapsing because Elizabeth was till that night an active drug user. By the following morning, she had started showing signs of withdrawal symptoms. The facility booked an appointment with the doctor that night. The nurse was on hand early to transport her to the doctor's office. The examination was thorough. She had been abused severely and had severe damage to her organs with the horrible beatings. Her jaw was dislocated and would need surgery. Her forehead had a permanent black bump, and she had a fractured bone in her right hand that could break at any moment. She was always in pain and used various illicit drugs to mask her pain. Ralph sometimes gave her strong narcotics as a reward for good behavior whenever the pain was unbearable. The doctor told her she would not have survived another beating. Incidentally, she was four weeks pregnant, which would have earned her another bout of severe beatings that could have ended her life, send her permanently to an early grave, and her mother might never see her again. It was a miracle, lucky to be rescued before her next beating.

The doctor explained the reports of the tests and his observations to Elizabeth and the nurse. More tests and reports were yet to come. Another appointment date was set for her. It was a welcomed idea that a nurse followed her. Her state of mind would make it impossible for her to comprehend or internalize all the health reports and information. He placed her on medications for pain and mental health and referred her to a dentist. Her dentition had to be evaluated. More of her teeth could be affected while a replacement would be needed for her chipped front tooth. Another referral was given to an orthopedic clinic for her fractured bone. By the time they returned to the facility, Ella was back with new clothes, sandals, and toiletries that she liked. They were once close allies and conversant with each other's preferences.

The doctor agreed to visit the facility daily to monitor her withdrawal symptoms. He would manage it as much as he could. If the stabilization was slow, she would be moved to a detox facility. The nurse started her medications in earnest. She had learned her lesson the hard way and was cooperative and compliant. Unfortunately, she lost the pregnancy, one too many. The pain of the miscarriage was enormous. The physical pain and withdrawal symptoms could have facilitated the miscarriage. At this point, she cared less. Her survival was paramount. Her body needed total healing, and nursing a pregnancy would make her situation worse.

She was safe, showered with love, care, and support by Ella, Francine, Carol, Amelia, and all the staff at the facility. She felt loved and cooperated fully with them. Carol met with her immediately after she returned to the facility from the clinic. She introduced herself as Ella's mother. Elizabeth was amazed. She never knew she had been released from prison. She hugged her tight and told her she was happy to meet her. Carol assured her she was in good hands, encouraged her to tap into all the opportunities and services rendered at the facility, and promised that the facility would take care of all her hospital bills, medications, and surgical procedures if any. She was happy she got away from Ralph's grip; she would never return to Ralph's house of torment, a torment chamber, drug hub, and jungle all rolled into one. She felt relieved and free, no longer restricted as she was. Freedom at Ralph's house was like being free inside a prison. True freedom would never be appreciated until lost. She unknowingly gave her freedom away and walked into a lion's den with her feet.

Francine would be returning to school the following day. She came to see Elizabeth, brought her flowers, and two novels to keep her mind busy and focused on regaining her physical and mental health back. Both novels were on the path to healing both physically and emotionally. Elizabeth thanked her for her love and concern for her well-being but was visibly ashamed of herself, for the hate she had shown toward Francine that spanned years. Francine was able to read her mind, body language, and facial expression. She quickly dissuaded her from regrets and shame and encouraged her to forget about her past actions and move with the present wheel of progress in the making. Elizabeth's medications sent her to sleep all evening and all night. Ella was happy that she was resting perfectly. Ella, Carol, and the clinicians agreed that she needed to agree to involve her mother in her recovery process most especially the impending surgery on her jaw. She was an adult, but no one could be too sure of the outcome of a surgical procedure no matter how little the procedure was. They needed her to consent.

Ella and Carol were happy for Elizabeth. She was in a better place, and in good and capable hands. Help was just around the corner for her. Elizabeth's prognosis turned for the worse a week into her stay at the facility. Her pain was excruciating. Withdrawal symptoms elevated. The doctor came, assessed her, and called an ambulance. He sent her to the hospital for admission. Ella and Carol encouraged her to allow Bethena to become involved in her health situation. She refused to sign an informed consent. Her love and care as a mother could be what Elizabeth needed at this delicate time. At Bethena's end, the investigators of the burglary at her former house had made an arrest and found some of the items he stole at a pawnshop. The owner of the store showed the video of the transactions to the officers who immediately arrested the culprit. He confessed to the burglary, the drugs, jewelry, heirlooms, and other items he stole. He led them to the other pawnshops and individuals that bought the stolen items from him. The individuals who bought the stolen items were arrested, charged, and some items recovered. Most of the items had been sold by the pawn stores. The officers needed Elizabeth to do a positive identification of the suspect. Her mother explained to them that she disappeared from their lives. She was happy for the items recovered, most especially the jewelry Jason gave her the first birthday they spent together. It was retrieved from the suspect's girlfriend. Bethena never thought she could be reunited with her family's heirlooms. They were priceless to her. She also wanted to pass them down to Elizabeth and generations after her.

When Elizabeth met Ralph, she was homeless. He came into her life when she was at her lowest ebb. Her stupidity, stubbornness, drug-ravaged brain, and entitlement mentality clogged her sense of reasoning. All entreaties from her mother, Jason, counselors, and law enforcement officers turned on deaf ears. Her headiness landed her in the lion's den. It was a stroke of luck, coupled with the good heart of Ella and most especially Francine, that saved her. Ella would not have been able to save her by herself. It was the quick thinking of Francine with her eagle eyes that made the rescue a success. Now at a safe house, she was too ashamed to involve her mother and stepfather. She was safe but already battered and emotionally broken. The scars had become a reminder of her horrors. The torment she went through in one year and the sadomasochistic experience she went through would forever leave an indelible mark on her. The residents at Carol's Ariel's Turnaround Center had stories of horror and unbelievable experiences in the hands of people they loved and trusted, horrible stories not only between lovers, married couples, parents to children, stepfathers to stepchildren, neighbors to neighbors, pedophiles, sex offenders, and stalkers. Over time, they developed mood disorders, such as anxiety disorders, manic depression, PTSD (post-traumatic stress disorder), SAD (seasonal affective disorder), ADHD (attention-deficit/hyperactivity disorder), eating disorders, bipolar disorder, schizophrenia, dissociative disorders, other psychosis, and more. The therapists encouraged them to share their experiences during group counseling sessions, verbalize, and begin the process of recovery and healing. Stories of individual life experiences were shared to help in the desired healing process. The experiences were barbaric, violent, and tingling to the ears. Erin, a mother of three boys, shared near-death experiences.

Erin met her husband when they were in their junior year at the university. He was a product of a broken home. His father was a construction site worker, a diligent worker who got tired and worn out at the end of every day. Despite his low income, his family was his number one priority. He would bring his paycheck home and handed it to his wife. His work lagged because of his constant tiredness due to the hard nature of his job. He feared losing his job and noticed that the other workers were active all day and never tired. At the end of work one day, he was in the company of a coworker who introduced him to drugs. It would keep him active all day, he explained to him. It was his first time seeing or doing drugs. His life changed and never remained the same after that encounter. When he got home that day, his wife noticed that something was amiss. She noticed a change in his behavior. He had a weird look, an unusual odor. She asked him, but he lied about it.

He had never smoked in his life; his wife was confused with the smell of the marijuana, the gateway drug he had tried. His situation catapulted into a spiral downward trend from that day. The following day, he worked hard and was not tired. He was happy. The site engineer noticed, was happy at his performance, and soon gave him a raise. The raise went into the purchase of more drugs. He gradually became involved in different drugs. His wife noticed minor changes that soon became major. He would return home late, drunk, and high. He enjoyed the company of his new friends than the usual loving company of his wife and children. His salary went to drugs and almost nothing for the upkeep of the home. He went to work daily but no money to show for it. He returned home under the influence daily. His good-natured behavior had changed for the worse. He became a beast, got irritated, and angry at the slightest provocation. The abuse started with his wife, verbally and subsequently physically. It soon extended to his children. He would beat them to a stupor. He once beat his wife until she went into a coma. She was admitted to the hospital for one week and almost lost her life. Her parents insisted she move back home with her children and asked her to file for a divorce. She eventually did. Life became unbearable for the wife. She left with her three boys who were all under the age of six. Her ex-husband abandoned them, became a deadbeat dad, and did not support her financially. She was at her parents' place when she learned that her ex-husband had died from a drug overdose. A few years later, she met another guy and remarried. The man during their courtship loved her children. He had no children of his own and seemed a good stepfather for her children. He took them out to the movies, Disney World, ice-cream parlors, ate out, and showered them with gifts. Her parents were happy for her and the children; unfortunately, his attitude changed the moment she said "I do."

He intentionally got a job out of the state they lived in, made his wife leave the children with her parents, and moved away. He did not want any child disturbing their love and freedom, and she agreed. She visited frequently alone after they moved away. The visits reduced and permanently died down. The grandparents became their legal guardians and took good care of them, but unfortunately, they died in succession within two years. She came for the burials, left them in the care of relatives, and returned with her new husband. The lives of the three boys took a drastic turn. They went from one relative to the other, bounced back and forth, and were abused both physically and emotionally. They ended up in different foster homes.

What Erin's husband went through in life toughened and scarred him emotionally for life. He lost contact with his siblings. The whereabouts of his two brothers were unknown. He was lucky to have stayed with a foster parent who saw his brilliance and supported him. He was offered a scholarship for his university education to study engineering and worked two jobs to support his room and board. It was not easy, but he managed. All relatives he knew died one after the other, was no longer in touch with any of his siblings, and tried to search for his mother without success. He wondered why a mother would abandon her children. The thought of it angered him, and he would displace the anger on anyone around him. He acted out and had a few altercations with friends, classmates, and roommates at the university. He got counseling for his behavior by the school authorities but was lucky that his actions did not involve law enforcement. When they met, he was loving and nice. He cared so much for her but displayed anger bouts intermittently. She saw nothing wrong with it especially when he told her of what he had gone through growing up. He would apologize afterward, and they would move on. She advised him to seek counseling, but he refused, brushed it aside, and told her he was fine. He believed that counseling was a waste of his precious time because the ones he did while in the university did not work for him.

They loved attending parties. It was the first year of freedom for both, but every party ended in a quarrel or fight. All the fun would turn to hurt for Erin. He had no friends, and Erin must avoid her friends too. He was possessive, never allowed her to dance with anyone except him, or be complimented by another person at a party. He would hit and kick her whenever his jealous bouts kicked in. She loved and allowed sympathy for him to overshadow her. She would beg and promise to stay clear of other people, then the beatings started. She blamed herself for causing the beatings. He was never at fault. The abuse went on for four years in the university, and despite the abuse, she married him after graduation. They were gainfully employed and welcomed a set of twins within the first year. The pregnancy was turbulent. He still laced it with occasional beatings. Her blood pressure shot up. It was a high-risk pregnancy and was delivered by caesarian section.

Not long after her discharge, she got the worst beating of her life because the middle name of one of the twins coincided with the name of a relative he hated very much. She was not privy that the relative abused him when he was young. He never raised an objection when the names were listed for the birth certificates. She bled so much from the stitches that she had to be readmitted and restitched. She refused to press charges or disclose what happened to doctors. She endured all the abuse with the belief that he would change. She believed he would not survive or cope with life if she divorced or turn him to law enforcement. He was damaged by his family. She must not add to the damage. She analyzed and reasoned that what he went through in his formative years was his reason for acting up. She believed what he needed was love and kindness. She would shower him with love, care, and kindness, and the combination would change his behavior for good. He simmered down for two years, and she got pregnant again and had another child. The innate behavior reared its ugly head again, this time for the worst. He never abused drugs or drank alcohol; his problem was anger, rage, and domestic violence. He would hit the wall, break the television, throw things, and hit her and the children for no reason. He was out of control when angry. It was as if the arrival of a child snapped anger, and hate embedded in him to the forth.

When the new addition to the family arrived, he insisted she resigned from her job. The dutiful wife that she thought she was, she obliged. He wanted her to stay at home and raise the children. He began to find faults with whatever she did. It was either an unclean house, plates in the sink, dinner too late, or even nothing and hell would let loose. One slap would lead to another. He would hit her head on the wall, turn her into a football, kick, and stomp on her. The children would run into the room anytime he arrived. They became reclusive. It was as if he was reenacting what he went through and wanted everyone to have a taste of it. Perhaps mirroring the way he felt growing up through them gave him closure and relief. To make matters worse, he began rationing money. He would give her what he knew would never be enough. He sold Erin's car with the excuse that they needed to cut down cost. Erin had to take the bus with three children.

They had a joint account and bought a house together when Erin was employed. Immediately after Erin resigned, he became the sole operator of the joint account, handled all the bills and mortgage, and kept all debit and credit cards with him. She dared not complain. The only time she summoned the courage to complain, he locked her up in the house all day and took the key and her phone with him to work so she would not call for help. Luckily, her friend in the neighborhood came around. Erin, through the window, narrated her latest ordeal. She advised her to seek help immediately before he killed her. Erin begged her to keep the information confidential. The last straw was the day he choked her, and she passed out. He revived her, gave her a thorough beating afterward in the presence of their children, he believed she pretended and was unaware of the gravity of the situation. When she was fully revived and conscious, she realized she just cheated death; the experience scared her and made her rethink what her life was worth.

She was happy when her friend and confidant called and told her about the new safe abode called Ariel's Turnaround Center. It was a safe abode for domestic violence victims on one side and treatment center for drug abuse on the other side. Her friend was always scared that Erin's husband would one day beat her to death. She had encouraged her to seek help for him or turn him over to the police. Erin had blatantly refused. Erin called the center and asked if she could come with her children. When the receptionist told her yes, she picked up her vital documents, personal effects, and ran to safety with her children. Every time Erin advised her husband to seek counseling, attend anger management classes, or get help for his mood disorders, it ended in a thorough beating. He took away the fun and bliss of marriage. She saw all the signs of domestic violence and dissociative mood disorder but was not willing to give up on him.

She loved him deeply, almost to a fault. What she had for him was a mixture of love and pity. Pity does not grow marriage. Helping him overcome his troubles was paramount in her heart but not worth losing her life for. She was happy she came out alive with the help of Ariel's center. Information about residents at the center was confidential, and the center notified law enforcement in case a missing person's report was filed with the department. Erin's situation was properly documented. Pictures of the scars and bruises on her body and the children's bodies were taken. She was checked by a doctor who wrote a report on her state of health and that of the children. Her gum was swollen. Her story and experiences were really touching. There was no dry eye in the group when she finished. Everyone cried. She told them what she shared was a tip of the ice bag of what they went through. The therapist asked members of the group to identify the signs of domestic violence from what Erin shared. Signs of domestic violence were glaring but often ignored out of misinformation, plain ignorance, or infatuation. Love does not hurt or hate. Anything capable of turning love and fun to hurt is a wet covering that must be totally avoided.

Erin had a degree in finance and worked at the bank for six years before her husband asked her to resign and stay at home. The facility's attorney wanted to file domestic violence charges against Erin's husband who frantically searched for Erin and his children; he had filed a missing person's report with the police. The lawyer contacted Erin to sign the appropriate paperwork to serve her husband, but she refused. The attorney reported to the facility. A meeting of the mind was set up at Erin's request, and the therapist, attorney, and other clinical staff were present at the meeting. Erin told the attendees that she believed her husband needed help, not incarceration. He needed help as soon as possible. His outbursts and animalistic behavior were a cry for help. She was willing to reform him, not sue or turn him over to the judicial system. Anger management, medications, and counseling for his PTSD would help him. She was not willing to make his situation worse by locking him up or making him lose his source of livelihood.

He had gone through so much in life, abandoned by his birth mother, lost contact with his mother and his siblings, passed from one relative to the other, abused both physically and emotionally, changed foster homes until he was able to settle with one, went to college with a dint of hard work, a loner almost all his life. He should not be subjected to more traumas. His PTSD had never been treated either with counseling or medications. If she divorced or sued him, he might die of a broken heart, commit suicide, or self-harm. He could become her "ex-husband" but would never become an "ex-father." She wanted him rehabilitated so he could be in the lives of his children. She would not want her children to grow up without a father figure in their lives or behave the way he behaved. She would be unhappy if her children became batterers of their wives. His experiences were the script he had been acting. If he was helped, they would have helped her children and generations to come, help them through the traumas they had seen and the abuses they had witnessed and experienced. His change and rehab would bring healing not only to her husband but to her and the children. She enjoined them to treat her husband's situation as an isolated and not a generalized case. Every situation would never be the same. She admonished Ariel's TC to support her to help her husband.

The therapist responded to Erin's submission. She reiterated that domestic violence was a serious criminal offense punishable under the law. The priority of the facility was the safety of the victim(s). The history documented during her admission to the facility pointed in no small measure to serious violations of her person and the children. The red flags were too many and obvious. He constantly put her down, was excessively jealous, battered, controlled all the finances, restricted her movement and association with others, hurt the children severally, had very low tolerance level, had anger issues, and almost killed her recently. She explained to her that it was normal when victims refuse to turn their abusers over for prosecution, but his behavioral traits and abusive tendencies needed to be curtailed. He should not be allowed to go free.

The attorney explained the law to her and told her it was not the intention of the law to separate couples or punish individuals arbitrarily, but the government had the right to save victims and punish offenders. Erin allowed all of them to share their thoughts, thanked them immensely for all their efforts, and expressed that she appreciated their support, care, and love but appealed to them once again amid tears that her husband needed immediate help. All those at the meeting were short of words. They promised to see what they could do to support her wishes while at the same time upholding the law. Erin was instructed to desist from any form of communication with her husband and anyone that could tell him her whereabouts. The twins had been transferred from the regular public school and began homeschooling instead. It would keep their location confidential.

C H A P T E R 1 0

Rude Shock

Gina had been in jail for a long time. The judge had refused her bail many times and kept her behind bars. She had not seen her mother since her arrest and did not know why she had not visited her. Benjamin had not visited her in over one year. He stopped visiting because Gina refused to see him on previous visits. Benjamin vowed to leave her in jail for as long as the judge wanted. Madeline's health had improved positively, but the relationship between the once lovebirds had turned sour. They hardly speak to one another. Her improved health status made her visit Gina at the jail. It was a big mistake. She believed that her daughter would be happy to see her but got the shock of her life. Gina saw her frail body, her visible health status with a walker that aided her movement. She did not ask why she was using a walker and told her in strict terms her visit was not appreciated. She vomited a lot of unprintable profanity and curse words on her mother in the presence of the inmates and officers. Madeline left in tears. She had quarreled with her husband for not visiting Gina more often, that he had not done enough to secure a bail for her daughter.

She had gotten a taste of what Benjamin had experienced severally. Every time Benjamin visited Gina, he returned upset, sad, and agitated. Madeline and Benjamin had a big argument that day in their living room. She vowed never to forgive her husband for being lackadaisical toward their only daughter. Benjamin was so upset and blurted out that he doubted if Gina belonged to him. He gave several instances that supported his doubts and buttressed his fears. Madeline was dazed. She could not believe what Benjamin had accused her of. Benjamin went further to tell Madeline that he would request a DNA to clear his doubts. Madeline, out of annoyance, told him to go ahead and threatened to file for a divorce the following day. Her threat made matters worse and more complex. Benjamin made good his threat. He took Gina's toothbrush and ordered a DNA. Madeline likewise contacted her lawyer to initiate a divorce against her husband. Both were adamant on their threats and pursued them vigorously. To make matters worse, Gina was 99.99 percent not related to Benjamin. He was infuriated. His loving wife had deceived him for over two decades. He had been raising someone else's child. A child that had caused him so much hurt, shame, and disgrace. He does not mind an adoption if they both agreed. Pinning another man's child on him was the last thing he expected from Madeline. They were sweethearts for years before they got married.

This development would turn into a big sensation with the media who had been on their prowl since Gina's case debut. Their personalities would become destroyed beyond redemption. Benjamin went straight to his office after he received the DNA report, locked himself up, and told the receptionist to cancel all his appointments for the rest of the day. He stayed in his office till almost midnight and wanted to be sure that he was emotionally stable and ready to accost his wife. If he had gone home immediately after he received the report, he would have aggressively accuse her, might hit, or do something he would later regret. At his office, he wanted his anger to subside before getting home. He had time to ruminate and ponder over many things, his life, marriage, career, Gina, Gina's troubles, financial losses, lost employees, and above all, the DNA report. He decided that he would redo the DNA test with another laboratory. There could be a mix-up somewhere. He decided not to ask Madeline about the result until he had done another test. When he got home, Madeline was already in bed, which was unusual of her. She would normally wait for Benjamin to return home no matter how late. Benjamin did not go into the master bedroom. He slept on the sofa in the family room.

The "good morning" Benjamin received from Madeline was a divorce document. She made good her threat. Benjamin collected the document from her without uttering a word. He went into his study, threw the document into his briefcase, picked up his car keys, and left the house. He was boiling inside with rage. He tried not to show it. When he got to the office, he called another laboratory to schedule another DNA. A divorce between them would be very messy and costly. The properties, investments, and wealth they acquired over the years would be a problem to share, thanks to Gina who had squandered a chunk of their resources. With his wife jobless and indisposed, he would lose his mansion to her. Whatever the case, his peace of mind was priceless. He needed a new DNA to show that his wife had been dishonest, untruthful, and unfaithful for more than two decades. He regretted his love and trust and wondered if his wife committed adultery all through the period of their union—maybe and maybe not.

The audacity that she brought another man's child into their marriage and refused to bore him a child tore his heart apart. He had begged her on several occasions for more children after Gina. She refused. He asked for adoption. She refused. He had trusted and loved his wife with all his heart. He had never cheated on her despite several love passes from women. He never acknowledged them. He had been truthful and faithful to his wife. Madeline called to ask if he had signed the papers. He told her no. He would go through and pass it to his lawyer. Madeline became angry. Benjamin advised her to remember her doctor's advice. He was not interested in nursing her again. He had more problems to contend with.

Madeline had ample time on her hand. She was at home full-time, and her mind was running wild. The devil finds work for the idle mind. Her mind had become the devil's workshop. Different ideas besieged her mind, good and bad. She took early retirement from her job because of her ill health. All she did was cause trouble and torment Benjamin. Madeline did not want a divorce. She wanted to scare Benjamin and make him beg. Their relationship had gone sour, but she knew Benjamin loved her very much, would appeal to her, and everything would gradually return to normal. Peace had eluded them. Peace in their household had turned to pieces. Peace of mind is far better than money or wealth. Without peace, happiness would evaporate, and the ability to make wealth would dissipate. Benjamin got a call from the diagnostic center that his test was ready for pick up. To his amazement a second time, Gina was 99.99 percent, not his daughter. Two tests from two reputable centers had confirmed the negative paternity of Gina, armed with the results. He was ready to ask Madeline about Gina's paternity.

Madeline was a revered pastor's child; her father was the senior pastor at the only church in the small city where they grew up. He was pious, highly respected, devotedly religious, and virtue personified. A man of integrity who preached the undiluted Word of God and was personable. His parishioners loved him. Her mother was supportive of her husband's work in the vineyard of the Lord. She was the women's leader and a Sunday school teacher and was religious, simple, and forthright. Benjamin attended service with his parents and siblings at the church regularly. The pastor and his wife loved them. The pastor and his family supported them when they moved to the city and joined the church as new congregants. Benjamin and Madeline became friends, inseparable since then. They studied together. Benjamin was brilliant and smart. He coached Madeline on subjects where she needed help. Their platonic relationship turned into a romantic one when they were in the university.

Madeline got a juicy job as soon as she graduated while Benjamin had his scholarship extended to law school, while Madeline also assisted him financially since she already had a job. When Benjamin graduated, they got married. Benjamin got linked up to his rich clients by both his rich benefactor, and Madeline who already knew some big connections through her job, his brilliance got him more clients; wealth smiled on them in a big way. Benjamin trusted her because of her upbringing, a child raised in a Christian home, a church girl with all the trappings of gentle disposition worthy of emulation. Madeline and her siblings were well mannered, disciplined, well behaved in the community. The qualities endeared Benjamin to Madeline from the time they were just friends growing up. He pondered over the results for long. What would he do? How would he ask her about it? What would her response be? Would she deny and defend herself?

What excuses, mechanisms, or defense would she put on? He was angry and sorry for himself. Where would he start from?

At almost fifty, he had no child of his own. His only daughter was make believe. When he got home, his wife was waiting in the family room. She accused him of not signing the papers on time. Benjamin ignored her, opened his briefcase, threw the two reports at her, and demanded an explanation. She walked past the two envelopes and demanded that he sign her divorce papers, She believed Benjamin had not signed them because he loved her. He would soon apologize and ask to make up with her. She was mistaken this time. A rude shock awaited her. Benjamin picked up the two envelopes, followed her to the bedroom, and asked her about the paternity of Gina.

Madeline's face lit up in great anger.

"What question was that?" she screamed. "Are you asking me about the paternity of our only daughter? Are you out of your mind? Over two decades? Is this an excuse not to sign the divorce papers? A ploy to waste time? Get out of my face!" she thundered.

Benjamin smirked, raised his voice as if it could bring down the roof, and requested an immediate, straightforward answer. Madeline was confused. She could not believe her ears. She insisted that the test result was a mistake. The test would be done all over. She would pay for a new test if needed. She then turned the table against Benjamin and accused him of embarking on a DNA test without informing her or Gina. He had no right to pull such a stunt on them. She would call her lawyer and sue him for all he's worth. Benjamin stood his ground and demanded an explanation. Madeline's first defense was denial. She refused to answer the question and subtly denied. She digressed from it by answering the question with another question. She then rationalized why her husband would even have the audacity and gut to insinuate that Gina was not his, even raise his voice at her.

Benjamin was dazed. How could she despite two results backed by science still lie to him? Her defenses were weak. She rambled and asked stupid questions. She had a lot of explanations to do. Benjamin was not ready to back down. He told his wife to sleep over the situation. He needed an explanation in the morning. She should think it through and come clean. He was angry but was not ready to aggravate her because of her health. He picked a pillow and returned downstairs to sleep on the sofa. Madeline, in anger, blurted insults at Benjamin as he went down the stairs. It was very unusual of her to use curse words, but their relationship had degenerated so fast. Madeline became scared and sat on the side of her bed, deep in thought. Why would her husband do a paternity test on Gina? Was it because she gave him a divorce paper (which she never meant)? She was never a wayward girl. She made an honest mistake that she had processed into the deep sea of forgetfulness a long time ago. She sent it to her long-term memory system, never to be recalled. She knew she was safe when it happened. It was a major mistake that she wished never occurred. This could be her total downfall; she might not survive this, she thought. On the few occasions when she remembered it, she had repressed the thought. They had insomnia that night. Benjamin tossed and tossed on the sofa while Madeline sat on her bed all night. The following morning, Benjamin looked tired from sleeplessness. Undeterred, he went to Madeline and questioned her on Gina's paternity. Madeline started crying, professed her love for Benjamin, that the divorce papers were a ploy to scare him in the bid to rekindle the real love they shared. She begged Benjamin to forgive her and would withdraw the papers. Benjamin listened. She paused. Benjamin waited.

She was not forthcoming. Benjamin became infuriated and asked about Gina's paternity again. He needed an answer. Madeline refused to talk, played dumb, looked at Benjamin, and refuted the result. Benjamin got angrier, insisted on an answer, took out the results from the envelopes, and read both out to her hearing since she had refused to read them. Madeline started crying again and begged Benjamin to allow her to perform the test at another diagnostic center. He agreed to her wish to fulfill all righteousness.

Gina had her day in court. The owner of the gun had been arrested. Luckily, he confessed to all the killings and exonerated Gina. Despite his arrest, she was still not off the hook. She had more charges pending but was lucky that the murder charge that could have sent her to many years of imprisonment had been taken off her docket. The charges were many but were minor compared to the murder charge. Gina's case moved swiftly after the arrest of the gun owner. She was in jail for so long because there was no evidence to show she was not a murderer. She thanked her stars that he confessed to all the killings. Her case lasted a week. Five years in prison without the possibility of parole was her sentence with credit for time served. She would be eligible for release in about two years, with six months' probation thereafter. For all the counts, she got five years each. The sentences would run concurrently. Gina was extremely mad at the verdict. Why would the only daughter of the most celebrated attorney in town be sent to prison! She saw no reason why she had to go to prison. She had high-caliber parents who had failed her. The revenge she planned for her parents would wait. They must pay, pay dearly with their lives. She would deal mercilessly with them her own way.

Her parents were not in court. They heard the news on television just like the whole of the community. The attorneys from her father's law firm refused to answer questions from reporters, and Benjamin was happy that they did not respond to any news media. Gina was not remorseful when led away. She pulled her tongue out at the judge and lawyers. It was disgraceful for Benjamin and Madeline who had their own fire burning on the mountain. Gina's situation changed from waiting in jail for a hearing to a prisoner. She was moved to another facility to serve her term. When she arrived at the facility, she met hardened criminals that scared her. She was a little kitten in the midst of lions. She got a taste of her medicine from the criminals. She was a superstar at the previous facility and quickly realized that she was a small fish in a big ocean. When she tried to assert authority, she was seriously rebuffed, for the first time in her life, she was scared.

*****

Carol being personable and friendly had her clients actively interested in a relationship with her. She was wary of people. Her experiences in the past made her skeptical of having a lover. She only needed platonic relationships. She refused to give her personal phone number to anyone and directed them to call her through the store phone number. Friends are good, but care should be taken. Everyone should have inner circle friends, minimum of two, maximum of three. Her inner circle friends are her mother and Ella, nothing more, nothing less. Friendship with more than two or three is already a group. To enjoy friends, keep the number few. A lot of friends would eventually constitute a problem. Do not to expand your circle of friends. Study your friends. Sift the chaff from the grain. Not all friends are friends. Some are after your secrets. Challenges in life are the best test for friends. It would show you who your true friends are. When you identify true friends, keep them, appreciate them, and guard them jealously. "So-called" friends are around you because they need something. The moment they get it, they would fizzle out like smoke. The next time you see them would be when they need another favor.

Amelia's experience during and after her illness was enough example of friendship, not to talk of the negative issues Ella incurred because of mingling with wrong friends. When Carol returned from prison, she returned with a "cap" of high sense and native intelligence. She was a very smart girl who derailed. Incidentally, her smartness cannot be taken away. It is inbuilt. She made bad choices before because of her vulnerability. She had learned her lesson and would not blame anyone or hold anyone accountable for her mistakes. She was a hundred percent responsible for her mistakes. She made the mistake and paid for the mistakes. She vowed to assist others to avoid her destructive past and mistakes.

*****

Most of Elizabeth's bruises, black eye, and marks were almost gone. They left scars as a reminder of her days in hell. She had followed the doctor's instructions to the letter, took her medications for her mental health diagnosis with great zeal, and got better. The staff at the facility took her to the dentist for a denture to replace her chipped tooth. She would return to the dentist in one week. Ella gave Elizabeth as much support as she could. She was a busy student with her own issues. As a recovering addict, she feared being overstressed to avoid a relapse. Ella was happy to support her but not to her own detriment. She took Elizabeth to the Department of Motor Vehicle to get a replacement for her driver's license. Elizabeth attended individual sessions with the therapist but had refused to join the group sessions because of classism, innate tendency, pride, and shame. The therapist counseled her against the notion, but she was yet to budge.

Carol visited the facility as she used to do every Monday. She visited weekly to have lunch with the residents. After lunch, she visited Elizabeth in her room to know how she was fearing. Elizabeth was happy to see her. She respected Carol because she was Ella's mother besides being the owner of the facility. Carol encouraged her to feel safe amid other residents in the facility. Carol deduced from their conversation that Elizabeth felt the others were beneath her due to her status. She advised her against classism. It is a destroyer. Classism had destroyed the lives of many people and hindered them from reaching their full potential. It is discrimination. No social class lasts forever. We are all born equal and need one another. There was no reason for her to feel superior or inferior to others. Looking down on people is pride, plain and simple. Destruction is the resultant result of pride. She admonished Elizabeth with the detail of her life story. Why she decided to use her wealth for humanitarian purposes, the discussion sank deep into Elizabeth's heart, whether she would change would be her decision.

*****

Francine's grandmother had another health scare. This time, she tripped and broke her ankle. When Francine heard, she dashed home with the next available flight. She was happy to see Francine. They talked all night the day she arrived. Francine slept on the sofa in Grandma's room and supported her back and forth to the bathroom. The two days Francine spent at home were her best days. Francine informed Ella of her arrival; they scheduled a visit to the facility to see

Elizabeth. She was happy to see them and had fun. Francine encouraged Elizabeth to follow through with her counseling sessions, medications, and determination to succeed. She had been clean since she got to the facility. Her therapist took a liken to her, strict with her drug screenings, and tested her three times a week. The facility allowed her to stay in the domestic abuse area but allowed her to join those in the rehabilitation section for group sessions also. She was on the right track though young and fragile in her recovery process.

Francine promised that she would call her often to check on her. Elizabeth pondered on why Francine was so nice and interested in her welfare and wished she had been friends with her instead of Gina. Francine was instrumental to the changes in Ella. If Ella could change her life for good, she would do it too. They went to the mall, then to a nice but inexpensive restaurant. The food was tasty. Elizabeth did not believe what they paid at the end of their meals. Such a meal would have cost them a fortune at one of the high-end restaurants. She posited on when she was living an unnecessarily expensive lifestyle on the bill of her parent. At her age, she should be in school or working on making her own money. She must learn to imbibe hard work, prudence, and independence. Francine talked about living a quality life within personal means. Elizabeth was amazed. She looked at Francine in awe throughout. When they returned to the facility, they sat in the lobby. Francine subtly introduced the issue of Elizabeth's mother and stepfather. She made sure the situation was appropriate. She studied Elizabeth's mood and composure all day and saw glaringly that she was subdued and ready for change.

What she had gone through had taught her an unforgettable lesson. Elizabeth heaved a big sigh and looked down. Hot tears dripped from her eyes. Francine was caught off-balance. She wrapped her right hand around her neck while Ella wrapped her left hand around her. Francine and Ella hugged her tight. She started to sob loudly. They pacified her. She eventually calmed down. Francine was the first to speak. She spoke about the importance of family, most especially the role of a mother, where possible a father or stepfather. She encouraged her to make amends with her mother. She admonished her that a person can choose anything in this world but not a mother. A mother is God's design. Her mother would forever be her mother, and Bethena loved her dearly. She needed to think of her future. Where she would move to when discharged from the facility? Even if released to an apartment, how would she pay for it? Living at the facility would not be forever. Ella shared the worry and stress that was visible on Bethena the last time she saw her. She buttressed it with the need to do the right thing, to right the wrongs and deviate from the destructive paths they embarked on before now. Elizabeth was depressed after Francine and Ella left the facility. She pondered over the discussion for a while, took her medications, and went straight to bed. She tossed and thought of her issues. Thank God for the medications she took. One of them was a sedative. It knocked her off within an hour. She probably would have laid in bed all night without any sleep.

*****

Francine's grandma felt better with her around. It was as if she was the medication she had been waiting for, and her spirit was livelier throughout the weekend she visited and joked that she might have to trip and break the other ankle so Francine would come home often. Grandma looked depressed when Francine picked up her luggage to leave for the airport. She held her tight and hugged her for a long time. Francisca and Francis sat in the car waiting for Grandma to release her firm hold and told her she would be back soon. Francine called before she boarded her flight and advised her to be careful around the house and avoid trips and falls. A fall for an elderly person could render them wheel-bound, if not dead, and the recovery process would take a long time. Grandma was happy to hear her voice again and wished her journey mercies.

Francine also called Elizabeth and encouraged her to make amends with her mother and stepfather. She must (not should) work on her self-esteem and rehabilitation. It was not a matter of should but a matter of must. Addiction and mental health disorders are two diagnoses that should not be treated with kids' gloves. They are fatal diseases but treatable. She needed all the determination and dedication she could muster to achieve sobriety and stability. It is an uphill task, but with patience and support from family, friends, loved ones, and professionals in the fields, she would attain her desired change. She promised to call her often. Elizabeth thanked her for the support and concern and promised to work diligently on doing the right thing. She mentioned that she would not want to end up like Gina. She heard about Gina's sentence on the news. It was the first time Gina's name came up since Elizabeth's rescue. Francine pretended not to hear what she said. She was not interested in glorifying the misfortune of others, hated gossip, and discussion of individuals was not her concern. Francine refused to be sucked into the world of backbiting and bitterness that Elizabeth loved. She ignored the statements and moved to the issue of Elizabeth's recovery. People with low self-esteem, jealousy, envy, and bitterness are those who indulge in gossip, bickering, and backbiting.

Elizabeth was torn on the issue of making amends with her mother. As for recovery, she had decided to make a spirited run for it and embrace it like Ella. The thought of Ella as a totally changed person became an inspiration to her. She used to be her partner in crime and drug abuse, and she looked healthier, sober, beautiful, focused, homely, and in the university. Ella's relationship with her mother was another major source of envy for her but in a healthy way. She looked every inch happy and glowed flawlessly. She talked about her mother and grandmother with so much love that made her skin raise with goose bumps. Elizabeth was too ashamed to call her mother or Jason. The thought depressed her. What would she say when Bethena picked up the phone? She was not aware of where they lived presently. Her phone number was one of the numbers she knew off-head, but she had no phone. Ralph took her phone and destroyed it in her presence. It was his ploy to sever her relationship with her contacts.

Ella came to see her at the facility. She encouraged her again on the issue of Bethena, that the support of loved ones is a key characteristic in the journey of sobriety. Her ability to effectively ace her addiction was because of the support she got from people. The motivation was necessary and vital. Her mother would be very handy to her in her journey to sobriety, especially in alleviating the pain of the trauma she had gone through. Ella knew Elizabeth would be nervous and struggle with the issue. She would continue to support and counsel her on the right path. When Ella got to Elizabeth's room, she met her sobbing and asked why she was sobbing. She reported that she missed her mom but could not bring herself to call her. Ella agreed she would call her and explain the situation but not in detail. Elizabeth would do the details herself. Elizabeth agreed, and Ella left for school. Elizabeth changed her mind again, called Ella, and told her not to call her mother. She would do so at her convenience. Elizabeth believed that her mother was responsible for what she had gone through in life and felt they had a toxic mother/daughter relationship and was not willing to forgive her or make amends at the moment. She had not gotten to the stage of accepting full responsibility for her actions. Her recovery would likely be impeded if she got in touch with her mother. Acceptance of her problems and readiness for a change was still hung on others.

*****

Erin had not called her husband. She followed the facility's instructions to keep herself and her children safe in hiding. She attended the daily group therapy session and met with the therapist for individual sessions. Erin believed her husband loved her and the children deeply but needed help for his PTSD, alcohol, and anger outbursts. Her husband, according to her friend, had become frustrated and depressed. She knew where Erin and the children were but did not tell him. Erin met with the lawyer again and agreed to sign the paperwork on the condition that her husband would only receive court-ordered anger management classes and help for his PTSD. He was a good husband and father. She would be a fulfilled woman to know that he got the well-deserved help needed to bring his senses back to normal. Erin was happy to know that her husband had begun anger management classes and had been on medication for his PTSD.

Elizabeth joined the group therapy session for the first time. In attendance were Erin, Kelly, and others. The therapist opened the session with the importance of the topic "self-worth". She asked each person to explain what self-worth meant. They all discussed self-respect, self-confidence, self-value, self-esteem, and self-understanding. She explained that all the above meant the same thing: respect, esteem, confidence, appreciation, and more. Self-worth is the internalized ability to appreciate oneself as good, worthy of love, and respect, in the same vein as others. We must love, appreciate, and respect ourselves. If we do not, others will trample on us and rob us of our worth. She then linked the word to the menace called domestic violence. Each of the residents shared how they gave their self-worth away and how they had paid dearly for it. Elizabeth was rooted to her seat when she heard the story of Veronica. She narrated how she got married to her second husband who was her boss at work. It started as an office fling that was not meant to result in a marriage. He was single while she was married and older. They enjoyed each other's company at work and would often seat together at the company's canteen. He loved to crack jokes, and Veronica would laugh and sometimes shed tears from excessive laughter. His jokes endeared Veronica to him. She loved to sit close to him to relieve the tension of her boring marriage.

Her husband was a quiet soul who loved her deeply but not a man of many words. They would be at home all day watching TV, maybe with a few sentences. He showed love through gifts, flowers, letters, and cards. He was very good with poetry, would write poems, stick them to her bedside, and watch her read them first thing in the morning. Veronica wanted him to express his love through effective verbal communication instead of writing. He would buy Veronica anything she wanted. All she needed to do was just ask, or even soliloquized. She would get the item/items almost immediately. Veronica knew he was a man of few words, very stingy with words, but believed he would change when they marry.

He hated being in the company of people, grew up a loner, and stayed a loner.

He moved away from his parents to seek greener pastures and independence. He had a good relationship with his parents, but his lone nature did not change. When he met Veronica, it was love at first sight. They fell in love deeply. Veronica was an extrovert while he was seriously introverted, but it did not deter them. He never bothered him when she chatted happily with others. Veronica loved wholesome fun, laughter, and spice. She was fascinated by her boss's jokes. His jokes had subtle insults and inappropriate comments that were overlooked because of "laughter." He would crack jokes with utter disrespect for other people's views, personalities, problems, and privacy. His jokes pointed at domestic violence, but Veronica was too fascinated with his comedy, never noticed, never bothered.

One thing led to another; they became lovers. The office romance soon became public. The establishment was against romantic relationships between employees, and both resigned instead of termination but continued the relationship. Veronica got another job sooner than the guy. She supported him financially without the knowledge of her husband and continued the relationship. He got frustrated, jobless, and always infuriated with the littlest of things. Veronica would calm him down and eventually got a job close to her new job. Veronica's husband realized she was cheating on him. The late nights and change in attitude gave her away. When he asked her, she told him the truth, apologized, and promised to stop the cheating. He filed for a divorce immediately. Veronica was undeterred, moved in with her lover, enjoyed the fun, and independence. She no longer rushed home to her husband. They had all the time to themselves. They clubbed, traveled, and on a sweet sunny day got married at a drive-through in Las Vegas while on a vacation to the Sin City.

Veronica had a job that paid more; she took care of the bills unlike when she was with her ex. Her new husband was never forthcoming with his money. Veronica wondered why she always had to pay all the bills. They both worked full-time jobs, and his pay was good too. The first time she asked, she got the beating of her life. It was less than six months into their marriage. She could not believe what hit her, a rude shock. She was ashamed to speak out even to her friends and family. They warned her about her cheating and remarriage, but she turned deaf ears. Her father told her she was leaving certainty for uncertainty. She bluffed him and told him she was an adult and knew what was best for her. She blurted that the marriage to her ex was a mistake. He was a bore who knew nothing about enjoyment. Life should be synonymous with enjoyment and not endured or managed. Her new marriage would give her fun to the fullest. She shut down all the advice one after the other.

The next few months were horrible. There was no week without a good beating. It was like she was in a dream world. He was no longer the amiable person she married. He became a new beast and blamed herself for turning him into a beast. She must have done something to trigger the beatings. She would refrain from what caused the previous beating, but her new technique would attract beatings and severe punishments. He would put her on time-out as if she were his student for a whole weekend. Veronica cut off her relationship with friends and family at his order. She went to work and back to the house and must not branch anywhere. He controlled all the money. She was a signatory to the account, but she dared not touch the checkbook. He did the groceries and even bought her undies, changed their apartment, and moved to another part of the city to avoid the prying eyes of family and friends. He cut off all forms of communication and would joke with her predicaments when out with his friends who were as mean and evil as he was.

Veronica lost two pregnancies in the three years they were together; pregnancy was not on the agenda, he reminded her. It was by divine intervention that she met her ex-husband, and as soon as he saw her, he knew something was terribly wrong. It was a destined coincidence. He knew her more than she thought. Her husband made her stop by the roadside, ordered her to alight from the driver's seat, took over, and zoomed off, leaving her stranded. It happened because she asked a question that infuriated him. She was in shock, and passerby looked at her in amazement. She was ashamed but tried to fake her composure. Her ex-husband was in traffic across the road, saw what happened, and realized it was Veronica. He made a U-turn. She wished for the ground to open and swallow her out of shame. He drove her to a parking lot and asked her what the problem was. She could not hide anymore. She opened up on her challenges and trials since the divorce and marriage to her new husband despite all warnings from family and friends.

They sobbed. He was more emotional than Veronica, blamed himself for the divorce, and should have given her a second chance. If he had, she probably wouldn't have gone through her ordeals. He took her to the police station and made her lodge a complaint of domestic violence against him. When the police saw the extent the of scars on her, they arrested him. The police escorted her to the apartment where she collected all her belongings, rented a storage, and quit her job due to shame, acute anxiety, and PTSD. The police told her about Ariel's Turnaround Center, and she became a resident at the facility. She showed her scars to the other residents with the permission of the therapist. The evidence and pictures from the hospital were too graphic to keep him in the public domain. It was wickedness in the highest order. The judge had no mercy on him. He was sentenced to twelve months in jail. Flabbergasted was an understatement for Elizabeth. She thought she knew about domestic violence. She never knew other people had worst experiences than hers. She was astonished but not too surprised. Her story had similar traits but would be for another day. The experiences touched each of them in diverse ways. No two experiences were the same, and the dynamics, severity, and stories varied. Violence in households is not peculiar to only the female gender. Men and children are also recipients of violence in the home. It was never an acceptable way to treat others. Love does not hurt.

C H A P T E R 1 1

Error

Madeline requested another test. The result was the same. Gina belonged to someone else! She knew it must be Kyle's. Kyle never missed any of the church programs and activities. He had a heart for God, but drugs were his undoing. Madeline's father loved him because of his great love for the things of God and counseled him on his addiction. Her father started the sobriety program in the church because of him. He was a functional drug user whose sobriety had always been an issue and had been to therapy and rehab but luckily had never been incarcerated or arrested. He had a full-time job, dressed decently, and always neat. A good portion of his money went to drugs and cigarettes. He was a chain-smoker, never married, had no children, and he was five years older than Madeline. His demeanor indicated he had a level of mental health issues, but when he spoke, it was difficult for anyone to ascertain his mental health status though some church members including her father believed he had mental and anger issues. He argued on trivial matters, and his understanding of the Bible was sometimes questionable and had an opposing view to biblical teaching and preaching. Many saw him as comical and dismissed him as a jester instead of an unstable person; however, he had his good side. He was very handy and good with his hands. He volunteered with the church's maintenance department, fixed anything that needed fixing, fixed them perfectly. He was an asset to the church. He helped many church members to get things fixed in their homes at no cost to them. He would sometimes buy the materials with his own money and would refuse reimbursement. He would joke that it was his own little way of showing God's love. His good heart and willingness to help at no cost endeared him to all.

Madeline had an encounter with Kyle two weeks before she wedded Benjamin. She visited home to discuss her impending wedding with her parents and siblings. It was that encounter that would turn her life and marriage into shreds years later. He liked Madeline and never hid the fact. Kyle occasionally shared his feelings for her, but she joked and brushed it aside. He was good-looking, no doubt, but Madeline was already in a committed relationship. Kyle knew Benjamin and his family. They attended the same church. Kyle disliked Benjamin because Madeline refused his advances, chose Benjamin instead of him, but he would occasionally summon the courage to tell Madeline his feelings and that he loved her dearly and love to spend the rest of his life with her. On this visit, she got home and found Kyle fixing the leaking faucet. He was alone in the house as the family treated him like a member of their household and had access to everywhere.

He could stay alone in the house without any family members around. The pastor's house was his second home. He was free with all of them including Madeline. He was happy to see Madeline. It was the first time he saw her since she moved away. They talked and shared ideas and experiences. He made so much sense and was logical in his discussion. He was articulate, a university graduate, but nobody knew any of his relatives. Madeline fixed a plate of food for herself and one for Kyle. They ate and settled to watch a movie together afterward. It was a romantic movie. They sat next to one other, one thing led to another, and the rest was history. She regretted it immediately, ashamed, felt violated, but he did not force her. It was consensual. They were both willing participants for the period it lasted. It was as if they were under a spell. Madeline was not a girl of easy virtue. She had a good upbringing. What happened was a big mistake. It happened impulsively. Mistakes happen in life. We sometimes do things we are not proud of. This one was a big one, a massive mistake! Unfortunately, the deed was too late. They were both ashamed of themselves. By Madeline's calculations, she was safe, not ovulating, reassured herself, and did the calculations over and over. Yes, she was safe. The secret would be a forever secret, never to be discussed. She miscalculated. She erred greatly. She married Benjamin two weeks later, moved on, and never entertained the thought again.

Madeline refused to show the report to Benjamin. She could not believe what just happened to her once-beautiful life, a life of envy with a name that opened doors, a life well sought after. She and her husband were the eyes of every event. She prayed fervently for the report to be different, to tell Benjamin "Didn't I say so?" but it was the same result. This was a shame. What would she tell her parents and siblings? They would never forgive her for dragging the name of the family in the mud. *Oh my goodness*! she thought. Her siblings had always said Gina was nothing like any member of the family. She had a behavior unbecoming of Benjamin and Madeline. She misbehaved at every family function, was rude, unhinged, spoke a thousand words in a minute, and totally out of order. All her cousins avoided her. None of them loved to be in her company. She lied every time and would never own up to her deeds.

Thanksgiving and Christmas celebrations were scary moments for the whole family. Gina would spoil everyone's fun, and when Madeline's senior sister and brother complained about her attitude, Gina cursed them out. Madeline and Benjamin were ashamed and gave excuses not to attend family gatherings afterward. Madeline's sister once saw Gina introducing her cousins to smoking. She cautioned her, and she cursed her out. The siblings stopped their children from associating with her. Grandpa and Grandma were not spared. They got a taste of her bad attitude. Whenever she visited, she would eat, refuse to clean up, always clumsy, would break, destroy items when angry, and never listened to instructions. Despite all, they loved her dearly. Gina tore Madeline's family apart. Her siblings, nieces, and nephews stopped visiting them. Gina would flaunt her parents' wealth and told them they were all beneath her and her parents. One of her sisters once told Madeline out of anger that she needed to take Gina to where she got her from. Madeline was angry with the statement and took offense at her audacity to talk ill of her daughter. She stopped talking to her sister and eventually stopped talking to all her family.

She withdrew the divorce paper from her lawyer. She begged Benjamin for a second chance, but he would not budge and stopped talking to her. He stayed away from home and had spent two nights away. She had scattered thoughts, scattered energy, could not sleep or sit still, and scared that Benjamin would leave or divorce her. She called Benjamin, but he refused to pick up her calls. At a point, his phone was switched off, which was very unlike him. She visited Gina, to tell her of the situation in the home, the DNA result, and probably a divorce from Benjamin. She did not want her to hear or read about it in the news in case Benjamin filed for a divorce, but Gina refused to meet with her. Gina had been transferred to another location that was five hours away. Her trip was a futile one. The journey to and from the penitentiary gave her the opportunity to think of the way forward. She needed to find Gina's father. She knew who he was, the only person besides Benjamin, the mistake of her lifetime. She had not seen him since her wedding. He was there as a solitary guest, though seen as a "family member." All the guests commented on his sad look and demeanor. Even her father joked about his sad disposition at the reception. Madeline made eye contact with Kyle at the wedding and quickly looked away. Madeline forgot about him since that day. She never for once remembered him. She had to fish him out and let him know he had a daughter called Gina when she returned home from her trip.

Benjamin had not shown up. He had been away for weeks. Benjamin eventually showed up, went inside the room, picked up a few belongings, and left again. He did not say a word to Madeline. She tried to block his way, begged, and appealed to him. He ignored her. She had no one to turn to. Benjamin had been her safety net all these years. Without him, she had no one else but her parents whom she had abandoned for many, many years. She desperately needed a shoulder to lean on and someone to talk to. She had crazy thoughts running wild in her head and thought of suicide but quickly ruled it out. Suicide was not a good escape route. Problems should be solved, not run away from. Her last option was to call her father who had retired from his pastoral work. He was surprised that she called. She seldom called them or her siblings. She needed someone to talk to, but when she heard his voice, she changed her mind. She did not know how to start her story and told him she called to say hello, talked to her mother briefly, and hung up. Madeline's health started taking the heat. She felt unwell. Her parents and siblings never knew she had two heart attacks and a stroke, that she was lucky to be alive, well, and still able to drive her car. She called her doctor to schedule an appointment. He made an immediate opening for her because of her recent health history. The moment he saw her, he knew there was an issue bothering her. He had been her private doctor for ages and knew her in and out, but the issue at hand was too big to divulge to anyone no matter how close the person was. A gigantic family secret that would die with her unless Benjamin disclosed the information. He assessed her, advised her on her health, and gave her prescriptions. Madeline was happy to talk to somebody. She had been in solitary for weeks. When she returned home, she took her medications and went straight to bed without any dinner.

All efforts to reach Benjamin proved abortive. He refused to pick up Madeline's phone. She became extremely worried about the situation. She had no one to talk to, and the situation was gradually killing her by installment. She summoned courage, swallowed her pride, and called her father. It was her last resort. When her father picked up the phone, she started sobbing uncontrollably. He was scared and asked her what the problem was. She could not even explain herself. Her father told her to come home. He could not drive to the city because of the distance, health, and old age. She promised to visit the following day. Madeline's father knew he had to inform all his children about the issue at hand. He had a close-knit relationship with all his children, except Madeline, who purposely took herself, Benjamin, and Gina out of the beautiful family setting. Her father was puzzled and knew the situation must be dire for Madeline to turn back to him for support. He told his wife that Madeline called again and sobbed on the phone and would come home the following day. They agreed to inform all their children about the situation and advise that they come home also.

Madeline for years forgot that her parents, siblings, nephews, and nieces existed. She no longer reached out to them, never picked up their calls whenever they called, and they lost touch with her. Her father called all her siblings and told them about Madeline's call. He had no idea of the problem but would love them to be around when she visited the following day. They declined and gave work schedules as excuses not to attend. Her father called Benjamin to inquire about what was the problem with Madeline. He picked the up phone out of respect for his father-in-law and former pastor but did not give a clue regarding any issue. He pretended like nothing was amiss.

The drive to the city where her parents lived was six hours long. Madeline set out very early in the morning and was there by noon. When she got out of the car, her parents were on hand to receive her. Immediately she alighted from her expensive SUV, her father noticed instantly that she was a stroke survivor. Her posture told the story. Her parents hugged her tightly. It was a reunion like the story of the prodigal son but surely not there to ask for her inheritance. She was rich. Her car and personality showed wealth, despite her posture and gait. They led her into the beautiful, small cozy home where she grew up. Her mother like all mothers dotted around her, kissed her, happy to see her lost adult child. Parents do not harbor offenses against their offspring no matter the hurt they caused them; most parents willingly forgive and forget. The love and bond between parents and children always stayed intact irrespective of distance or hurt. Seeing the hurt in Madeline's eyes automatically brought down rivers of tears from her mother's eyes. Her father went into his bedroom and made a frantic call to all his children. They all arrived within two hours. Their father would never call an emergency meeting without something very important. They loved their father and appreciated his judgment. Madeline and her mother calmed each other down. When her siblings arrived, she could not face them out of shame. She abandoned them like bags of trash along a dirt road, but the love in their eyes when they hugged her one after the other melted her fears and shame. Family would always be family. A loving family is priceless. Her parents and siblings saw her interviews on television, pictures on pages of newspapers, hear about the flamboyant life she lived with her husband and horrible news about Gina, but they kept to themselves since she was the one who cut them out of her life. This reunion seemed priceless and long overdue, though no one besides Madeline knew the reason for the visit.

Madeline apologized for all the years she had disappeared from their lives, missing-without-action (MWA), with no calls or visits. She was devoid of love and affection toward the welfare of her parents, sisters, and brother, even nieces and nephews. After a late lunch, they all settled down to know the reason for the emergency meeting. Madeline's father apologized to all his children for summoning them at such short notice. He reported that Madeline called a few days ago and again the previous day. Things seemed not right with her. He was not aware of the situation, but her sudden return and calls seemed scary to him. He would love all of them to treat the situation as one big, loving family that they were. His pastoral gene took over with a sermon on forgiveness, forging ahead in love and in the spirit of oneness. Madeline took over amid tears and appealed to everyone to forgive her for abandoning the family for years, stating that the reasons were part of what she was about to discuss. She professed her love for all of them and never loved them less. Madeline was a strong, independent, opinionated, loving, and hardworking sister they grew up with. Her sobs and tears baffled them. What could be the problem? Her sisters switched positions with their parents who sandwiched Madeline on the sofa. They held her hand on both sides and wrapped their other hand around her shoulder. She looked down for a while, blew her nose on a tissue, and cleaned off her tears. As soon as she cleaned off her tears, more hot tears trickled down her face in a torrent. Her emotional state affected her loving family. All eyes were suddenly in accordance with Madeline's.

She began with the state of her health, shared the two heart attacks and a stroke that almost killed her, but left out what led to the stroke and heart attacks. She took early retirement from her job because of her health. The heart attacks were well managed, but the stroke made it impossible for her to continue with her job. She was in physical therapy and had to learn how to function effectively all over. She discussed the state of her marriage. Her one-time loving marriage had turned into a mirage and nightmare, and love had become an illusion to her and Benjamin, all thanks to Gina. She recalled how Gina's behavior had always caused rancor at events, linked it to the last time she attended the family gathering, how she decided that staying away was the best option, painfully opted for it, and she refused to pick up calls from all of them to avoid being questioned on her absence at family gatherings. They all looked at each other, puzzled, short of words. Gina was a handful, but they never hated her or her family and never meant for her family to distance themselves. Gina's undefined behavior was not a good excuse for her to abandon them, most especially their old parents who needed love and care from all of them in their old age.

She recounted all the nefarious activities that Gina embarked upon, her drug use, criminal activities, the shame, the litigations, the pay-off monies, and above all, the crime that earned her five years behind bars.

All her actions and overbearing attitudes were of concern to her and Benjamin. She was court-ordered to rehab many times but to no avail. Her attitude wedged a big rock between her and Benjamin who had stopped talking to her and was likely to divorce her. They were all alarmed when she mentioned divorce and could never believe Benjamin would divorce her. He adored her. She reported that he had virtually moved out of the house to God knows where, refused to pick her calls, and hated her with passion. Madeline's father choked and coughed uncontrollably. His son rushed and got him water to sip. He was so dazed that he drank the whole cup of water.

"Divorce? Why?" he muttered aloud. "Why would he divorce you because of a child's unruly behavior? We would all support you to get her reformed, pray, fast, and lead her in the right direction."

All her siblings and mother nodded in affirmation. They all promised to support, reform, visit, show that they love her irrespective of her behavior and win her over with love. Madeline sighed heavily, looked at all of them, wiped, blew her nose, and told them there was more to it.

They all chorused, "What more?"

Madeline then dropped the bombshell! The glass cup her father held dropped to the floor and shattered.

"What did you just say? Benjamin was not Gina's father?"

Her mother went pale. Her father looked disoriented. Her sisters withdrew their hands. Her brother quickly went to their mother's aid. She was almost falling off her seat.

It was as if the blood in her body drained out in a second. Madeline fell to the ground, sobbing uncontrollably. For a few seconds, nobody attended to her. They focused on their parents who were visibly in shock and could suffer heart attacks. Her brother later reached out to her, pulled her up, and got her seated. "I am so sorry" was all she could mutter, her voice in and out. Her father got up and went to the window. He needed fresh air. The air-conditioner that was on seventy degrees in the house seemed like in the nineties. The room became hot. They were all sweating inside a fully air-conditioned room. Her father looked up and said, "Oh my god, please do not forsake me at this time." Everyone was shocked. They looked at Madeline with disgustful eyes. All of them short of words. Madeline sat in shame and could not utter a word. What could she say? What apologies could she render that would wipe off the shame she had brought on her family? How would the congregation and community accept her father? She had castigated the revered pastor who worked all his life to preach holiness, consecration, purity, and the bed undefiled. Though retired, he still attended the church he pastored, and as a member, the congregants knew him and all his children.

The dust settled after about one hour. No one uttered a word. They tried to internalize the bombshell, had lots of questions to ask, and had a big decision to make. Her father who could not get his thoughts together sat quietly by the window and sweating profusely. Her mother sat quietly by her husband and could not look up or utter any word. Her brother lowered the air-conditioner to sixty-five degrees and assisted his parents back to the sofa. He asked how and what led to a DNA test. It was not the right question, but that was what first came to his mind. Madeline explained that Gina's outright outlandish behavior and drug abuse made Benjamin question her paternity. She recounted most of Gina's atrocities, how she almost shot her with a stolen gun over a pricy bag she did not order on time that led to her second heart attack, recounted her several misdeeds in school, suspensions, numerous fights, DUIs, accidents, rehabilitations, and more. Benjamin became confused, and so was her. Madeline recounted how she erred only once. It was a grievous mistake that she regretted immediately after it happened. She never thought it was a problem, but she miscalculated. She never thought she got pregnant for another person until the test result confirmed it. She had to redo the test after Benjamin did it twice, and the result was the same.

"Who then is the father? Do you know him?" her father roared.

It was the first time the children would hear their father raise his voice. He instantly apologized. Madeline looked down in shame and prayed silently for the ground to open and swallow her up. She fidgeted, nervous, anxiety written all over her. He never raised his voice at her when she was young, talk less of now that she was an adult and married. She could not blame him. She blamed herself. She nervously said yes. Her sister asked who the father was. She mentioned Kyle's name lamely.

"Kyle? Which Kyle?" they all chorused. "The Kyle that used to attend the church, the Kyle that was like an adopted son in this house, is he a Kyle we know?"

She looked up and mumbled a weak "Yes." Her father went pale and almost fainted. He loved Kyle like his own son. He had only one son and three daughters. Kyle was his church member. He had a soft spot for him and took him like his son. Why would he violate his daughter and rub shame over him like a perfumed lotion. Madeline explained how it happened. It was an honest mistake. It happened within the twinkle of an eye. They did the unthinkable. It was a stupid momentary passion. She hated herself but confessed to being a willing participant. He did not force her. Both could not explain how they became carried away by what they watched, and they regretted it immediately. He had always professed love to her, and she had always rejected him. The silence was thick. Nobody spoke a word. If a pin fell to the ground, the noise would be thunderous.

"Kyle?"

They were all stunned, lost for words. Her father got up and left for his room. Everywhere was quiet. Thoughts running wild in each head. About fifteen minutes after her father left and did not return, Madeline's mother and brother got up to check on him. They found him on his knees, praying by the side of his bed. They knelt and joined him, knew he was broken. He did not look up. He just kept praying. He got up after another fifteen minutes and wiped his tears. It was the first time they saw him cry. He was a man of strong faith and believed so much in the Lord and the Word of God. He touched his wife's shoulder and beckoned to them to get up. He exited the room, and they followed. He sat on his vacant seat, heaved a heavy sigh, and was silent for a moment.

He then began to admonish them, "Judgment is for the Lord. Only Him can judge us. There was no reason to judge anyone."

He spoke on faith, forgiveness, and accepting the will of God. What happened was God's will, and no one can query God's will. "His ways are not our ways. His thoughts are not our thoughts." He was ashamed of the situation and felt let down, but Madeline was of an utmost priority now. Her emotional well-being was paramount. If God could forgive us for all our sins, there would be no moral justification to judge her on what she had done. Nobody is above mistakes.

Only God is. We are all human and tend to make mistakes. As a family, they would find a way around the issue, but they must lift Madeline up and not let her sink in her guilt. Her shame would be a shared shame, but God would wipe away the shame. Madeline would have to personally seek God's forgiveness while they intercede on her behalf. They would get Benjamin on board to proffer reconciliation, believing that God would show them how to intervene. As for Gina, they would all support her rehabilitation when released. For Kyle, God would direct them to where to find him. He must be aware of the situation. He had to know. Madeline had a sense of relief, a family to support her and fall back to. She stayed with her parents for the week and tried to put the pieces of her life together. All calls she made to Benjamin went unanswered, Her father was able to talk to him, and he promised to attend a family meeting with his in-laws later. Gina's paternity issue would be kept within the family for now.

The last time anyone saw Kyle was the day Madeline got married. He was exceptionally quiet, absent-minded, and unhappy. He wore a sad look that was glaring to all the guests, but nobody knew why he was sad. He left town that night and had never visited, called, or returned to the church or city since then. Kyle had issues but loved by everyone. He was a great helper in time of need in the community and in the church. His disappearance was visible, talked about, and eventually forgotten. Madeline's father missed him so much, but they knew he was alive because no one heard about his death. Madeline's marriage to Benjamin hit him like a rock. He moved away, lodged at a hotel in another city for a while, got a job, and tried to start afresh. It was an uphill task for him. He relapsed mentally because he stopped using his psychotropic medications, went back to doing drugs, and later admitted to a psychiatric hospital for over a year. Stabilizing him was difficult. He was manically depressed, nonconforming, and noncommittal. He left when he became stabilized and committed to his treatment. He moved to another state, started life afresh, picked the pieces of his life, and tried to piece them together. He got over her, began a new on-and-off relationship, and happiness returned to his life. He never joked with his treatment and medications since then. He had been on his job for almost two decades and advanced in positions. He never married and had no children. Locating him was a priority to Madeline's family.

*****

Elizabeth changed her mind again about contacting her mother and stepfather. Ella agreed with her. She needed her mind to fully embrace the need for a change before a change could happen. The change was for her and not for her mother. Recovery is first and foremost for the individual involved. It is never to benefit or make another person happy. Sobriety is beneficial to the person addicted. You do not change for another person. You change for yourself, for your well-being. She could take her time and needed to be fully stabilized emotionally to face her. She was ashamed of the behavior she meted on her mother who loved her to pieces, but that was their family issue. Ella continued to convince her to attend both therapy groups. The attendance would equip her with the way forward, on making better choices.

She looked at Ella and smiled cynically, nodded her head severally, and looked at her sternly but in an effective way and asked, "Who did this to you? Francine? Your mum or grandma? Who? All the above?"

Ella smiled back, sighed heavily, and said, "Nobody but me. I did it for myself. I had the greatest support from Francine, my mother, and my grandmother. I chose to do it for myself. The importance and necessity for a change overpowered me. I needed the change. I needed to love myself. What I was doing to my body was nothing but hate. I changed the hate to love, changed my hurt to love. I needed to be useful to myself, to get off the destructive train and joined the train to freedom, needed a better life devoid of drugs, clubbing, partying, and the many ugly things that trailed it. My life was on a roller coaster to destruction and death."

She sighed again. "I was hurting myself thinking I was enjoying. I hated to tow the same lifestyle that destroyed my mother. Thank God she had a second chance. This is my second chance. I grabbed it with both hands, all thanks to Francine who showed me the right way. I did it for *me*, for *myself*, for my *future*. I want you to do the same. Let us face it. What did we gain? Look at the number of years we wasted roaming the streets, spending money we did not work for, lavishly spending money at other people's expense. If we worked for money, would we spend it the way we did? It was easy to spend because it was cheap money. The money we never worked for. We messed up big-time, thinking we were enjoying "life."

"The life I have now is a million percent better than what we were doing previously. I am a new person. The Ella that you knew before was far gone. I wake up every day with a clear head, and it's getting clearer by the day. I am healthier, assimilate better, slept better, think positively, changed the things I could change, and move on one day at a time."

Elizabeth looked at her in disbelief, She was truly a changed person, so different from the Ella she knew, a better, nice-looking, clean, and kind. She coveted Ella's new being.

Ella looked at Elizabeth and helped her wipe away her tears. She hoped her speech made an impact. Elizabeth looked at her and told her how she admired her guts. She knew it must have been difficult for her initially and praised her for embracing change. The most difficult thing for many people to embrace in life is change. It is like pulling a tooth without an anesthetic agent. A destructive lifestyle formed over many years would be a daunting task to erase overnight. She wished she were Ella, to get changed with a magic wand, but no magic could make change happen. Only an individual could do it with determination and dedication. She extolled Ella for her insistence, for the pain she went through overcoming her withdrawal symptoms. She had truly done well for herself. Elizabeth agreed to begin attendance at group therapy sessions. Ella was happy. She stayed a little longer with her and left for her classes at the university.

Elizabeth attended the domestic violence group session after Ella left. She was amazed at the discussions and testimonies of the clients during the session. She never knew there were people that had gone through the type of violence described. The openness of those at the session made her share some of the experiences she went through at the hands of Ralph. It further amazed her that she could share without shame. Sharing brought out the pain she harbored in her heart. The things she thought were demeaning, it was like a burden lifted off her shoulder. Some of the things Ralph did that she could not even tell Ella about were made open. It was an eye-opener for the group. Ralph was king. She was his subject. She was demeaned, humiliated, and violated. Elizabeth shared the experience of the night she lost Ralph's priced drugs when a commotion suddenly happened at the nightclub. They were together having a supposedly nice time when a fight broke out. She had her "wares" on the table to deal out when suddenly a big fight started. She scampered to pack all her drugs but did not get everything before dashing to safety, when Ralph realized some drugs were lost, her head became his ball. That was the day she almost lost her front tooth.

When they got home, she got the most bastardized beating of her life. He tied her up and beat her so mercilessly that her mind told her she was dead. The beatings were intermittent, with higher and greater intensity in succession, and she bled from her mouth, nose, and private part. She lost a pregnancy that night. The pain was too severe to describe. He cared less, left her on the floor bleeding, and went to sleep. He woke up to use the bathroom about four hours later, saw her writhing in pain, kicked her, went into the bathroom, and kicked her again on his way out. He realized something was terribly wrong when he stepped on blood and the urine she released during the severe beatings. He flicked the light switch, saw lots of blood, and realized she was in and out of consciousness. He made a call to somebody. When he arrived, he untied her. They carried her into the bathtub, washed her, and the stranger administered medications on her. Only Ralph knew who the person was. She knew the person had medical knowledge the way he treated her or a quack who had perfected his enterprise over time. Ralph paid him cash before he left, which angered him the more. He roared loudly for days that she lost his drugs and lost more money to the person that treated her. She was sore for weeks. The beatings and punishment for losing the drugs continued despite her pains. She begged and apologized many times before he warmed up to her.

Elizabeth felt better when she shared part of her story. It was as if a miracle happened to her. She felt her burden lifted and could not believe that she shared her experience with total strangers—people she always thought were "beneath her." She felt the love, empathy, and the spirit of togetherness in the room. Everyone had a story to tell, similar stories. They were in the same boat, all abused seeking healing, male and female, and realized that domestic violence cuts across gender. Verbalization helped her. She felt no shame afterward and felt validated. If sharing only one of her experiences could make her feel relieved, she needed to push them out of her mind and get better.

A male in the group shared his story. Men statistically find it difficult to verbalize in domestic violence situations. He was different. He ran for his life like the women, verbalizing helps, alleviating the pain and burden, and giving hope for a better future and opportunity. Adam was one of the two males in the group. His wife battered him for years. He had a respectable job, a senior managerial position, had a wife and children, and a loving home filled with love, fun, and bliss—a situation he knew nothing about became his undoing. There was a case of theft in his department. As the manager in charge, it was his responsibility to oversee his subordinates. He was suspended and later terminated, and the investigation exonerated him, but his company let him off because they believed he was negligent.

Initially, his wife was highly supportive emotionally, financially, and otherwise, she was a dutiful wife until Adam's paychecks ceased. She took care of all the bills since she was the only one working. Adam tried to get a job, but luck was not on his side. The months progressed, and apprehension set in for both. His wife changed. She became a total stranger to Adam who had suddenly become the house engineer, house husband, cleaner, cook, and baby minder all rolled into one. He never complained and did all the chores with gladness of heart, but nothing he did was appreciated by his wife who tongue-lashed him at every opportunity. His situation turned from verbal abuse to physical abuse in no time. The first time, she hit his head with a saucepan for not getting dinner ready on time. The intensity graduated from saucepan to anything she could grab or lay her hands on. She would slap, kick, refuse his conjugal rights, and then began to sleep out of the house. She gallivanted the streets with her friends who were solidly behind her. She was the breadwinner, should do whatever pleased her, and he could leave if he was uncomfortable with her newfound fun. What was the importance of a man who could not provide for his family? She once asked him. Her friends supported her cheating ways and clubbing. Adam cried in secret, ashamed of telling anyone, and how could he tell his family and friends that he was a punching bag for his wife? She became demon-filled, different from the woman he married years ago. The last straw was when she almost stabbed him with a kitchen knife. The first two times, he thought she was joking, persuaded, calmed her down, but the third time was one too many. He escaped through the kitchen door and ran for his life to Ariel's Turnaround Center for solace. His short stay at the center had helped him regain his lost dignity and self-esteem, and sharing part of his experience lifted the burden off his chest. He had filled out applications, interviewed, and would start a new job the following week, kudos to his case manager.

*****

Francine called Ella as usual. She was her greatest encourager that walked this planet Earth, a kindhearted lady with a reservoir of kindness to share. She later called Elizabeth who was happy to share the interaction she had at the group session earlier in the day. Francine was happy at Elizabeth's attitude toward her recovery and rehabilitation. She sounded optimistic. It warmed Francine's heart and encouraged her to turn her life around as Ella did. Elizabeth told her that she would try her best. Her spirit was willing, but her body still yearned for drugs, and the withdrawal symptoms were torturous on her body and brain. Francine shared coping mechanisms with her, encouraged her to talk to her therapist, follow up with coping skills they shared before, advised her to follow her treatment plan, attend AA/NA, and pair with Ella to work on ways to stay clean and sober. Elizabeth thanked her for all her efforts. The discussion hit a cord in Elizabeth's heart. She had a rethink of her decision concerning her mother and stepfather. When Ella visited her again, she informed her that she was ready to contact her mother and do the right thing. Ella was happy with her decision; it was the best decision. She called Bethena immediately and informed her of Elizabeth's whereabouts.

Bethena was on top of the moon. She leaped for joy and told Ella she was on her way. Bethena called her husband who was out of the country on a business meeting and informed him of the good news. He encouraged her to get her back home as soon as possible. Bethena was overjoyed when she met with Elizabeth. Her look was horrible, but that was nothing to the joy of seeing her daughter alive. The counselors advised Bethena to allow Elizabeth to continue with her recovery process at the center. Moving her away would hinder the progress the facility had made so far. She agreed with the professional advice the counselors gave, discussed it with Elizabeth, and they had a meeting of the mind to remain at the facility to continue her sobriety journey. By the time Bethena left, both mother and child had come to terms on the way forward. Bethena and Elizabeth stayed together all day. By the time they parted, both hearts had been mended with love. One week later, Jason visited Elizabeth in the company of Bethena. They agreed to family therapy sessions biweekly. It helped build them up emotionally and psychologically. They supported Elizabeth in her recovery process. She made great strides and made her family proud. She, however, was yet to be at peace with Jason but working vigorously on it.

Jason was happy with the new development and progress made so far by Elizabeth. He was excited that a woman saw the need to start such a facility in the community to support other people with her money. He organized a meeting with Carol and donated $1 million to her NGO. Carol declined it, but he insisted and told her it came from his heart and was a token to appreciate the great work she started in the bid to help total strangers. She collected it and thanked him for his kind gesture and deposited the money into the NGO's account. Bethena and Jason allowed Elizabeth to stay at the facility, finish her individual and group therapy sessions, and learn all the skills to begin life on a better platform. She had become accustomed to all the residents and staff at the facility and was happy to be part of the great facility. Francine and Ella were thrilled at the development, Elizabeth's change of heart, as well as her recovery effort. She stayed a total of ninety days and was discharged from the facility. Bethena and Jason were on hand to get her home. She was in the shock of her life when they arrived at the mansion where her mother and Jason lived. Her mouth was wide open when she stepped out and saw the opulence of the front area of the property. If the entrance was this captivating, how would the inside look? Bethena and Jason welcomed her with balloons, a big cake, and an array of food. She laughed and asked if she was a prodigal daughter. "Where are the guests?" she asked jokingly. A part of Elizabeth they never saw. They had never seen a smile on Elizabeth's face before, not to talk of a joke or laughter.

"Did you do all these for me? I feel so loved. I am sorry for all I made you pass through, but believe me, I went through hell before my rescue."

"Rescued?" Bethena and Jason exclaimed.

"Rescued, yes, rescued. A story for another day."

They ate and had an enjoyable time. Elizabeth looked around in dismay. Everywhere looked so posh, luxury at its peak. It was elegance personified, beautiful to behold, rich with all the trimmings of opulence. She knew her mother could not have spent that much on a mansion of this magnitude. They all retired to bed after midnight. She promised to intimate them with her story and experience. Elizabeth was aghast when she got to her bedroom. It looked like a princess's room. Her first night was superb. She slept like a baby and dreamed like Joseph the dreamer.

Elizabeth did not know that Jason donated $1 million to the facility where she resided for ninety days. It was a secret. When she heard, she knew her mother would not have personally donated such an amount. She was convinced beyond doubt that Jason must genuinely love her and wanted her progress. He must really love Bethena to have donated such an amount of money to the NGO. She also learned he promised a yearly donation of $1 million to each of the programs. Who was this man called Jason? What was his source of wealth? What enterprise was he involved with? She had to know. She started to search the internet and needed information on her so-called stepfather. When she woke up the following morning, her mother was the first person to say good morning to her with a broad infectious smile. The table was set for her breakfast. Jason made breakfast before he left for an early meeting with foreign investors at his manufacturing company.

Her mother beckoned to her to sit, but she insisted she wanted a tour of the mansion and had questions for her mother to answer. She wanted to know the level of her mother's investment in the mansion and how her investments in the mansion would affect her inheritance. Bethena told her to freshen up. She would take her around. She could read her mind. She knew she had questions to ask her. Elizabeth took her shower, freshened up, and came downstairs for the tour. The dress she wore was a bit revealing. She forgot about her scars. Her mother saw the scars and screamed. Elizabeth was shocked. She never expected her mother to see the scars. She made a mistake with her choice of clothing. She calmed her down, promised that she would tell her story at an appointed time, dashed to her room for a change of clothes. Bethena was shocked.

"Tell me immediately," she requested. Elizabeth smiled and told Bethena to give the tour of the mansion she promised. Her story would come later. Bethena agreed. She did not want to stir the hornet's nest.

Bethena gave Elizabeth a tour of the mansion. She was astonished, speechless to say the least. The opulence and wealth displayed were astounding. Elizabeth saw family heirlooms stolen from the previous house and inquired how she got them. She said that the items were recovered after the arrest of the robber, and Jason bought more on their honeymoon. The case was pending because of Elizabeth's disappearance. She quickly informed her she was not in any trouble regarding the case. What the law needed was for her to seek rehabilitation for her drug issue. She had done part of it at Ariel's. The tour lasted over an hour. As soon as they returned to the table, Elizabeth told Bethena she was no longer hungry.

She needed information on Jason, his wealth, and businesses. Bethena smiled and persuaded her to eat first. She would give all the details she wanted after breakfast. She delayed the breakfast for her so they could eat as a family, famished, and needed to eat to enable her to take her medications. Bethena was always in a decent health shape to Elizabeth's knowledge. Bethena never took time off from work, was always punctual, worked late, had never been admitted to the hospital, or complained of any form of ailment; in fact, she hated medications. It baffled Elizabeth when she said she needed to take her medications.

"Are you sick? Are you okay? Why are you on medications?" With an emphasis on the plural, she asked.

Bethena pretended she did not hear the questions. She started apportioning the scrambled eggs Jason made. He was a good cook, and even Elizabeth commended his skills. As they settled to eat, she asked about Jason again. Bethena knew her daughter too well. She knew it was about her inheritance. She was quick to let her know she had no dime in the purchase of the mansion or anything inside or outside. It was all Jason's money.

All she said was, "Whoa, I can't believe this. What does he do?"

Breakfast was quick. Elizabeth needed answers to her questions.

*****

Ella and Francine were happy that Elizabeth had returned home to her parents. They knew she had a lot of explaining to do besides the catch-ups. She had been clean for at least sixty days to the best of their knowledge. Though she could relapse if tempted or in a compromising environment, they agreed to allow her "alone" time with her family for at least one week. Francine was already in her third year and had performed way above expectations. She had received numerous awards of excellence, but nothing compared to the good deeds and kindness she had shown across the board to everyone, most especially Ella, Elizabeth, and their parents. Her kindness were unquantifiable. She was a selfless giver. She gave time in abundance and resources where applicable despite her busy schedule at school. "Help" should be her middle name. She spared nothing when a person needed her help.

*****

Bethena was surprised when Elizabeth cleared the table after breakfast and did the dishes. She could not believe what just happened. She dried the dishes with a napkin and figured out where to place them. Bethena was astonished but said nothing.

When they retired to their seats in the family room, Bethena said, "Thank you for cleaning up, well appreciated."

The singular act made her believe she must have gone through hell. She refused to be disciplined at home and got a load of discipline from outside. No matter how enormous the training at home seemed, they are to be imbibed as fortification toward the future. As soon as they settled down, Elizabeth asked the same question again. Her selfish, greedy disposition was yet to be dealt with despite what she went through. It was always about money. She was too much in love with money she never worked for. She never worked to receive a dime she could call her own sweat and labor. All she did was spend and spend. Why should she work when her grandparents and mother had worked to amass money all their lives? They had worked for her. All she needed to do was to spend the money. In the event of her mother's demise, everything would become hers. Why should she work? Why should she attend universities like Ella and Francine? Her thought process had suddenly changed again, totally screwed up, Bethena knew she needed to educate her on the basic things of life.

Ella's discussion about the value of money and spending money lavishly went through the right ear and exited through the left ear immediately. All Elizabeth wanted was a good life at other people's expense. Bethena saw glaringly through her and was ready to cut her to size with love. She did not want to jeopardize the reunion but at the same time needed to set the records straight and set her daughter on the right path in life. It baffled Bethena how Elizabeth became so greedy for money. She feared that without good financial value inculcated in her, she would squander her inheritance in a fleeting time. Thank God that her parents knew the value of money and good education. They added a clause that forbade Elizabeth from receiving any inheritance until after her university education or attaining the age of thirty. Bethena was quiet. She sipped her orange-flavored drink and set the cup on the side stool. Elizabeth did the same. She was busy rolling her eyes all over the house assimilating the opulence. She was in awe with what her eyes saw. As Bethena voiced the first word, her phone rang. It was Jason. He would be returning by evening. He was delayed because his private jet was still in service, and he would set out as soon as they finished. Elizabeth's awe rose to a higher level. She eavesdropped on her mother's discussion and could not believe that Jason whom she labeled a gold digger had a private jet. As far as her brain would let her, it was Bethena's money and her inheritance that Jason was spending.

Madeline's parents were supportive of her. They pampered her like a baby the whole week she was with them. They made sure she ate and took her medications. She emaciated so fast, lost weight, aged overnight, and they feared for her health. Her father called Benjamin and had a long talk with him. He shared that she had betrayed the trust he had in her. Madeline's father explained the grievous mistake she made two weeks before their wedding and that she regretted it. She had never stepped out of their marriage and never knew the mistake resulted in a baby. He was forthright with Benjamin, and he believed him. He was a good pastor who shared the Word of God undiluted, practiced what he preached, and trained his children in the way of the Lord. Benjamin could attest to it, his teaching and preaching helped shaped Benjamin's life. His youthful days were spent in the church he pastored. He respected him, admired him, and wished his children would turn out like his children, wished he were not in the boat he had found himself.

Madeline's father minimized the details and invited him to the house so they could deal with the situation face-to-face. Benjamin agreed, and a date was set. Madeline's father invited all his children to the meeting. When Benjamin arrived, he looked worse than Madeline. His eyes were sunken as if he had cried for days. He had lost weight also and was not as boisterous and confident as he used to be. When he entered and saw Madeline, he busted into tears. The two of them had become shadows of themselves. A minimum of twenty years had suddenly seemed added to their respective ages. All the siblings started crying too, including Madeline's mother. The only dry eyes were that of Madeline's father. As a pastor, he had seen it all, heard unbelievable stories in his lifetime, and his pastoral profession had made him hear, witness situations, trials, and challenges in the lives of parishioners.

Madeline looked sober, broken, and subdued. All she could utter was "I am sorry." She explained her side of the story. Benjamin knew Kyle from the days when they attended church together and knew he had mental issues as well as drug addiction. He perfectly and immediately understood where Gina got all the traits she exhibited—genes she inherited from Kyle. Gina needed help; they would give her all the support she needed when released from prison—psychological, medical, and emotional. If they had known what they knew now, they would have been initiative-taking and offered help sooner. They would have rehabilitated her a long time ago. They thought her behavior was youthful exuberance, never opined that she had inherited issues. Benjamin thanked them for their love and support and told them he had come to take his wife home. He loved his wife and had never loved her less. He was only disappointed that he had to do a DNA to find the truth. He believed now that his wife miscalculated and did not intentionally deceive him. They would deal with the situation as a family. If they needed help, they would reach out to them. They would appreciate it if the situation remained within the family and kept confidential.

As for Kyle, he would look for him, inform him of the situation, and allow him access to Gina if he wished to be part of her life. Everyone was happy and thanked Benjamin for his understanding and maturity for being a good husband, brother-in-law, and son-in-law. The happiest persons were his pastor and his wife. In all his pastoral years, the best family he had been able to unite back succesfuly was his daughter's family. He was full of kind words and prayers for Benjamin. They had dinner together as a family, and Benjamin took Madeline back home. They drove home in one car; Madeline's brother drove Madeline's car back to the city for her.

Benjamin and Madeline knew they needed to take care of themselves. They flew out of town on a two-week vacation. All they did was rest, sleep, eat, and use their prescribed medications. They put off their phones and needed rest more than anything in this world. When they returned, their haggard looks had disappeared to a satisfactory level. They looked well-rested, gained some of the lost weight, refreshed, and well-nourished. They were able to catch up on lost times during the vacation and rekindled their love for one another. Benjamin used his professional skill to search for Kyle. It was not difficult to locate the state, city, and address of where he lived. He also got his phone number. He waited a few weeks before he called him and used the period to think deeply about the best way to present the situation. Kyle hesitated to pick up the call when the phone rang. By his nature, he does not pick up phones with no indicated number on his caller ID. He changed his mind on this particular call for no reason and quickly picked it up before it rang out. To his dismay, it was Benjamin. He had not thought or heard from him in a long time. He was surprised when he heard who was on the line. They exchanged pleasantries. Kyle once hated Benjamin because of Madeline, but that had changed with time. They chatted as former acquaintances. Benjamin told him he would like to meet with him when he visited his city during the weekend. Kyle was happy and accepted the offer for a meeting—men's hangout probably. Benjamin and Madeline created time for couples' counseling before the meeting. They met with a clinical psychologist for a few weeks. They needed counseling to buttress the faith-based counsel from Madeline's father. The sessions were also to equip them for the meeting with Kyle.

Kyle was oblivious to the news about to hit his ears. When the conversation was over, Benjamin was more confused than before he called. He expected an uncoordinated man on the other line, but his utterances were intelligent and confident, and he seemed to be doing well. Benjamin researched him more and dug out more information on Kyle. His lawyers would have done it quicker, but he avoided them to keep his family secret. He had a live-in girlfriend who was always in-out of his life and had no children.

Madeline appealed to Benjamin to allow her to attend the meeting with Kyle, and he agreed. Kyle was happy to see them. He hugged, exchanged pleasantries, and discussed life in the community where they once lived, politics, law, current affairs in general. He avoided questions about his job when Benjamin asked him, turned to Madeline, and asked questions about her father, mother, siblings one after the other. He knew them personally, was once free with all of them, and she answered, but he could sense that she had something bothering her. She was not the usual lady he knew and fell in love with. She seemed quieter. He also asked Benjamin about his family. He knew all of them also but was not close with them. He welcomed them once again to his home. He had declined Benjamin's offer for them to meet at the hotel and told him his home would always be open to him for old times' sake.

His home was cozy, beautiful, and in an upscale subdivision. His house was tastefully furnished, neat, homely, and inviting. He had two new cars in front of his two-car garage home. When they arrived and saw two cars, they thought his girlfriend was around and thought they should not discuss the reason for the meeting. They wanted the discussion with him alone. When Kyle told them she left months ago, they were relieved. His on-and-off girlfriend was luckily out of the picture. He cooked food and had the table set with a sumptuous meal whose aroma filled the air. He offered them drinks, which they gladly accepted but declined the meal until after the discussion on why they visited. He was awestruck, more than surprised. They had nothing in common. What could be the reason for their visit? He had forgiven Madeline for marrying Benjamin instead of him and had even forgotten it. He felt cheated at that time but had overcome the feeling, had pushed the thought to his long-term memory system a long time ago, and had never recalled it. What could be the cause or reason for their visit? He looked scared and looked at the two of them as if to decipher from their countenance the reason for the visit but had no clue. He sat down. Silence enveloped the room. No one spoke for about five minutes. Kyle broke the silence, timidly with his voice shaking, asked why they visited him.

C H A P T E R 1 2

Tough Love

Bethena came back to her seat after talking to Jason. She looked at Elizabeth who was busy inspecting beautiful artworks around the house. When she saw her mother making her way back, she turned and returned to her seat. Bethena ignored her at first and responded by asking where she had been, how she got all the scars on her body, and what happened since she left the treatment center that Jason paid so much money for. Elizabeth smiled and at the same time looked puzzled. Instead of answering her, she asked her questions about Jason again. Bethena told her that, as the parent, she needed answers on the welfare and whereabouts of her daughter. She would tell her everything she needed answers to after she had explained herself in detail and encouraged her that her explanations would determine her response on her life and new husband. She reiterated to her that as her mother, rehabilitating her was paramount in her heart more than anything else.

Elizabeth looked at her with contempt, got up in furry, and walked out on Bethena. As she walked away, she promised to dig to the bottom of whatever she was hiding from her. Bethena shook her head in disbelief. She thought Elizabeth had changed after her recent ninety-day stay at Ariel's Turnaround Center. How mistaken she was. She knew her daughter was callous, self-centered, selfish, and a money monger. She never knew she could be so heartless to her happiness. She had taken her selfishness to the highest level anyone could think of. She needed real help, professional help. All she wanted was money to spend. She squandered it as if money was going out of fashion. Bethena loved her but was poised to show tough love to Elizabeth, her only daughter. With her marriage to Jason, she had promised herself to be a good mother to his three children and had gone to parenting classes to learn how to function effectively as a mother. She knew she blew it with Elizabeth and was ready to be a perfect example of a mother to her four children. When Jason returned, Bethena told him about the aborted discussion with Elizabeth. He advised her to let the matter be for now. When he saw Elizabeth, he treated her with love and tried to warm himself into her heartless heart.

Bethena watched Elizabeth like a hawk around the house. Besides, the mansion had security cameras all over. The robbery at her former house had taught Bethena a lesson. The house was extra wired. Elizabeth noticed it and knew she had to be extremely careful. Her mother had not given her an allowance for her upkeep. She told her everything she needed was in the house. Bethena had decided not to give her pocket money anymore. As an adult, she needed to learn the importance and meaning of dignity in labor. If she worked, she would know the value of money. She knew she could pilfer things of value from the house to sell so she could have money to spend, show off, use drugs, live life on the fast lane, and return to being her usual, notorious Elizabeth.

Bethena promised to support her reformation and advised her to follow in the footsteps of Ella, her friend, but she ignored all entreaties. Her first week in the house seemed like walking on eggshells for both. They showed love to one another but with civility. Elizabeth had no access to any of the cars or money. Bethena was no longer willing to give her hard-earned money to frivolous things and or drugs. She poised to starve Elizabeth's drug addiction. Without money, she would not be able to purchase drugs or visit the club. Jason took them to dinner at an exclusive, patrons-only restaurant. When they approached the restaurant, Elizabeth was awed by the treatment they got right from when they drove into the premises to when they were seated. It had the touch of royalty and privilege. She was confused and daunted about who Jason was. She was too intimidated to eat her food. The service was top notch. The food was palatable, but she was too distressed to eat. Jason could read her countenance and tried to ease her distress. She had to find out who Jason was and what he does for a living.

Jason left home early the following day, allowing Bethena to have quality time with their lost-and-found daughter. Normally, he would have gone with Bethena. He hated to leave her alone at home. Bethena had turned into his "twin" after the wedding. They were always together. They understood each another and blended well together. Bethena informed the police department of Elizabeth's return and turned her in for the case against her. The robber-cum-drug dealer was eventually arrested. He confessed to the robbery and that Elizabeth was complicit. She invited him to the house, and an assortment of drugs was recovered from her nightstand. Some of the stolen items had also been recovered. He sold some and gave some to his girlfriends, but the police recovered most from the buyers and girlfriends. Jason told them to forget about the remaining items.

Elizabeth was found guilty after three court appearances. She would attend a six-month rehabilitation or serve twelve months in prison with six-month probation thereafter. She agreed to the former and would go to the rehabilitation program from home instead of a residential facility. With the case over with, Bethena sat Elizabeth down for a strict mother-daughter talk. Bethena gave her strict instructions that must be strictly adhered to. She was firm, uncompromising, and merciless. She told her that it had to be her way or the highway. She would support her to the best of her ability but would not spoon-feed or babysit her. Her court-ordered program must be totally and strongly adhered to, or she would send her to prison to finish her term. Elizabeth could not believe her ears.

She was free to go to any facility of her choice to do her program, but if she wished to stay under her roof, she must be disciplined, respect her home, respect her and her husband, abide by all her rules, do house chores, be of good behavior, get a job or return to school, and test negative to all drug tests. She must never bring any visitor to the house, except Ella and Francine, no clubbing, and no cigarette smoking. Bethena paused for a few minutes. The silence was deafening.

She went further and said, "You have the free will to make your decision. You do not have to follow my laid down rules. You are an adult and can make decisions that you feel will favor or be beneficial to you. The decisions are yours. Feel free to do what best suits you. This is my house. I make the rules here. I am not forcing you. It is a free world."

Elizabeth was dazed, could not believe her ears, could no longer decipher if the person in front of her was Bethena or someone else. Bethena informed her that she needed a response from her by midnight; if not, she would be on her way to any residential treatment facility of her choice in the morning or to prison. Elizabeth underestimated what her mother could do. Her voice indicated she meant every word that came out of her mouth. Elizabeth's days of using defense mechanisms were over. There was no room for rationalization and distorting reality. She either stay on board or get off the board. Her bloated ego had finally been deflated by no one else but her once and former enabler-in-chief.

Elizabeth was short of words. She had a court order to respect. If she does not, she would be on her way to prison. She feared prison. A whole twelve months? Scared of her mother's tall order, had a probation officer to also contend with, her mother's demand was tall but doable. It was better than being behind bars. With her drug offense, she would be a felon when out of prison, so prison was not an option at all. She returned to her room sluggishly, ruminated on her mother's demand all day. She came down to dinner herself instead of Bethena calling her. The first sign that the effect of the tough love had started. She looked lifeless, dejected, and without energy. They ate in silence. After dinner, she cleared the table and did the dishes. She returned to the family room, sat on the sofa across from Bethena, and told her she had agreed to her terms.

Bethena told her she would have her append her signature on the agreement. She agreed, looked sad, and nervous, and Bethena was unperturbed. Bethena had a movie playing on television. Elizabeth sat there, lost in thoughts. She watched a two-hour movie with her mind drifting a million miles away. They sat silently for two hours. They hugged each other and said good night. When they retired to bed, Bethena was the happiest. It was her best night's sleep. She slept like a baby. Her child seemed ready for recovery. It was the best news to share with Jason who was the architect of the tall order. He explained to Bethena that only tough love could reform Elizabeth. She had gone far and deep into drug and criminality. To reform her would have to be strict and stringent, love with a dint of mercilessness.

Bethena woke up late. Breakfast was ready, prepared by the almighty Elizabeth. She could smell the aroma from her bedroom. Elizabeth got up early, prepared breakfast, and made coffee. She had never cooked all her life to Bethena's knowledge. Who taught her? When and how? Necessity, they say, is the best teacher, the mother of invention, she thought. Bethena could not believe her eyes to see the table already set. They ate breakfast in silence. Elizabeth cleared the table, did the dishes, and cleaned the kitchen. Bethena told her to get ready. They needed to be somewhere by 11:00 a.m. They returned to their respective rooms to shower and freshen up. By 10:00 a.m., they were both ready. Bethena drove. Her countenance was not appealing. Nobody spoke for the forty-five minutes ride. When they parked, Bethena informed Elizabeth they were there to meet with her parents' lawyer who eventually became her personal lawyer. She wanted Elizabeth to meet with the attorney concerning her inheritance that she always referred to. A small smile permeated her lips. She quickly turned her face so that her mother would not see the smile. She already did, pretended she did not.

Elizabeth's inner mind jubilated. She would be free from her mother. With her inheritance in her possession, she would be free to move out, live her life the way she wanted, out of the prying eyes of her mother and her stupid, fraudulent Jason of a husband. Who knows where he got his money? She would no longer depend on them, most especially her brain-washed mother. Her money was eventually coming to her. Yes, yes, yes, she won at last! They entered the attorney's office and exchanged pleasantries with the receptionist who ushered them into the conference room. She offered coffee or soda; they declined and thanked the receptionist.

The attorney ushered them into his office. He had with him a sealed big old envelope. They shook hands. He signaled to the seats. He was far older than her mother, a famous attorney. Elizabeth had seen him on television on occasions, never knew he was the family lawyer. Bethena introduced Elizabeth to him and discussed the mission for the visit. Elizabeth needed information on her inheritance from her grandparents. He shook Elizabeth's hand again and told her he was happy to meet with her at last. They exchanged pleasantries. He asked her about her schooling, but she had no response to offer. He picked up the envelope and turned both sides to Elizabeth and Bethena and made them confirm that it was sealed, never opened, with the court stamp and seal, and never tampered with. He proceeded to open the envelope.

Elizabeth was happy that her wealth was ripe, about to fall on her laps, the latest and youngest millionaire. She was happy, jubilating inside her heart without any outward inclination or disposition. She was a guru in the art of pretense and deception, knew how to fake her attitude, and made situations look real when it really was the opposite. The attorney read out the content of the last testament of her grandmother to her. Elizabeth's grandparents were die-hard advocates for education. They instilled the importance of education in Bethena, and she truly made them proud. The last testament to Elizabeth bothered on education also. She was to inherit 10 percent of their wealth at the completion of her first university degree or when she turned thirty years of age, 25 percent when she had her second degree; if she did not further her education after high school, 1 percent should be her entitlement at the age of thirty. All other grandchildren were to inherit the same. In the situation of no other grandchildren, the remaining percentage in varying order should go to three medical research centers to further research on medications to treat three diseases namely: mental health, substance abuse/drug addiction, and cancer.

Her grandparents left an inheritance for children unborn, children they were not opportune to meet—the same clause applied to them also. Bethena got her inheritance years ago. Elizabeth was a year old at the time. Her mother knew about the contingent in the last will and testament when she got hers. The attorney kept the envelope for the grandchild(ren). That would be when Elizabeth was at least a degree holder. That was the main reason Bethena always encouraged her to study hard. It was as if Elizabeth's grandparents projected into her future. Thank God, the contingent was arm twisting for her. Elizabeth sat rooted to her chair. She could not fathom what had just befallen her. She was confused and disoriented and instantly hated her grandparents to the core. Bethena was aware of the clause. The clause was in her copy when she got it years ago. It never bothered her because she worked hard to make her own wealth and believed her daughter would do the same. The attorney gave a copy to Elizabeth and told her she had the right to confirm it at the probate court where it was registered years ago. Bethena thanked the attorney, and they took their leave. Elizabeth left depressed, unhappy, sad, and dejected.

On the drive back home, Bethena told Elizabeth about her parents. They were die-hard advocates for quality education, hard work, discipline, and hated laziness. The word "lazy" does not exist in their dictionary, never condoned it. They worked hard for their money. They were great philanthropists who donated a lot of money to medical research, colleges, and gave out scholarships. They taught her to be upright, studious, hardworking, disciplined, to never rest on her oars, never depend on other people's money, and imbibe the right value for money. Their slogan was that her education was the best inheritance they could bequest to her. The best wealth a person should enjoy in life must be the wealth the person worked for. They taught her dignity in labor, never to depend on handouts or other people's wealth.

She built her life around their advice, studied hard in school, had her master's degree, got an excellent job, and rose on the ladder to success, and the rest was history. The attorney they just left his place was now her personal attorney. Her last will and testament were with him. In case of any eventuality, Elizabeth should reach out to him for her last instruction. She had instructed him to donate 100 percent of her wealth to various charities. Elizabeth was bewildered. She looked confused. No wonder the attorney had a weird look on his face when Bethena introduced her to him as her only daughter. She had built her life on a castle with no foundation. It had crumbled on her. All her hopes, yearnings, and aspirations had been dashed; she had placed all her hopes on her inheritance, not knowing it was all a ruse she had played on herself.

Bethena told Elizabeth that the information she needed on Jason would be best discussed by Jason himself. He would meet with her on his return from his overseas trip. When they got home, Elizabeth asked for the agreement, signed it, and went straight to her room. She knew she had been boxed into the corner by both her grandparents and mother. No wonder her mother always emphasized education. She just turned twenty-five, with no admission to any university or a degree on the horizon. Ten percent? Ten percent might be a lot, but that would be after four years of learning in the university or 1 percent when she turned thirty. In order words, she has five years before she could receive a dime. It sucked, really sucked. It was not her money. She had to wait and had good thinking to do on the way forward.

*****

Benjamin and Madeline looked down and did not know how to begin the conversation. Kyle asked again. His question jolted Benjamin who seemed lost in thought and absent-minded. He cleared his throat and told Kyle that Madeline needed to intimate him with a development.

"A development? I am listening."

Madeline narrated her story and refreshed Kyle's memory of the onetime escapade they had weeks before her wedding, how regretful she was, how she calculated her cycle, and thought she was safe but miscalculated. She had a daughter named Georgina.

"Gina's behavior became highly unbecoming. Benjamin decided on a DNA test, and the DNA result proved that Gina was not his biological daughter."

The negative result for Benjamin meant a positive result for Kyle. Madeline paused while Kyle opened his mouth in disbelief. He suddenly went pale, as if he were about to pass out. He suddenly felt ashamed, never wanted Benjamin or anyone to know they had the onetime fling. He found it difficult to assimilate what Madeline just shared and asked her to repeat herself. Madeline was ashamed of herself and found it uneasy, but she shared it again. Kyle became light-headed, bemused, and unable to comprehend the situation. All seemed like a dream to him. He pinched himself to wake up and asked Benjamin to wake him up from his deep slumber despite his eyes wide open. Benjamin kept mute, utterly deaf and dumb. Kyle started to cry, unable to withhold the news. He knew he had ruined Madeline's life, marriage, and the lives of all her siblings who were upright, disciplined, and well mannered, talk less of her parents' lives, most especially her father, who was a revered pastor. How would the church members who knew him feel about him? They would view him as a traitor who violated the pastor's daughter. As he cried, Benjamin and Madeline began to sob too. They sobbed for a long time, cleaned their faces, and proffered on the way forward.

Benjamin cleared his throat and thanked Kyle for allowing them into his home, for listening to the news of an adult daughter he never knew existed. They needed a way forward. Kyle needed to tell them what the way forward would be. He was the biological father of Georgina, and they thought it was wise to let him know he had a child. They would love to keep the paternity a secret, if possible, but everything depended on him. Kyle got up, paced back and forth, speechless. He never wanted a child, vowed never to have one, and never wanted a child to inherit his mental illness. He inherited his mental illness from his severely deranged mother who died in a mental institution. His mother was a loving wife who dotted on her husband and child. His father's addiction got her depressed due to loneliness. His father was an alcoholic who would roam the streets when drunk and kept late nights daily. His addiction aggravated her mental disorder that was salient. Her mother suffered from bipolar disorder. It was hereditary in her lineage.

Kyle had effectively managed his illness because he was well-educated, learned, and read a lot on how to manage his illness. The stigma of mental illness was too much to place on a child. He never wanted any. Besides, his personal doctor once told him he had no chance at procreation because of an accident he had when he was young. The news about Gina got him confused and caught him unawares. He trusted Madeline and knew she was never a wayward girl. Madeline mentioned that Gina's behaviors and attitudes were unbecoming. Kyle needed more information. What does she mean by unbecoming? He composed himself and sat down, asked Madeline to expatiate on the word "unbecoming."

Madeline gave a detailed account of the atrocities of Gina, as many as she could remember, but was careful not to scare Kyle away with too much information. She would allow the information to unfold to him gradually. He listened attentively with rapt attention. When Madeline finished, Kyle got up again. It was evident that he was deep in thought. Neither Benjamin nor Madeline was able to ascertain whether he was enthused or not at the news that he had a grown-up child. He paced back and forth again, went to the refrigerator, poured himself another cup of cold drink, sipped the drink, sighed deeply, came back to his seat, was about to speak, paused again, looked at them, and started talking. Kyle explained his family background, his father's drug and alcohol addiction, his mother's mental health disorders, his upbringing, education, his mental health challenges, alcohol and drug addiction, all the support Madeline's father gave him through the church to attain sobriety, his desire not to have children, and his love for helping others was his avenue to fight off his demons. Gina's troubles were hereditary. She got it all from him. His genes and lineage were responsible for her addictive behavior and illness but not the criminality. He had never been involved in any criminal acts and was unaware that his father partook in criminal deeds. Madeline and Benjamin became fully aware of where Gina's issues came from. She inherited her addictive and mental health genes from Kyle's lineage, drugs, and mental disorders led to her criminal activities. Kyle agreed to be in Gina's life but gave Benjamin and Madeline the honor of being her legal parents. He apologized to them for his intrusion into their well-planned life. He saw them on television all the time and knew they were the doyen and cynosure of society but never thought of them beyond what he saw. What happened between them was a big mistake. It happened impulsively, a mistake to be regretted for the rest of their lives.

*****

Jason's overseas trip was an immense success. He was able to sign the contract of an airline business he had worked on for a decade, and he returned home incredibly happy to the loving arms of Bethena. The joy and happiness were too much. She decided not to distract the joy with Elizabeth's issues. Jason was the first to get out of bed the following day. As usual, he went straight to the kitchen and started preparing for breakfast. He was whistling a popular song when Elizabeth walked in. She told Jason she would take over the preparation from him, but he declined. Cooking was a passion to him. His late wife loved cooking. She made homemade meals for her family daily. He cooked with her mostly in the evening after work. When she passed, caring for his three children taught him to excel in cooking. Elizabeth insisted. He agreed, left the kitchen, and told her to shout his name if she needed help. He smiled at her as he left.

Elizabeth responded with a weak smile. He could tell that she was brooding over something. Bethena would later explain the situation to him. They ate breakfast in silence. Jason loved table manners to the core. No talking while eating was a table manner his late wife inculcated in him and their children. After breakfast, Jason and Bethena returned to the room. Bethena shared all that happened while he was away, showed him the signed agreement, and he was amazed.

"Are you sure she would abide by all these?"

Bethena smiled and nodded in affirmation. "Let us wait and see."

Jason told Elizabeth after lunch that he would like to have a word with her whenever she felt comfortable discussing with him. She told him she was available anytime he was available. They agreed to the evening, before dinner when Bethena would have returned from her doctor's visit, the words "doctor's visit" puzzled Elizabeth. Was her mother having health issues? She has been on medications and now doctor's visit? What was wrong with her?

In between lunch and dinner, Jason sat by the pool, enjoying the cool breeze while reading a vital document. He saw Bethena drive into the driveway and waved to her. She joined him by the poolside after fixing a jug of iced lemonade, got two cups, and called Elizabeth to let her know she was back. Elizabeth decided to join them by the poolside. Bethena apologized to her that she should have gotten an extra cup for her. She dashed back inside and returned with a cup for Elizabeth. By the time she returned, Jason was already discussing with Elizabeth who was visibly nervous. She lively up a bit when her mother returned, lemonade poured, and an especially important discussion began.

Jason looked at Elizabeth and spoke directly to her, "My darling wife here told me you wanted to know who Jason is. What exactly do you what to know?" he said with a broad smile.

Elizabeth seemed taken aback. She had asked her mother severally and would prefer that her mother shared the information with her instead of Jason. When her mother told her that Jason would tell her himself on the way from the attorney's office, she thought she was joking and tried to deflect from the topic. She was on the spot, facing Jason directly. For the first time in her life, her confidence failed. She felt belittled, felt totally subdued, and could not say yes or no. Jason asked her again and told her to relax and feel comfortable to ask whatever she wanted. Elizabeth felt a calm breeze blow over her after her mother signaled to her to talk. Her confidence level returned a little. She told him she would love to know everything about him.

"Everything? If you want everything, I will share everything with you," he said jokingly.

Jason told Elizabeth how he was born into a family of have-nots. His parents were poorer than the church rats. Feeding and clothing were a big problem. They fed on the little they had and shared clothes among the siblings. His father worked at different construction sites and took him along to support him at the various sites. He got remnants of food from the other construction workers and would keep leftovers as to-go for his other siblings and mother. Life was unbearable in the city they lived, so they moved to a bigger city with more job opportunities. In the new city, his father got more jobs and improved wages because he was well-skilled, and things got better with more jobs. Jason was able to sharpen his construction skills.

After school, he would join his father at the site and supported him with his job. His father's situation changed for the better. He was able to save money, bought land, and built it with Jason's input. The construction was done by the two of them from start to finish. That was how he cut his teeth in the real estate business. He saved from his menial jobs, bought land, built, and sold it. He made money, bought another land, built, and sold it, another and another and another. The rest was history. He made his first million when he was in the university where he studied civil engineering. His parents were both gone to their graves. They taught him the value of money, challenging work, discipline, and respect. They taught him that family is everything. His siblings are all millionaires. As the first child, he pulled all of them up and are all doing well and progressing in their chosen fields. He hated hand-outs to people and would rather teach people to fish than give them fish to eat. He was a life-changer who had supported people to change the course of their lives, became well known in the real estate business, ventured into the manufacturing of beverages, then into pharmaceuticals, insurance, and in the process of establishing an airline business.

Without waiting for Elizabeth to ask further questions, he discussed his love life with his late wife, her undying love for him and their three children, her support for his businesses, her illness, and death. Bethena rubbed his hand as he became emotional. He choked up. It was usual of him to tear up anytime he shared thoughts about his late wife. Elizabeth told him to accept her sympathy and condolence. For once, she really meant it. Her countenance showed sympathy.

He braced up and continued, "My late wife was a therapist who loved helping people without any reservation, treated everyone with merit and respect, and would go the extra mile to render help."

He discussed his children individually, shared their individual qualities, God-given talents, and how proud he was to be their father. Elizabeth suddenly felt jealous. The way he described their qualities with affection and pride made her turn green with envy. He was swift to tell Elizabeth that he had a reservoir of love waiting for her to tap into.

He looked at Bethena and then to Elizabeth, "Let me effectively address your constant innuendos in an effective way, not with any form of disparage. I am not a gold digger. In fact, I dug diamonds and gold for myself, never dug gold for anybody. I worked hard all my life and made my own money. I started at an early age, made money early in life, sustained it, and presently making enormous money. I am wealthy, but I do not flaunt my wealth. I learned to be a silent billionaire. I keep my cool and hated to be noticed. I have never taken a dime from my wife, Bethena, or a dime from your inheritance. I have made enough money to go around, with you inclusive. I am married to your mother. I love her dearly. She was godsent to me. I thank God every day for bringing her my way. I love her with every fiber of my being. My children love her so much, and she loved them to death. I love you as one of my children. I do not love you as a stepfather. I love you as a daughter if you would allow me. Let me into your life and heart, but as an adult, you are free and old enough to make your decisions whether to allow me to be your father or stepfather. I promise to support you one hundred and one percent in your recovery process, but you must imbibe the right attitude, behavior, discipline, and respect. You must have and show the right value for money. If you do, the sky would be your limit. Your sobriety must be the first thing for us, most especially for you to work on. My wife and I are ready to spend any amount of money to get you the best therapist money can buy."

Elizabeth sat still and could not utter a word.

Elizabeth eventually got her composure together, thanked Jason and her mother for their love and support, and promised to begin her recovery process in earnest. She had no choice anyway. She had either therapy or prison, no other option. Jason and Bethena got up and sandwiched her in a bear hug. It was a long hug. Elizabeth and Bethena shed tears of joy. Jason consoled them and told them he loved the two of them dearly and reiterated that he had so much love for Bethena and any offspring from her. Elizabeth thanked them again and promised she was ready for therapy. Dinner was late, but it was worth it. The big issue was finally resolved. Bethena and Jason were happy that Elizabeth willingly accepted without any insistence. They presumed it would be an uphill task convincing her. The court order had to be followed to the letter. Elizabeth had always been a hard nut to crack. They were happy at the outcome of the meeting and her response. Jason chose his words well; he was a man of the people and knew how to deal with different situations to get the desired result. Jason took the ladies out to dinner at an upscale diner to appreciate Elizabeth's acceptance to willingly go to therapy. The dinner was good. They had a good time. Elizabeth tried to blend with the flow. It was difficult. Her confidence level had suddenly evaporated. She felt intimidated despite the outpouring of love shown to her. She was ashamed of herself, of her behavior, most especially the name-calling and disrespect toward Jason.

It baffled her that he never said a word or responded to her and her insults. Most people of great substance like him are not as humble as he was. The thought hurt her the most. She saw firsthand that Jason loved her mother deeply, dotted around her, so caring and loving. She was happy for her mother. She found love. At last, her story was like that of the patient dog that got the fattest bone. The fact that love found her made her overjoyed for her. She saw happiness in her eyes. She radiated, and her skin glowed and happiness was visible in her. Everything about her had changed. She had become homely unlike when she rushed out early, only to return late in the night. Her job had a firm hold on her.

She was enjoying her newfound independence from her VP job, all thanks to Jason.

When they returned home from dinner, Jason informed Elizabeth that he would call one of the best addiction treatment centers in town to book an appointment. The following day, Jason called and scheduled an appointment for her at an outpatient treatment program. The appointment was set for that afternoon. She was scheduled to meet with one of the best therapists in town. Incidentally, her probation officer came in the morning on an impromptu visit. It was his first visit. He met with Elizabeth and subsequently with her parents. The officer was happy to know she was on track. He would visit again in one month to assess her progress; he told her she would be called randomly for drug tests. When Elizabeth woke up the following morning, Jason was in the kitchen. She took over from him. After breakfast, she apologized to both for her behavior and all she put them through.

*****

Benjamin and Madeline were relieved. The visit was a success and uneventful. Kyle invited them to the table. It was past lunchtime. The discussion took a long time. Madeline and Benjamin were full of joy. Food was not of importance. Joy and happiness had filled their tummies. They could not turn down Kyle's offer. He had gone the extra mile to prepare the meal. They ate as one big family and shared stories from the church and the community where they once lived. Kyle explained to Benjamin how he loved Madeline and wanted her as his wife. He wanted her for two reasons: the first was because of her discipline and upbringing; the second was her kindness and personal disposition toward everyone. With his condition, he needed a kind and compassionate lady who would be lenient and loving toward him. Madeline's personality fitted the ideal wife he wanted. That was why he made advances at her. With the way the family loved and cared for him, he believed that his chances were good.

Unfortunately, Benjamin swept her off her feet with his love. Their encounter was once, never planned; in fact, it was his first encounter with any lady. He had never mated before. Incidentally, that one encounter resulted in a child. Benjamin should please forgive Madeline because she was not a promiscuous lady. She was a reserved and well-behaved lady, and her attributes endeared him to her. He should also forgive him. He used to love her but had moved on. He would love to meet Gina, but her parents would forever be Benjamin and Madeline. He was her father biologically, but it takes more than biology to be a parent. They agreed to visit Gina together at the prison. They would fix a date that would be convenient for all of them. Information about paternity would, however, be discussed with Gina at a time conducive after her prison term. The atmosphere and timing had to be right for such a discussion. Kyle was very civil and understanding, and he agreed to keep the news a secret between them. When they decided to take their leave, Kyle saw them off to the car. He had a long handshake with Benjamin, gave Madeline a brief hug, turned to Benjamin, and once again apologized for the situation. He was a fine and wonderful gentleman.

CHAPTER 13

A New Identity

Carol was the focus of the community. Her NGO made her a well-known figure, and it had impacted the community positively. She was a mystery to the community. They knew her mother and daughter, but nobody knew her or the story behind her sudden appearance. She surfaced and became an unknown celebrity overnight. She started a flourishing floral business and an NGO—all doing well significantly. Her mother was a well-known figure, but her sudden appearance puzzled people. Rumor mongers were at work, gossiped, but none bothered her, and she minded her business. Carol was an industrious worker with a heart of gold. She never left a stone unturned when it came to doing good and being kind.

Ella followed suit in her mother's footsteps. She had changed significantly, and people who knew her before were amazed by the transformation that happened in her life. Carol took her out to a nice restaurant for her birthday in the company of Amelia. She commended her for her passionate effort in turning a new leaf. She would have been heartbroken to return home to a dysfunctional family with a daughter who was a crackhead criminal roaming the streets. Her change of attitude and behavior had made her a happy and fulfilled mother. Amelia thanked Carol and Ella for making her proud, making her a better mother and grandmother. Ella shared her therapist's session on making amends and seeking forgiveness from people they hurt in the past when possible and necessary. It was the second time she shared information on the topic. The first time she shared it with her mother, it had a profound impact on her. The guilt of what sent her to prison came to the fore. The guilt erupted in her conscience. It ate her up. Discussing it again hit her hard, and now bent on doing the needful. She must search for the family of the lady she killed and make amends. She had a sleepless night and needed to do something about it. Restitution was what she needed to liberate her soul, and ease her guilt. She had a moral inventory of her actions, ready to do the right thing.

A week after Ella's birthday, Carol informed her of her plan to visit the city where she was born and to look for the family and friends of the lady she killed. She intended to seek forgiveness and make amends. Ella discussed the topic further and emphasized to her that amends and seeking forgiveness were only when deemed safe by the offender. Carol agreed and promised to keep herself safe. She needed to clear her guilty conscience, convinced Ella to go with her, and convinced her that she would keep them safe.

She explained to Ella how the guilt of killing the lady had impacted her thoughts in the last few weeks, grinding her ability to move on to a halt, and tormenting her. Amelia was to stay behind to take care of the store and supervise the staff. Two days later, they set out on the seven-hour drive. Carol marveled at the development that had occurred while she was away. She had a vivid recollection of the city she once roamed and wreaked havoc. It was a small city at the time but now had high-rise buildings, malls, banks, gas stations, tarred double-lane highways, and more. The journey was long, but being in each other's company made it worth the while. They chatted, shared memories, catch up on time lost. Ella did all the driving; she was not sure of her mother's ability to drive on the freeways. They stopped two times on the way to rest at the rest areas, once to fill up the gas and once to eat at a restaurant close to the highway. When they arrived at the city, they went straight to the hotel, rested, and freshened up. They drove around the city. It was easy to locate the house where she grew up. It had been remodeled and looked like a masterpiece at the corner where it stood. They drove around and retired to the hotel when it was getting dark.

They got up early the following day and drove around until they got to the location, but everything had changed. She was sure of the location but at the same time confused. Instead of the club, a high-rise building was in its place. She knew the club owner. He lived not far away and knew some of his mistresses also. If she could not find him, she would search for them and find a way to locate them. He was in his late forties or early fifties at that time and must be an old man now. The mistresses must be old also. They were older than her and often chastised her for being too wayward at her age. A visit to the club owner's house yielded a positive result. When she introduced herself, he immediately remembered and recognized her.

He looked stunned and could not believe his eyes. The last time he saw her, she was young. Her assertive, aggressive nature and bad temper made her a shrewd highly feared girl by the patrons. She frequented the club and had turned the place into her second home. He ought to ban her from coming to the club because of her age, but he never did. She had a big frame and could pass for an adult. He offered them seats, made them comfortable after pleasantries, offered them alcohol, and they declined. They told him they do not drink. He looked at Carol with disbelief and joked that he could not believe she no longer drank alcohol. To open a conversation, they discussed old times at the club, the occurrences that had happened over the years, and the situation that sent her to prison. The mood was light. They jokingly discussed Carol's waywardness, her atrocities, about things they recalled. He was happy to see her. He told Carol that a big company bought the club from him. The offer was too good to overlook. He was getting old, worn, and tired of all the nefarious activities at the club and the late hours he had to endure daily. He sold the club and the land, took the money, invested, and retired early. He began playing golf to while away his time. Carol was happy for him, but in her mind, she thought of the many lives ruined at his club, including hers, the many shady deals, drugs, violence, and prostitution that took place at the club. To him, clubbing was the business where he got his livelihood; he was good at it and had a great passion for it. He was a shylock, unforgiving, uncompromising, and a no-nonsense club owner.

Carol seized the lively atmosphere to ask for information on the woman she killed. He was quick to ask why she was looking for her family and friends. She explained that she wanted to see them, atone for her sins, apologize, and make available financial contributions if necessary or possible. She paid her price at the state's penitentiary for twenty-five years but would love to do something nice for the family if she was able to locate any of the family members. He asked her if what she intended was necessary. She told him it would help her erase part of her guilt. She was out of order to have taken the woman's life. She was not in her right senses. If she were, she would not have done it. In retrospect, she wished she had behaved otherwise on the night of the incident. Her speech and notion seemed genuine to him. He agreed to make inquiries and told them it might take one or two days or even more, and they agreed to come back the following day. When they stood up to leave, he asked her about the beautiful damsel with her. Carol told him to pardon her manners and introduced her as her daughter. She had her while in prison, and her mother took care of her during the period of her incarceration. He nodded in disbelief; never knew she was pregnant on the day of her arrest; he saw her at the back of the police car and had no inclination that she was pregnant. He looked at Ella intently. She resembled someone he knew. The resemblance seemed too outstanding, but he kept quiet. He greeted Ella and told Carol he was happy for her.

"Your daughter has grown into a beautiful young lady. You must be proud of her," he uttered.

Carol nodded in affirmation, and thanked him, and they retired to the hotel for the night.

Carol shared more stories of her escapades when she was young, the many things she was not proud of, the drugs, criminality, sexual immorality, lying, cheating, stealing, and gangsterism. She messed up big-time but was happy that she could now use her experience and resources to better the lives of others, to liberate those she could from the pangs of addiction, mental disorders, domestic violence, and intimate partner abuse. The city had too many bad memories that were difficult to forget. The flashbacks were too much to contend with. She was bad, out of order, out of control, and acted in many bad ways.

Her vulnerability opened her to the floodgates of evil and criminal activities. She wished she could take her actions back. Ella told her to forget about the past and forge ahead. The past should be in the past, the present is now, and the future is tomorrow. Moving forward should be her priority. The past needed to be relegated to the background. She should use the lessons learned from the past as a compass to navigate the present and future. She had gotten on the right track with the NGO and opening the assortment of problems of the past could be detrimental. Her focus should be on how to remain the better person she had become, build on her new image, and continue to channel her energy on the excellent work she started when she returned from prison.

She needed to forgive herself, release herself from the shackles of guilt and unforgiveness, and forgive herself for the actions of when she was ignorant. She knew better now. Unforgiveness would lead to frustrations, anxiety, depression, stagnancy, other disorders, and relapse. She referred her to the Serenity Prayer she learned at therapy and meetings. She encouraged her mother to allow serenity (peace) to reign in her life. She should not flog herself over the things that had happened and could not be changed, needed to embrace the things she could change, and accept wholeheartedly the difference between what she could change and what she could not change. She had made a step in the right direction to make amend. Whatever the outcome, releasing herself from the guilt would be the next step. She smiled, and the two of them recited the serenity prayer in unison.

God grant me the Serenity
To accept the things
I cannot change
The Courage to change the things I can, and
The Wisdom to know the difference.

(Reinhold Niebuhr, an American theologian)

After reciting the prayer together, they embraced themselves. They had become mother-daughter that seemed like best friends. Carol learned the serenity prayer while in prison. It was one of the prayers she recited daily. They discussed the words: serenity, acceptance, change, courage, wisdom, and difference each in its entirety and encouraged themselves with the words. It was quality time spent together. The night ran a race. It was morning before they knew it. They had breakfast and drove around the city. Carol showed Ella places her parents used to take her.

At noon, they had lunch at a diner, sat outside, enjoyed the breeze, drove around the city again, and stopped at the club owner's house at around four in the afternoon. He was happy to see them again and told them he had not been able to get the desired information. The period was too short to get information on the people. It was a long time ago. Most had relocated to other places or died. He would keep seeking the information they sought. They discussed other issues. Carol shared her experiences in the different prisons where she served her term and learned from fellow prisoners, both good and bad. She had turned her life around, deviated from her bad experiences, and embraced the good ones.

She got her GED, learned different crafts, and excelled in them. She opened a floral store after her release and had started an NGO to support other people, to encourage them to avoid prison. It was her little way of giving back to society and depopulate the place called prison. He listened attentively. It was evident to him that Carol had changed. He marveled at her new dispensation, fully convinced to support her in searching for the family she was looking for. He was happy to share that he had also turned a new leaf after he sold his club, changed from his old ways, now well vested in church activities, and no longer mingled with the wrong crowd. He had asked his higher power for forgiveness, became a community leader, used his past experiences to mentor and advise the youth, and had turned to a pillar reckoned with in the community.

He had a great interest in Ella and asked about her father. Carol told him she had no idea. She could not figure out who impregnated her. He nodded and looked at Ella again. It seemed like he had an idea of who her father could be from the resemblance, but he said nothing. He wanted to be sure before uttering a word. He invited Carol and Ella to the golf course the following day. He had a game with one of his friends. They agreed to meet at ten in the morning. They called it a day and left for the hotel. Ella asked her mother why the club owner looked at her so intently. Carol told her she had no idea. They prayed, recited the serenity prayer again, and called Amelia before retiring to bed for the night.

The following day, they met with him at the golf club. They had fun watching the old men golf. It was a good exercise for Carol and Ella, and they trekked so much on the golf course. He introduced them to the patrons at the golf club who knew Carol's mother, but they had no recollection of Carol. After the golf session, they had lunch. Carol and Ella sat at the outer section of the clubhouse; they avoided the areas with alcoholic drinks. They returned to the club owner's house, settled, and resumed the discussion that brought them there. He informed Carol that he had called all the people he knew that could give him information on the slain woman but was told that the lady lived with her grandmother who was her legal guardian after the death of her parents. She had no children; unfortunately, the grandmother died of a heart attack weeks after her death. Nobody had information on any of her friends. They were mostly fair-weather friends, acquaintances, and doing the same illicit trade together. Carol was sad that she erased a lineage. She decided to immortalize her by erecting a recreational center in the community to enhance the youth, girls, and boys alike. They left the following day and promised to stay connected with the club owner. Amelia was happy to have them back at home. She was happy that they came back safe and thrilled with Carol's decision to erect a place in the community for the youth. Carol's generosity made Amelia fulfilled. It would be money well spent for the benefit of others. What is the essence or usefulness of money when not shared? Money is meant to go round, support others, help humanity, touch people's lives, and impact others. A cheerful giver gets more reward than a miser who spends only on himself/herself.

*****

Madeline's family, especially her father, was relieved when they learned of the outcome of the meeting with Kyle. Madeline's father decided to call Kyle, but Kyle called him first. He apologized to his former pastor for what happened between him and Madeline. He wanted to explain his side of the story, but he told him it was not necessary. He, however, thanked Kyle for his understanding and civility. He encouraged him to be involved in any way he wanted, asked him to return to the "sonship" relationship he had with him in the past and that he was welcome in their home anytime. Kyle thanked him for forgiving and welcoming him back into the family. He told him that he loved and would always love them. Benjamin who had stopped reaching out to Gina after she had refused to see or talk to him on occasions scheduled to visit her. To his greatest surprise, she agreed to meet with him. He informed Kyle, and the three of them visited Gina. She had changed, lost weight, and seemed remorseful.

The training and discipline she refused to imbibe at home had been impacted on her by the jail system. She looked different, subdued, and humbled. Pride had dealt a big blow on her, humbled to the level of timidity. She had forcefully learned that destruction was the best teacher to pride. She looked a shadow of herself. Her big mouth had suddenly lost its reservoir of words. Immediately, she saw her mother. She knew her mother was a stroke survivor from the way she walked and that she was the cause of her mother's ailment. It broke her spirit, and she sobbed. She asked Madeline what was wrong with her. She told her not to worry that it was a long story but presently fine.

Benjamin introduced Kyle as a friend of the family. Gina greeted him nicely but was puzzled. In the first instance, she was not expecting them to visit her for the first time with a visitor, not used to seeing visitors in their home. Why was the friend visiting her? She noticed that he had two birthmarks, one on his nose and one on the back of his left hand. Gina had the birthmark on her nose and the other on her right hand. She was confused and puzzled but kept mute. When they were ready to leave, she commented about the birthmarks, the coincidence, and they joked and glided into another topic. It, however, dawned on Benjamin and Madeline the correlations of the birthmarks on Gina and Kyle, they also noted that they had the same dimple on their cheeks whenever they smiled. They never noticed it until the day of the visit. Kyle informed them that Gina had all his traits. He saw the birthmarks. They were visible. He suspected that Gina would figure it out sooner than expected. He loved her but would prefer not to visit her again to safeguard the paternity issue and not cause more harm than good for all of them. He, however, promised to visit her through other means. He could have access to the facility at his convenience through his job but would try not to usurp anything that could cause her to suspect anything, however, did not tell them what he does that could give him such access to prison facilities.

Jason registered Elizabeth into one of the best rehabilitation centers in the city they lived. She opted for outpatient instead of a residential treatment facility. Jason and Bethena were happy that she would be at home with them to bond and normalize their tumultuous relationship. Jason was willing to do all he could to warm himself into the heart of Elizabeth. To him, family was everything. Happiness and joy must reign in their abode. Bethena needed peace of mind for her health to stabilize. Bonding with Elizabeth might normalize her raised blood pressure, and medications with incessant milligram increase. Jason was not ready to lose his wife a second time. Money was not a problem to Jason; he would spare no stone in rehabilitating his daughter. His love for Elizabeth knew no bounds. He loved her the exact way he loved his biological children. Bethena was the love of his life, and so would Elizabeth. The therapist was an experienced professional with years of therapeutic service to individuals, families, and the community. She met with Elizabeth for the psychosocial assessment. She encouraged her to be open, verbalize, and truthful in her responses as it would determine her assessment and the best treatment plan for her. She discussed that all her answers and counseling sessions would be confidential. HIPPA law forbids sharing of medical and personal information with anyone unless agreed in writing and signed by the consumer.

Elizabeth was initially uncooperative, faked her desire for rehabilitation, and untruthful in her responses. She knew the right answers to make it seem she was ready for treatment. She had been in and out of treatment and would not have gotten involved in this one if not court-ordered. Treatment had become a revolving door for her. The therapist knew she lied, noted her untruthfulness during the first session with Elizabeth, counseled her on "truth vs. lie, how they affect sobriety and the rehabilitation process," and told her she would not have to task her memory if she was truthful. Lying would make her task her brain before every response, make her look stupid, build more lies upon the initial lie. Jason and Bethena shared daily activities with Elizabeth as a form of support. They knew she would lie on many of the answers she gave to the therapist, and they encouraged her to be truthful and fully forthcoming to the therapist so she could offer her the best therapy and treatment. When Elizabeth got to the facility the following week, she told the therapist the whole truth and nothing but the truth. The therapist told her she knew she lied on the answers and would have eventually extracted the truth from her. Elizabeth asked how she knew. The therapist discussed her mannerisms, facial expressions, choice of words, composures, and distractions. Elizabeth smiled, knew her game was up, and promised to be truthful and open. She did a new psychosocial assessment and a new treatment plan for Elizabeth.

Elizabeth shared her family history, medical history, educational background, alcohol/drug use (types of drugs), psychiatric history, traumatic issues, criminal history, eating habits, personal preferences/associations, and more. Elizabeth was forthcoming. She told the whole truth. A new treatment plan was developed. Elizabeth participated and gave her input and was pleased with the plan. Her treatment plan included the following and other items deemed fit for a smooth process:

1. Individual counseling sessions three times a week
2. Group therapy sessions three times a week
3. Family therapy sessions once a month

4. Attendance at AA/NA meetings two times a week
5. Get a sponsor for the AA/NA meetings
6. Urinalysis once a week on demand, randomly
7. Assignments are to be submitted as at when due
8. Follow-up
9. Aftercare

Elizabeth worked with the therapist on the treatment plan, signed it, and the therapist started the counseling sessions in earnest. As usual with addicts, she became disinterested again. She would arrive at the sessions tired. She participated minimally, deliberately avoided questions that are personal, looked sleepy, yawned often, had minimal attention span, and weaved between interests and disinterest. The therapist allowed her to work at her pace, knew she was not prepared, and had seen the tactics before with other clients when mandated by the judicial system or forced by their parents. She encouraged her to be involved for her liberation and not for anyone. She jokingly asked why she yawned often. She did not respond verbally and responded with her shoulder and eyes down. The therapist asked why she looked tired, if she had a good night's sleep, was bored of the session, or needed oxygen in her brain. She looked puzzled with a wry smile, giggled, and asked if those were the reasons for yawning. The therapist responded that they are reasons for excessive yawning. Elizabeth then responded timidly but with a frown "all the above." When her eyes met that of the therapist, they both laughed aloud. The therapist was able to break into her difficult, cold attitude, and shared the importance of a good night's sleep on the brain to avoid boredom, tiredness, inactive participation, and adequate oxygen for the brain. From that moment, she began to actively participate in the sessions and started enjoying the sessions as they progressed. The first few weeks were stressful for her; she kept the pace and gradually became engrossed in them. When the stages of addiction were discussed, it dawned on her that she was truly an addict. She recounted how her initial use turned to abuse, built a tolerance to the abuse, made her become dependent and addicted, and led to many relapses over the years.

Elizabeth recounted how she became initiated into drug use by Gina. She had never tried any drug in her life (not even cigarettes) before she became Gina's friend. Not that she was a saint, she was a troubled youth, but her notoriety never delved into the area of drugs. Gina smoked cigarettes, encouraged her to do the same, then marijuana, the gateway drug. It was her first use. Gina convinced her that she would like it. She did not like it the first time but needed to do it again in the spirit of belongingness to Gina's world. Gina was the coolest new student in the school, beautiful, fashionable, and rich. Everyone wanted to be her friend. Elizabeth saw herself as the chosen bride when Gina became her friend. She was happy and felt on top of the world as an associate of Gina who already was friendly with Ella. Gina was a bully. Nobody crossed her path without repercussion. Being Gina's friend meant no one could mess, disrespect, or bully her. She liked that a lot. To remain Gina's friend, she followed her instructions to the letter, drugs inclusive. The first few times of experimenting with marijuana, she disliked it. The side effects were too much for her to bear but forced and coerced by Gina to continue. She encouraged her that she would get used to it with time. She eventually got used to it. It became regular for them to smoke cigarettes and marijuana daily. Gina was the provider. She brought the drugs and knew where to buy them. They graduated into other drugs, abused more than one drug daily, and would top it up with alcohol.

It became recreation. When they got into trouble for drinking alcohol at the back of the cafeteria in their senior year in high school, they were undeterred. It was supposed to be a wake-up call, but the risks and punishment were nothing compared to the desire to use and get high. They were already dependent on drugs. They had turned drug use into a game to affirm superiority and the best person to use most was applauded. They became hooked on drugs by the time they left high school. They had built tolerance levels that needed daily sustenance to function effectively.

As rich kids, drug purchase was not a problem. They had unfettered access to easy and cheap money from their parents and guardian, and they had excess money at their disposal. Gina was no longer the able supplier; they could purchase drugs as much as money could buy. Anytime supply was short, there would be problems with anyone they had contact with; fortunately, they all had absentee parents who were not vigilant enough to notice or curtail their excesses until it became too late. Even when they had the first altercation with Francine, their parents were too busy to secure effective supervision for them. Several of the evils they committed attracted just slaps on the wrist from their parents. Criminality followed suit, in school, outside of the school, in the malls, in different clubhouses, the DUIs, stealing, fighting, and all the attendant factors of drug-addicted individuals. Elizabeth disclosed all the negative activities the trio did. With an emphasis on her input, she shared elaborately the hatred, envy, malice, bullying they meted on Francine, and the unwarranted disdain for an individual that led them deep into addiction and criminality. She shared the opportunities they blew because of jealousy and envy while their classmates received tutorials/support from Francine. They saw her beneath them, unworthy to teach and support them academically. Fashion, outpacing, and bullying Francine were of utmost priority to them. Graduation from high school with no admission to any college or university compounded their problem. They had nowhere to go all day, so they roamed the streets, use drugs, club, and stole things they could afford for fun. Ample time on their hands led to more criminality and drug use. They became good tools in the devil's workshop. They terrorized people mostly at the malls and clubs. They were the untouchables. The wealth and names of their parents were their shields.

The therapist listened with rapt attention. She did not disturb her thought process and verbalization. She was happy that she spoke out, sometimes with chuckles and sometimes with vents. Her admission of drug use, reasons for use, people she used with, places where they used, behavioral trait attestations, and criminal acts showed she had gained something from the therapy session. It was a step in the right direction for both. The therapist led her to accept that she had a problem. Acceptance was a key factor in the recovery process. Elizabeth became willing to work on herself after her admission at a crisis point. She asked the therapist the way forward and what she needed to do to attain sobriety. It was the first time she admitted she had a problem. All the previous treatments were a joke to her. The therapist discussed why a change was urgently needed to salvage her from personal destruction.

Weeks into the therapy sessions, the therapist noticed that Elizabeth had performed above her expectations. She had effortlessly glided through the stages of change. She had surpassed the pre-contemplation, contemplation, preparation, and action and was already at the maintenance stage. All her random urinalysis had been negative. She had put in a hundred percent of her time and effort into the program, fully ready for the desired change. Her probation officer was happy to receive the report from the treatment center on her urinalysis. Every time he met with her, he saw a renewed individual who had become personable, respectful, clean in outward appearance, healthier, and in good spirit and shape. Jason and Bethena made themselves available monthly for the family therapy sessions. They were Elizabeth's greatest support. They made sure there were no alcoholic beverages in the house, drove her to and from sessions, took her to her AA/NA meetings, made her comfortable, made sure she attended her psychiatric appointments, and reminded her of her medications, which she used accordingly.

Her sponsor was a dependable soul. She supported her as needed. At the end of the court-ordered six months, Elizabeth was in decent shape. She finished her recovery process with a clean slate to begin life afresh. The aftercare and follow-up sessions went smoothly; she maintained her sobriety, and her life changed drastically with great hope for the future. Elizabeth learned a lot at the treatment center. In her personal assessment, her therapist was the best. She was heaven-sent to her. She pulled out the best in her through the CBT (cognitive behavioral therapy) technique. She would be forever grateful to her for the changed person she had become.

She had not touched alcohol or drugs for one year, knew the triggers to avoid, people/friends to mingle with, places and areas to avoid as well as things that could arouse her interest in drugs. She kept her support system small, made no new friends, in touch regularly with Ella and Francine who had become her mentor and lifesaver. She attended AA and NA meetings and had become a sponsor to a new lady at the meeting. Looking back, she knew she had erred, failed herself in so many ways, and truncated her progress in life with no one to blame but herself. She took full responsibility for all her actions, regretted her excesses, ready to put the past behind her, and open a new chapter for her future. Bethena had followed the process her parents laid down for her. She went to school, graduated from university twice, got a job, excelled, climbed the ladder to success, and she would do the same. Her life's aspiration took a dire turn when she became friends with Gina. Her determination now was to excel, retract her steps from the wrong way, follow the right direction, keep her sobriety, and be dedicated at over a million percent. The change was for her and not for anyone else. Change to impress anyone besides yourself would never work or be productive.

With the treatment program behind her, she enrolled at the community college. Returning to school was never too late, and learning never ends until a person becomes interred in the grave. Francine and Ella convinced and encouraged her to return to school. Education is the only endowment a person can bestow on oneself. No one can take away what you have learned. It is yours forever, your personal embedded keepsake within you, your enlightenment and power. She embraced the idea with both hands and heart. Jason and Bethena were the happiest. They gave her all the support she needed. Support before, during, and after treatment was particularly important. Francine and Ella were not left out. They had been her support through thick and thin.

Ella and Francine visited Elizabeth at home, and they saw firsthand the love and affection Jason and Bethena showered on her, and they advised her not to blow the opportunity for anything under the sun. Bethena had more vigor and stability, her health had stabilized drastically, her last three doctor's visits showed great progress, and her blood pressure had normalized, thanks to Elizabeth's return and recovery.

The milligram of her blood pressure medication was reduced after six visits, which showed her pressure had stabilized. Jason was happy at her renewed health. Elizabeth's stability and sobriety were key to keeping his wife alive, and he would do anything to make them healthy and safe. Bethena was full of appreciation and joy that Jason came into her life at a time she needed his support. If he had not been supportive of her, she would have died of a broken heart because of Elizabeth.

*****

Carol returned home from the visit to her birth city unfulfilled; she would have been happier if she found a relative of the lady she murdered. Amelia encouraged her not to be anxious and depressed. The club owner would find someone in her lineage soon. In the meantime, she should focus on her NGO and helping other people. Her plan to build a recreational center for the youth of the community to immortalize her was on course, soon to be executed. A few days after her return, the club owner called. Carol believed she got the breakthrough she awaited. He told her there was no added information on the lady, but he had other information to share with her. Carol listened attentively after pleasantries. He reminded her of the man he introduced to her at the golf course, the elderly man with a squint on his left eye. He apologized for describing him with the squint, not that he wanted to be derogatory, but it was the best way to make her remember. Carol recollected the man because of the description. He told her that he might know the father of Ella from the resemblance he noticed on the day they visited. Carol was short of words. She did not know whether to continue the conversation or to discontinue. Her brain went into sleep mode. Would Ella want such information? How would she receive or respond to the information? Would seeking her father disrupt their lives and bond? What if the person was an addict who could reverse her recovery process? Her brain went quickly into overdrive in an instant. She was confused, lost for an answer. After a few minutes, the club owner asked, "Are you there?" Carol summoned courage and said, "Yes, I am listening."

The club owner sensed her reluctance. He thought about how she would receive the news but also thought that not telling her of the likelihood would be a disservice to Carol who he undoubtedly saw as a changed person. He told Carol to sleep on it and call him if she wanted to proceed with the information. Ella came in as soon as she dropped the phone. She saw her face and could tell she was upset. She persuaded her to share what the issue was. She did after dinner.

Ella and Amelia agreed that there was nothing to lose by exploring the issue. Carol agreed with them reluctantly. She feared opening an assortment of problems that could destabilize their perfect relationship. She pondered over the issue all day before dinner. They eventually agreed that no matter the outcome, the bond between them would stay intact. Carol called the club owner the following day. He gave her the number of the man they met at the golf course. He was a constant patron at the club at that time. He was not an addict. He was a big spender who loved clubbing to relax and "kill" boredom. He was rich and had businesses that gave him good returns. He was a bosom friend of the club owner, a social drinker who loved to enjoy himself after a hard day's job. His wife died early, never remarried since the demise of his wife, a family man to the core, took good care of his children, and catered for them alone.

His first son worked part-time at the club. He was not a drinker and never drank or used drugs. He was always at the back washing cups and plates. His father allowed him when he asked for permission to do a part-time job at the club. He allowed him to work so that he would know the value of hard work and money. His father and the club owner kept an eye on him. His son, Baron, chastised her severally for being around a club. They liked each other, attended the same school. He was seventeen while she was fifteen. He hated seeing her at the club. He liked her and wanted to see her change her lifestyle. He was broken when he learned that she was arrested for stabbing someone who eventually died. That was the last he heard about Carol.

Carol called him. He told her that Ella had a great resemblance to his first son and would like to investigate the matter. When he saw her at the golf course, his intuition was that Ella belonged to his family. If Ella was his grandchild, he would love his son to be in her life and would like to have a relationship with her. Carol remembered his son, mated with him, and others, and would not want to search through the likelihoods. He asked Carol for permission to give her number to his son. He would reach out to her, and they could explore the truth about Ella's paternity. Carol thanked him and told him she would expect the call from his son. He reached out to his son whom he had shared the information previously, gave him Carol's phone number, and told him to reach out immediately. A few minutes after the discussion, his son called. He promised to be at her store the following day. Incidentally, he lived in the same city as Carol and Ella. He had been to Carol's store countless times, but they never met, did not pay attention, or probably were not observant nor cognizant of the resemblance. He arrived before nine the following day. It was a long night for him; he eagerly waited for dawn to see Ella, whom his father had described as his spitting image.

*****

A new era dawned for Gina after the last time her parents and Kyle visited her at the penitentiary. She suddenly wanted a relationship with her parents and called them often on call collect. They had also warmed up to her, and the relationship began normalizing from civil, platonic to more of parents and child. Her stay at the prison had made her realize all her follies. She had been drug-free because her prison location had zero tolerance for drugs, but illegal drugs still trickled in. Gina learned to stay away so she could get early release due to good behavior. Sensibility had set in for her. She had not heard from her bosom friends who had gotten their lives in order, progressing with meaningful life alterations. They were no longer the drug heads she knew them to be. They were clean, stable, and sober on the right track to success. Benjamin and Madeline made it a point of duty to visit her at least once a month and deposited a reasonable amount into her commissary account. The era of big pocket money no longer existed. She was to live like any other inmate. Gina inquired about the man that came with them. They gave her excuses. The time was not ripe to let the cat out of the bag. Gina learned crafts to keep herself busy. She had only a high school diploma that she got at the exact GPA to graduate. Her brain had rested from the bombardment of drugs. She could think better, reasonable with a high level of morality, and her change was notable. She was recommended for early release due to good behavior and report and might be released in a few months all things being equal. To her greatest surprise, her uncles and aunties paid her visits. It warmed her heart but puzzled her. Her parents severed relationships with them a while ago. Why the sudden change? She was happy when they no longer visited each other. They were a pain to her and were unhappy that her parents spoiled her. They hated the way she lived as if there would not be a tomorrow, hated the way they looked, and chastised her. She asked her parents but got no tangible explanation.

*****

Francine was on the way to another major accolade, this time a giant feather to her cap. She had the highest CGPA (Cumulative Grade Point Average) in medical school. No student had gotten such a high score. She was on the news for almost one week before her graduation for interviews with the top TV and radio stations. Her parents planned a surprise graduation party for her. Ella and Elizabeth with their parents were not left out. Besides the party, Jason had another surprise for her and her friends. He planned to fly them out in one of his private jets to an island for a weekend getaway in appreciation of the support she gave Elizabeth from time to time. It had changed Elizabeth in ways immeasurable. Francine's boyfriend, who also was her classmate and study partner, was a few points lower than her. He complemented Francine so much in many ways. He was brilliant, kindhearted, unassuming, humble, likable, and handsome. He loved and adored Francine so much and planned to marry her someday. Their relationship while in school was platonic though Francine knew he wanted more than friendship. She never encouraged him. Books and studies were her priority. Francine's grandmother wanted her to get married as soon as possible. She wanted great-grandchildren. Francine laughed every time she blurted out her wish. She planned to work on her residency and then on a specialty. The first time she met Francine's friend, she told him her wish. Everyone present busted out in laughter.

*****

Carol and Amelia got to the store at a quarter to nine. They came in through the back door. A staff came in to inform her that someone was at the reception to see her. When the staff was about to leave, she blurted out that Ella looked every inch like the visitor. The staff members had opened the store and let him in. Ella had an early morning lecture and was not available. Carol signified that the visitor should come into her office. When Carol saw him, her jaw dropped. It was as if another Ella came into her office. He introduced himself because Carol seemed lost, rooted to her seat, and looked as if she saw a ghost. When Amelia came into Carol's office and saw him, she almost fainted, quickly got her composure back, and introduced herself. Carol got up, shook his hand, and offered him a seat. When they made eye contact, the old memories flooded their brains, and they started chatting, forgetting the reason for the visit for a while. Amelia returned to her office to give them privacy and time to discuss the pertinent issue.

When Carol saw him, she knew a DNA was not necessary but would oblige one to put the riddle to rest, to confirm all doubts, cross all Ts. Ella's full-blown picture was on the wall in Carol's office. He marveled at the resemblance. He thought within himself, *If this child is not mine, I wonder whose child it would be*. He knew his father frequented the club, but he would never touch a teenage girl who was the same age with his children. Ella finished her lecture early and returned to the store in case her supposed father was still around. True to her thought, he was still there. When Ella entered, her mind seemed to have played a trick on her. What she saw threw her off-balance. She was nothing but a replica of the man sitting in front of her mother. Her first instinct was, "This is my father!"

A person's first instinct is mostly the right one. She had never seen such a resemblance in two people before. She jumped on him. She had done it intuitively before her brain kicked in. *What if he is not your father*? After hugging him for a long time, she released her grip and asked, "What if you are not my father? Where did this resemblance come from? I have never seen two people with such a powerful resemblance. If you are not my father, I would love to know you more. I have heard stories that God made two people in the same unique fashion but that He puts them in distinct locations or continents, and here are the two of us in the same country and city."

She said jokingly, "Someone in my school once told me she saw a man that looked very much like me. I discarded the statement and moved on. She was right."

The mystery man just laughed. He got up, gave her a bear hug, longer than the one she gave him. The hug was so touching. They both felt the family touch, a blood bond. He released her, looked at her again, and saw how beautiful she looked. She had a beautiful blouse that almost matched her skin color with black dots on it. She looked dainty and extremely beautiful. Her clothing hugged her skin perfectly and beautifully. He thought within himself, *If this is my daughter, I have lost beautiful years of her existence*.

He looked at Ella and said, "I have something to say here and now. I am not aware I have a child. I am not a deadbeat father. This resemblance tells me you are mine. I am a zillion percent positive. Even without a DNA, my instinct tells me you are my child, the moment I saw your picture, even before your arrival, my inner being confirmed it. This is my submission."

Everyone reeled with laughter. He paused for some time. "Let me tell you my story. I met your mother when we were very young. We attended the same school. I didn't know what love was because I was a child, very young, but I knew I liked her a lot. She was very beautiful, still is, full of life, and always alone. She always looked bored by the street corner after school. She would roam the streets endlessly. I would come outside to play with her since I lived blocks away. My mother died when I was about ten years old. My father never remarried. He devoted all his energy to raising me and my sister. He had mistresses who wanted to become his wife but never married any of them. My father was neither rich nor poor. He was an average man, comfortable enough to cater to his family. He took care of us and provided all we needed. We lacked nothing. I loved making money in my spare time to augment my pocket money. I decided to take a part-time job in the evenings at the club only on weekends. I worked only two days a week, Fridays and Saturdays. The owner who knew I was hardworking and disciplined happily employed me, gave me hours at the club on weekends, and paid me a stipend. My father allowed me to work after I persuaded him that I would never touch alcohol or do drugs. His friend promised to keep an eye on me. My father, who was a frequent patron at the club, also kept an eye on my activities.

"Your mother loved the club. She was always around the club. I warned her on occasions about it as well as her association with the old people at the club. On an occasion, one of the old men, as I called them, gave me a hard knock on my head because she ran home when I lied to her that her mother was looking for her. I had a terrible headache for days from the knock. It was a ploy to get her away from the old men whom I thought could take advantage of her. Your mother ran to the house only to return minutes later. She fumed that I played on her intelligence, lied to her, and vowed never to believe anything I tell her again.

"One day, her mother was searching for her. I ran and told her, but she did not believe me. When she found out she was at the club, hell was let loose on the owner and patrons. She wanted to involve the police but was dissuaded. She probably disciplined and restricted her. She stopped coming to the club, but it was short-lived. We showed affection to each other and mated only twice. We were just mischievous, wrong, and carried away by youthful exuberance. We were not boyfriend/girlfriend per se, but we liked each other genuinely. She would bring me cookies, and I would bring things from my house to share with her. We loved each other's company and shared gist. I was not at work the day the incident that sent her to prison happened. Nobody knew she was pregnant at the time. She hid it so well from everyone. I saw her a week before then, and she looked normal to me.

"The club owner and my father told me the police arrested her. That was the last I heard of her until my father called last week when he met you ladies at the golf course. He told me that I needed to contact you, that we had something in common. He would not tell me what it was until I confessed to him that I had dealt with your mother. He would have killed me at that time if he knew I was sexually active. He gave me her phone number yesterday, and I contacted her immediately. When your mother was arrested, her mother, Amelia, moved away. In fact, it was not long after the death of her husband. Everything happened so fast."

Amelia was in the adjacent room. She heard everything. She was not eavesdropping but heard all the story because the excitement was high. The pitch of Baron's voice was high. He was not a loud person naturally, but the joy of seeing Ella, his replica and probably his daughter, was not the type of joy that could be hidden, discussed huss-huss. Carol cleared her throat loudly to call the attention of everyone and to calm the high tension. Ella looked incredibly happy, enjoying, and assimilating every word. All eyes turned to Carol for a second. Baron smiled and continued his story with a dream he had years ago. In the dream, he saw Carol running back to the house after school. She dashed inside and out, called Baron, and told him she had a present for him. He stretched out his hand for the present only for her to dash back inside and shut the door. When he woke up, he wondered what the dream meant. He was at the university and had not seen Carol for over ten years. He seldom dreamed, but whenever he dreamed, it usually came to pass. His dreams were most times infallible. He pondered over it, forgot about it, and moved on with his life. The moment his father told him about Ella, the whole dream came to the fore as if he just woke up from a slumber. Ella was the gift Carol refused to give to him in his dream. Amelia joined them as unlimited laughter took over the room. It was an outpouring and joy and love.

Carol asked Baron the way forward. She wanted DNA to confirm the paternity of Ella, and Baron agreed. Ella was happy and ready. Baron offered to take them out for lunch, but Carol declined. She wanted more information on Baron and was not ready to mingle with anyone with drug or alcohol issues or problems, not willing to jeopardize both recoveries. Barons spent a good four hours with Carol and Ella. It was a great reunion and felt as if they had known each other forever. He shared his life story. He finished high school with flying colors and proceeded to the university where he studied biochemistry. He was hardworking, worked for two years, and returned to school for a master's in business administration (MBA). After graduation, he worked for a medical research company for five years, left for a clinical research company, and worked for another five. He then started his own clinical research company. His company had been in existence for a decade. It was one of the top five clinical research companies in the city. He never smoked cigarettes, never did any drugs, and was a social drinker. He had not been inside any club since he left the club where he worked as a teenager. His biography soothe Carol's heart. She had learned her lessons the hard way and was not ready to let her guards down. Her sobriety and Ella's meant so much to her than a father-daughter relationship. Ella grew up without a father. She could live her life without one if the relationship does not seem right. Anyway, Ella knew better and knew what she wanted for her sanity. She wanted a father, not a father figure. If it would be a father figure, she would not be interested.

Ella was not willing to waste any time. The anxiety was too much for her to bear, so an appointment date for the DNA was the following Monday. Francine was marvelously surprised and happy for her. She called daily to calm her nerves while waiting for the result. Francine was her best confidant. She hid nothing from her. Baron took Carol and Ella to lunch when they left the diagnostic clinic. Everyone they encountered at the restaurant commented on the resemblance between Ella and Baron, embarrassed at a point, but Baron was happy. Ella would be his only child if the test returned positive. He had been too busy with work and business than with marriage and procreation. He would be the happiest in this world if Ella turned out to be his and had promised himself that he would make up for the years he had lost. *How do you make up for the absence of over two decades?* he thought. God will teach him to be his best.

Francine came to town on the day the result was to be received. She wanted to be there for Ella whatever the result turned out to be. The result was open with everyone present. The anxiety was sky high. It was a joyous day. Baron had a daughter. Ella got a father. Carol was extremely happy. A chapter of her life suddenly read out the word "positive." She was happy the dark area of her life suddenly lit up with illumination that could no longer be dimmed. Ella's stigma got lifted. She now had a father, a father to walk her down the aisle on her wedding day, a male figure to advise and counsel her on the way to toe. The joy was infectious. Merriment marked the day at the store. Carol had a person to call the father of her daughter who was already a grown woman. Baron would bring a new meaning to their lives. It was a chapter beautifully rewritten to solve the untouchable riddle of their lives. The irony and miracle of the situation made it worth the joy and happiness. They were in search of restitution but got a miracle in return. Carol never thought of opening the chapter of Ella's paternity, and Ella was not searching either. They were at peace with the issue. As for the restitution, the latest development had given it greater relevance. Baron promised them he would not only step up, but he would also make up for all the lost years.

*****

Francine was top of her class despite her busy schedule. She attended clinical and hospital runs, volunteered at NGOs, taught classes to her coursemates and juniors, and was always on hand to help the academically needy. She became a force to be reckoned with in school. Francine was respected for her intellect, brain, and brawn. She got great recognition at her graduation. Her name became a household name. Her parents and grandmother had a special place reserved for them on the podium because of Francine's accolades. She shone like the stars in the sky and made her parents, community, and university proud. Ella and Elizabeth's family were all in attendance. It was a day filled with joy. Francine was the latest medical doctor in town. Baron was the icing on the cake at the reception, he came to join Carol, Ella, and Amelia. He looked perfect with Carol. They had become good friends, and Jason was happy to meet the much-talked-about Baron. Francine's grandmother gifted her a brand-new car. It was a surprise present to Francine. She was the proudest grandmother in town. The good report on Francine's honorable deeds, integrity, and humility made everyone swell with pride.

Francine was beauty, grace, brain, and kindhearted rolled into one. She was an embodiment of special talents and vices. She was well-built in character, well-equipped, and sustained it. She guarded her character and integrity jealously. She was down to earth. No atom of pride could be found in her. She was an epitome of humility. Her humility helped Ella and Elizabeth break their prideful life and lifestyle, a life of feeling on top of the world whereas they were at the bottom of the ladder. Pride made them believe they did no wrong. The world and the "just" was the wrong ones. Francine may not be from a family as rich as Ella and Elizabeth's but rich in diverse ways. True riches cannot be measured in wealth/money but "in who you are, what you are, and in the lives touched. Posterity should be the focus and not in the number of zeros in a bank account." Jason made good on his promise to Francine and the girls. They got a getaway in one of his private jets to an island to celebrate Francine's graduation, all expenses paid. It was a wonderful time of bonding and rest for Francine and the girls.

C H A P T E R 1 4

Concordia

An early release was granted to Gina for good behavior. It seemed unbelievable that Gina got a report of good behavior. Gina? The bully, hater, proud, intimidator, and the reservoir of uncouth tongue and manners? She had a naturally sharp tongue with smart responses to issues, Gina of all people? She truly did. She returned home to no friends. Ella and Elizabeth had moved on, sober, doing well in school, changed and different from the personalities she knew. They kept their distance but were willing to give her support if she was willing to toe the line of sobriety. Freedom was good, but old habits do not die easily. She wanted to begin clubbing. Her parole officer was strict, and she dared not misbehave. Gina had succeeded in wasting her youthful years. When she heard that Ella and Elizabeth had become friends with Francine, her hatred boiled over. She always wanted the last laugh, but Francine had the last laugh, always had the last laugh.

Francine was never a hater. She learned at an early age to always rise above the noise. She was never discouraged when stones are thrown at her, used the stones to build masterpieces and bridges. No wonder she excelled above haters. People talk about an individual when there are good happenings in the person's life, when they see good things and impacts of the individual. Francine had all it takes for myopic-minded people like Gina to hate her. Francine rose above pettiness. Haters are inconsequential to her progress. She thrived on hate to succeed and kept doing good, never distracted. She had her focus on life, always followed through on her plan, and never deviated. A hater's main goal is to truncate a person's progress. One must learn, devise ways to make their aims/goals untenable, do not allow haters to dim your light, do not permit them to hurt you. To listen to their rhetoric is permitting them a space in your head, use your brain correctly, turn your head in the right direction, and raise it high. Haters are under. They love to keep you at the same level with them, refuse to look down, look up, for they are nothing but dirt. Dust off the dirt, shake the beast they had become into the fire to burn off. Francine was poles apart from Gina. Francine stood for love; Gina stood for hate. Francine was love. The word "help and support" was in her DNA. No matter the level of hate Gina exhibited, she cannot erase love from Francine's DNA.

Francine knew Gina needed help; she ran into her at the restaurant when she rushed to pick up her to-go lunch in between patients. She was in a hurry but could spare a few minutes. The look on Gina's face was that of a person highly depressed, marred with hate and disdain. Francine greeted her, but she did not respond. She sat in a corner alone, isolated from all the patrons eating and chatting happily on tables far from hers. There was no clear reason why she was there. She did not order anything, and there was no sign that she ate anything. She looked haggard, unkempt, and unapproachable. Patrons at the restaurants sat far away from her. Francine moved closer to her and said hello again.

She responded reluctantly. Francine asked if she could sit with her. She nodded with her shoulders wiggled up, not signifying approval or disapproval. Francine sat with her anyway, tried to begin a conversation, and asked if she was okay. There was no response.

She sat with her for about five minutes without any utterance from her. Francine eventually summoned courage, told he she could call her anytime she needed someone to talk to, left her phone number on the table, and left. Two days later, Francine saw her at the same spot, all by herself again. She looked troubled. It was evident that something was eating her up, morose, and dirty as if she walked on foot to the place. Her usual bubbling persona was missing. It seemed she had not showered for many days. The restaurant was not busy. It was past lunchtime. All had left except her. Her look was scary. There was nothing to indicate she ordered or had eaten anything. Francine went to her and sat with her without uttering a word.

Gina looked at her and asked why she bothered about her, why she should talk to her.

"What is your problem? You are not my therapist?" she snapped.

Workers at the restaurant heard her. They looked in the direction and saw someone sitting with their lone visitor who had recently turned the spot into her daily abode. Francine kept her cool and did not respond. Minutes later, she asked if she could get her a cup of coffee or tea. She declined the offer. When Francine rose to leave, she gave her number again.

She said, "I bet you threw away the number I gave you the other day. This is my number again. You can call me anytime you need me. I know you have a lot of things bottled up. A problem shared is half-solved. I promise to give you a listening ear. I would not judge you whatever the situation was. I would render support to the best of my ability. That's what we are created for, to support and help one another. Don't let what you are going through eat you deeply. Share it. You would marvel at how better you would feel afterward. If you cannot share with someone you know, share with a stranger. You would appreciate the power of verbalization. Life is full of challenges. There are good and troubled times. Life is never fair. Difficulties are an integral part of life. Nobody can live life without a period of challenges. How we wiggle through them would be a testament to who we become. Life cannot be life if it is only on a straight line. There are curves, corners, bumps, hills, valleys, mountains, and potholes on life's way. They are challenges of life. If a person's life seems too straight, the catastrophic event that could spell doom could be waiting by the corner. The blind spot that is not visible. No matter how rich or poor a person is, challenges of varying degrees will come. Challenges are no respecter of persons or status."

Gina uttered nothing. She looked at Francine as if she was talking to the wind. Francine got up, went into the restaurant, paid for a meal, and asked that it be given to Gina. Francine took her to leave and returned to work.

*****

Baron checked on Ella and Carol daily. A wonderful relationship had begun between the three of them, and Ella visited him often. He asked Ella to meet his family, to know them, and have a relationship with them. Carol allowed Ella to travel with him to meet his family. It was a great reunion. Ella's grandfather, whom they met at the golf course, gave her the best welcome of her life, took her around the city, and introduced her to everyone. It was as if he was rushing to catch up with all the lost time. The club owner was also at a reception organized by Ella's grandfather. He gifted her a piece of jewelry owned by his late wife, Baron's mother. At the reception, Baron's only sister brought her children. She was happy to introduce Baron's nieces. They joked about Baron's chronic bachelor status. He joked that though a bachelor, he is the father of a beautiful grown woman. He was proud of his daughter and sang her praises to all present. When Ella returned home, she had lots of juicy information from the trip about Baron's family and all the people she met. It was an unforgettable lifetime experience. Baron truly stepped up. He was a doting father and loved Ella to bits. Ella shuttled between two homes, which made her mother and grandmother lonely. They were inseparable before the "good" intrusion of Baron. They were, however, happy for Ella but missed her absence whenever she went to Baron's place to spend time with him.

Baron's constant presence at Carol's place dug up the affection and love that never materialized in the past. Their platonic relationship soon turned into slight pecks on the cheeks to quick lip kisses and eventual kisses. Carol was initially careful but gradually realized that the affection was getting deeper. Baron invited them to dinners often. The closeness and discussions flowed freely between them, and they started dating. Carol feared that her past would hinder the love brewing between them. She dragged her feet on occasions. Baron read her mind and assured her he was truly in love with her. Carol asked how he felt about her past as an ex-convict and how his family would portray and view her. Baron told Carol to allow the past to remain in the past. Everyone has a past, a learning curve for everyone to learn from, and told her that she was a victim of circumstance. She was naive, and people took advantage of her naivety. He encouraged her to leave the past behind and face the present and future.

He posited why people who had gone through the prison system return to society and be segregated by the same system that had already punished them by stigmatizing them again. He promised to love, cherish, shield, and honor her. Her mistakes were in the past and would remain in the past. They were both matured, respected each other, were comfortable in their own rights, and parents to a grown beautiful woman. Amelia and Ella gave Carol the go-ahead to date Baron who was visibly head over heels in love with her. He loved Carol for who she was and never judged her former flaws, character, and mistakes. He wanted a family with her. Nine months later, he proposed, and she said, "Yes." They had a small wedding with only twenty guests. It was the best day in Ella's life. She witnessed the wedding of her parents after decades of teenage affection that died and resurrected. They had a two-week honeymoon; it was a time of refreshing for both. Carol was in her early forties, returned from the honeymoon pregnant, a high-risk pregnancy for her age. She was scared and could not believe she could get pregnant though she used no protection. Children were no longer in her plan or agenda. That chapter in her life closed a long time ago. Baron was happy, and so was Ella and Amelia. Ella would become a sister to someone in nine months. They all promised to nurse Carol throughout her pregnancy, and they sure did. It was difficult for her to carry the pregnancy because of her age. She had issues but managed to scale through. She had support from her family and had back pain throughout because of the weight of the twins on her body. She had Ella over two decades ago as a teenager. Pregnancy was strange to her body and had two Braxton hicks in the last trimester but was sent back home that they were false labor pains.

Nine months ran so fast. Carol delivered a set of twins, a boy, and a girl. Ella joked that the children were hers. Her mother was just the carrier. The morning sickness was over. Carol had acute hyperemesis gravidarum (HG) and threw up till she was five months pregnant. A baby shower was organized for her, courtesy of Ella, the big sister. She declined the bridal shower before her wedding, so Ella insisted on the baby shower and organized it. The few guests attended with nice presents for the expected babies. Carol become a shy person since her return from prison. Her lifestyle had changed. Nothing really impressed her. She had seen the two sides of the coin in her life's journey, the good and the bad. Ella and Baron decorated the room for the babies, bought baby items, and filled up the room. The decor was on point for the prince and princess on the way, and Francine supported them with the decorations.

Amelia had input in the plans. She spared no expense to await her grandchildren. When Carol went into labor, Baron was at a conference in a city a few miles away from where they lived. Ella called that the twins were on the way. He came at the exact time Carol pushed out the first baby. He was happy to witness the birth. The twins were fine. No health challenges as expected with delivery at Carol's age. Carol heaved a sigh of relief when the doctor gave the twins a perfect health report. Ella was the babysitter, minder, and caregiver to her mother and the twins named Baron and Carol. Baron's house was a three-bedroom house as a bachelor. Carol moved in with Baron after the wedding while Ella stayed with Amelia. He sold the property after the wedding and bought a mansion that would accommodate all of them. Carol made sure the mansion had a mother-in-law suite to accommodate Amelia. Baron was rich and could afford it. He paid for the property without any contribution from Carol or Amelia.

The property had both his name and Carol's name on it. Amelia sold her property, and they all moved into Baron's mansion at his insistence. Life together was blissful for all of them. The arrival of the twins made Carol cut down on her attendance at the store. She devoted her time to the children and vowed never to be an absentee mother like Amelia. Ella took over the running of the two floral stores. They had become big, catered for expensive weddings and celebrations, and had become a million-dollar revenue-making outlet in a short space of time. Carol employed two nannies to assist with the children. They had more than enough hands caring for the children with Ella in the first position.

*****

Gina stopped the visit to the restaurant, Francine checked with the employees, and they said she stopped coming to the place. She refused the meal Francine paid for, left, and never returned. Francine shared both encounters with Ella and Elizabeth. Ella visited Gina's house and was told by Madeline that her whereabouts were unknown. She left home two weeks after she returned from prison, and they had not seen her for close to one year. Ella thanked them and left, promising to contact them with any news or sight of her. Gina moved away from home when her paternity issue was disclosed to her. Benjamin and Madeline waited for two weeks after she was released. She initially thought her parents were joking, but when they told her that the visitor who came on the visit to the prison was her biological father, she went into a rage, destroyed items in the family room, and left. All entreaties to explain the full details fell on deaf ears. She called Madeline unprintable names worse to describe a loved one not to talk of her biological mother. She left the house on foot that day and had never returned.

Madeline became heartbroken and cried bitterly. Benjamin consoled and advised her to take it easy because her health was fragile. Benjamin explained to Gina that DNA or no DNA, he would remain Gina's father. Gina was not interested in whatever he had to say. She did not spare him with her foul mouth. He had to dodge an expensive flower vase that she threw with the intention of breaking Benjamin's head. With Gina's precarious behavior, Benjamin and Madeline agreed to adopt another child, a child that would be different from Gina, a well-behaved, well-trained child that would bring glory and honor to their name. They began the paperwork for the adoption. The paperwork and procedure were cumbersome, with several hurdles to jump and no possibility of light after the tunnel. After much deliberation, they agreed that surrogacy would be much better, easier, and faster. The child would be a hundred percent theirs and cut off the waiting time to pursue an adoption.

Benjamin and Madeline agreed to have a baby through surrogacy. They found a woman who perfectly matched the criteria they desired, and with the plan finalized, they would hear the cry of a baby or babies in their household soon. Gina would, however, forever remain their first child; they would do everything to find and reform her. Kyle was aware of the development. He also had machinery in motion to find Gina. He kept his distance but worked hard to find Gina on his own and gave Madeline and Benjamin space to manage their family issues but told them to reach out to him whenever they needed him. He emphasized his promise to do whatever made them happy. Mr. and Mrs. Wiggins thanked him for his love and understanding. The doctor announced the good news to them that the surrogate mother had become pregnant. The plan was for a set of twins or triplets, they wanted to push their luck. Benjamin's law firm had bounced back. Business was on a roll again. He had new attorneys and many of the big firms they lost in the wake of Gina's numerous troubles had returned. They realized there were no other firms better than Benjamins. Besides, Gina's issue had been long forgotten. There was no reason to punish him further for the atrocities of his daughter. The relationship between the Wiggins had improved tremendously. The lost love had returned, bigger, better, and healthier. The only pain they had was Gina. Finding and turning her life around would make their joy complete. They had devised ways to cope with Gina's issues and pushed them to the back burner. The surrogacy issue was now on the front burner. The joy of new babies would totally rekindle the sorrows of the past. Madeline's health had a good jump, and her prognosis became better and progressed positively every day.

*****

Francine's grandmother had another fall. It was not a bad fall. She broke no bones but was bruised. Francine rushed home to see her. Grandma was elated when Francine told her that she might be getting married soon. She jumped up and danced around the house ecstatically. It was the same guy she knew; he came to study at the university she attended. He came with full scholarship from his state, got a full ride because of his brilliance, and he was Francine's coursemate who became her study partner. They became friends, inseparable, liked each other a lot but kept their relationship platonic. Only school issues, and nothing else attached. After graduation, he summoned courage, told her he loved her, and wanted their friendship to move to the next level. A love relationship ensued, and now had decided to become steady with each other, she agreed to be his "official" girlfriend. He loved the fact that he would be married to a sapiosexual lady. Francine was old-school when it came to the issue of dating. She was very conservative.

Craig respected and loved her conservativeness. He waited patiently until Francine was ready for a relationship and knew she would be a good wife. Craig took Francine to meet with his parents and family members. She was homely, respectful, and blended easily into the family throughout the one week they spent in Craig's hometown. They fell in love with her instantly. He took her to meet all his relatives. They all noted her humility and kind heart. Craig's father passed away when he was young. He was single-handedly raised by his mother. He was brilliant, the doyen of his mother's heart. He made his mother proud with his brilliance, good nature, and manners. His mother never remarried and concentrated on the upbringing of her children and their academic exploits. She worked two jobs to train her children and toiled day and night. His mother received Francine with both hands and total love. His senior sister was at hand to receive her. She got married years ago and had two children within five years, a boy and a girl. She brought them with her to meet Francine and brought flowers and presents for her. Craig's mother poured her heart out to Francine and told her how happy she was to have her as her daughter, not a daughter-in-law. Francine hugged her and promised to be a good daughter and wife. She would not be a wife who would keep Craig to herself. Craig would be a good son and dutiful husband to both, that he would be "mine, yours, and ours." She presented gifts to her new mother; she reciprocated with gifts also. Craig's relatives gave her gifts and welcomed her with both hands into the family. Craig loved Francine so much, understood Francine well from the years they related as friends, knew Francine loved to live close to her parents and grandmother, and conceded to live wherever she wanted. His love for Francine knew no bounds and would do anything to make her happy.

Craig proposed to Francine three months after they became official. She requested a small wedding. They agreed that all gifts be in cash and donated to Ariel's Turnaround Center and a homeless shelter in the town. They chose where the donations would go together. He knew she had a heart for others. Francine had a small wedding. They invited only fifty guests, twenty on both sides and ten friends. Her wedding dress was beautiful to behold, gorgeous, and classy. It fitted perfectly on her figure-eight body. She looked ravishing in her dress. Ella was her maid of honor. The day was perfect, and the sun shone all day for the most beautiful bride in the whole universe. The bridal shower was organized by Ella and Elizabeth two weekends before the wedding. It was a day to remember. They had lots of fun and showered Francine with gifts. It was the best "thank you" to the selfless Francine who went to great lengths in supporting and helping other people. Francine literarily supported them to turn their lives around for good. The shower was nothing compared to the great deeds she had done for them. The shower was for only close friends and colleagues.

After the wedding reception, Grandma handed a big envelope to Craig and Francine. She instructed them to keep it safe. It contained very vital documents. It contained documents of the inheritance her grandfather left for her, her endowments, and more, Francine and Craig were appreciative of Grandma's kind gestures. They would go through the documents after their honeymoon and gave the envelope to Craig's mother to keep. Grandma told them jokingly again that she needed great-grandchildren as soon as possible. Francine also jokingly responded that she needed to enjoy her marriage before children. They all laughed. Elizabeth and Ella were part of the wedding. They supported Francine throughout the preparation and wedding day. Ella and Elizabeth were with Francine in the hotel room when Elizabeth soliloquized that she wanted to get married too. She fancied the idea of a wedding, the preparations, the wedding dress, and more, wished she were the one in Francine's shoes. Francine told her to be patient. Her time would soon come, and everyone has an appointed time. She admonished them that patience and endurance are like Siamese twins. They walk hand in hand. Our expectations may not come when we want, but with patience and endurance, the expectations would happen. The saying that "Rome was not built in a day" was true, precept upon precepts, one after the other the blocks were set. It took time to put a structure up not to talk of a city. The journey of a lifetime starts in a day with the first step. Sometimes it seemed like baby steps but would progress with time. With time, the baby steps would become stronger, faster, and eventually steadfast. We learn to walk as babies with a wobbly rise, stand, fall, stand again, and fall again. With resilience, we take the bold step and gradually move with great strides. Life gives chances, sometimes more than once, guard your chances with both hands, hold them firmly, and refuse to let the opportunities of life pass you by or slip through your fingers. Opportunities lost once would attract double effort to regain or sometimes never regained, never lose hope, and nothing is ever too late. It was as if Francine saw a crystal ball of what awaited them. They got their lucky break at the wedding. Both met guys who swept them off their feet. Doors of relationships opened for them.

Time will tell if the relationships yielded fruits. Francine encouraged them to endure and be patient.

Francine and Craig had their honeymoon on an island. It was quiet and refreshing for them. Their relationship was built on friendship. They were best friends, classmates, study partners, confidants, and knew each other like the back of their hands. They got each other's backs and understood one another perfectly. The enviable relationship they had made the preparation for the wedding easy and hitch-free. Everything went smoothly without any problem. Both families, especially the parents and grandparents, united as if they had known each other for ages. They spent two weeks on the island and returned home to rest for one week before resuming back to work. The week after the honeymoon was for house hunting. They opened the envelope Grandma gave to Francine after the wedding. The inheritance ran into millions. Grandma had invested the monies into ventures that yielded great interests. New millionaires by inheritance. They have enough money to buy their dream house with surplus left.

Craig and Francine agreed to donate $100,000 from the inheritance to Ariel's Turnaround Center and a homeless shelter. The money would be equal parts between the two places. Craig and Francine are medical doctors by profession. They are already high-level earners in society. Francine resumed work three weeks after her wedding. They moved into Craig's apartment and started searching for a place to call home where they would begin their lives together. The thought of Gina never escaped Francine's mind. It bothered her every time she recalled it. The encounters at the restaurant left an impression on her mind. Francine discussed it with Ella who also had her mind on searching for Gina. Francine's ward round at the hospital on the day she resumed suddenly became eventful. She noticed a female homeless individual on the bed at the end of the room. She was fast asleep, thanks to the sedatives given to her. She was admitted the previous night for an undisclosed ailment. She had a very high fever. Her prognosis was not good. The paramedics who brought her to the emergency room said she was picked on the side of the road. She was unresponsive. Passersby thought she was dead, and a store close to where she lay on the ground called the authorities to pick up a dead female body, when the paramedics arrived, they realized she was still breathing. She was in and out of consciousness. They resuscitated her and transported her to the emergency room. Francine could not disclose Gina's ailment to anyone due to HIPPA laws. She shared her identity with the hospital so they could contact her family about her admission. She had no identification on her. Francine recognized her immediately she saw her on the bed although she had changed and emaciated tremendously. Francine waited after her shift so she could talk to her, but she slept all day. Francine was sad about the way Gina looked but happy to see her alive though in a precarious situation. She kept an eye on her and instructed the nurses to do the same. An IV drip was on her left hand. She woke up intermittently and slept off again. She was sound asleep when Francine left for the day.

She could not take her mind off the fact that Gina turned herself into a homeless individual despite all the opportunities opened to her. She deserved better and needed a turnaround for her own good. Excessive anger coupled with mental health that had gone untreated for years had severely affected her. She needed an intervention fast, but who would offer it? Who could reach into the deep depths of her heart ravaged by years of negative emotions? Negative attitudes formed out of ignorance and self-volition. She was ignorant with volition to perpetrate evil and chose to live in her own illusory, self-destructive, and deceptive nature. Failure to identify such traits could erode a person's achievements in a lifetime within the twinkle of an eye. Gina needed help right away. She could do better, deserved better. She had the best opportunities at her beckon and call. Misuse of the opportunities had been detrimental and had spelled doom for her. It was never too late to avert the doom if only she deviated from the destructive paths she had towed for years. Gina had everything mapped out for her but chose to mess up. Wealth and riches would destroy an individual if not well managed. It messed up her thinking and eroded her brain, Name recognition destroyed her life. Nobody chose the vessel of transport to the world. One's vessel to this world is chosen and designed by the Maker. All an individual needed was to embrace the vessel and make good of the journey. What would have happened if her parents were poor? Would she still turn out the way she did? Francine, however, was in the dark about Gina's paternity, but her profession made her know she needed serious mental health evaluation.

When Francine resumed duty the following day, Gina was awake but drowsy from her medications. The IV fluid was still dripping into her veins. She was semiconscious but was able to see a doctor walk past her bed to another patient. The doctor looked like someone she knew. She espied, but everything looked blurry. She tried to turn to see the person again, but Francine exited into the other room before she could get a better glimpse. She believed it was Francine but also thought her brain and eyes played a trick on her. She slept off again. Francine went through her hospital chart and ordered a series of tests to follow up with the ones already ordered by the doctor who admitted her. She would look at the test results to figure out what her prognosis was. Francine's first task was to stabilize Gina and get her high fever under control. The laboratory called with the test result. Her organs were damaged, most especially her liver. She needed more tests to ascertain if she had liver cirrhosis. Her kidneys was not functioning effectively either. Gina returned to heavy drinking and drug use when she left the house. She did whatever it took to get her drug and alcohol. She had no permanent home address and slept wherever night found her. Francine knew Gina was in trouble. Her prognosis was not good. That was why she collapsed on the street. Her homeless comrade left her on the road and disappeared into thin air. He feared getting into trouble with the law if found with her. He would be made to answer questions he knew nothing about. They were homeless together and formed an alliance. They knew nothing about each other.

More test results came in for Gina. Her liver was not functioning effectively because of years of drugs and alcohol abuse. It could regenerate if she stopped drugs and alcohol use, allowing the liver to heal, but could become fully damaged without urgent intervention. Further drugs and alcohol use could totally damage her liver and make her a candidate for a liver transplant. It could also affect other organs. The medical team met on the best treatment plan for Gina. Foremost, she had to clean up her act, stop drugs and alcohol altogether, and become clean and sober. She had constantly felt blue, depressed, always looking sad and morose. She had used illicit drugs to treat her sad and depressing situations instead of getting professional attention. The medical team wanted her to become stable, explain her prognosis, and involve her in the process. Francine needed to talk to Gina as soon as possible and counsel her as an acquaintance who wanted her alive, not dead. Gina was not responding to treatment. She had been in the hospital for over twenty-four hours, and the hospital contacted her family. Madeline and Benjamin were happy to know about her whereabouts but sad that she was semiconscious. They rushed to her bedside and asked for the best treatment money could buy. They ran into Francine, were surprised to see her, and knew instantly that she gave the hospital their information since they were told no identity was found on her. They thanked her profusely and knew she would do everything in her professional ability to support Gina with her clean and kind heart. They knew she was not vindictive and would never take Gina's hateful behavior against her to heart.

When they saw Gina, they could not believe their eyes. She looked different from the daughter they nurtured all their lives, emaciated and boney. They met with the professional team of doctors to decide the way forward since Gina was not able to make decisions for herself. She was in between consciousness. Her state of health bothered her parents. They informed Kyle about the development. He drove hours all night to be there the following morning. He saw Gina for the second time. She looked totally different from the woman he saw on the visit to the prison. He could not get any information from the medical team because they had no inkling of his relationship with Gina, so he did not even bother to ask. Madeline and Benjamin explained the situation to him. Gina's eyes opened when they got to her bedside. She was too sick and not very conscious to recognize them. Kyle stayed two days to support Madeline and Benjamin and visited daily with them. He tried not to arouse any attention to himself. He returned to his base when Gina was awake. She saw Kyle but uttered no word to him. With Gina's whereabouts known, Madeline and Benjamin could fully focus on the surrogacy. Her disappearance had been burdensome on their minds. They feared Gina's reaction if she eventually returned to the house with a set of twins in the nursery. They wanted her to be fully aware of the twins on the way. Her siblings and biological children from the loins and blood of Madeline and Benjamin, carried and delivered by a surrogate mother. They never planned to relegate Gina in any way. She would forever remain their first child, but they needed to prepare her mind for the arrival of the children. Kyle had agreed to let them have Gina and would even sign her over to them if needed. His name was not on her birth certificate. By law, Benjamin was the father, but what if she wanted her biological father in her life? Those were issues Gina needed to decide personally but was presently indisposed. Her health was the number one issue. Other things would follow when the time arrives. The babies are due in weeks. Plans were in top gear for their arrival. They kept the pregnancy secret. Only family members knew about it. Kyle was aware. He was happy for them and knew they would never treat Gina as an outcast. Francine saw Kyle on visits to the hospital in the company of Gina's parents. She noticed birthmarks that corresponded with distinct marks on Gina but had no clue of the situation. She had always wondered why Gina had such an eccentric egoistic trait that trampled on all forms of natural human behavior. Gina destroyed others with zeal, unaware that she was also destroying herself.

Gina had a twisted soul, a narcissist to say the absolute. She did evil with zeal and had no conscience or remorse. She behaved poles apart from her parents who were highly revered and respected in the community. They were professionals in various fields and successful. Gina was nothing like them, different as if from another planet. If Francine knew what her parents are now privy to about her paternity and what she inherited through birth, she was positive that they would have sought professional help earlier to avert her years of negative outbursts, drug/alcohol use, and criminal activities. Francine never hated Gina; she hated her unruly behavior and character. She knew that rich privilege and situational factors affected Gina's excessive and uncultured behavior. If Gina attended treatment and counseling sessions, a refined individual would be the resultant product. The visits with Kyle puzzled Francine. Gina's parents introduced Kyle with only his first name and no further description of the relatedness. Gina's medical chart showed no clue except her liver prognosis. There was nothing to indicate any form of mental illness. Gina's health had improved in the last few days. She had started talking and alert. She narrated her ordeals, drug use, homelessness, and family background to the doctor on duty. She, however, omitted what led her to move out of her parent's home. Her medical history was not complete. She had no knowledge of the mental health issues she had inherited from Kyle, her biological father.

When Madeline and Benjamin tried to inform her of the truth about her birth, she refused to listen to them, stormed out, and left home in annoyance. The doctor explained her liver prognosis to her in detail. The prognosis scared her to death and the fact that her situation could lead to organ failure and eventual death if she does not act fast. Effective treatment would be expensive and time-consuming. She needed full determination, dedication, and financial backup from her parents to become healthy and back on her feet. The information meant that her parents had to be involved, and the money aspect would be the responsibility of her parents. Initially, she resisted. She wanted nothing to do with them. The medical team explained to her that her existence was at risk. With a liver not functioning effectively, she would become sicker. Life would be difficult, and daily activities would be in jeopardy. Francine stepped in and advised her on the implications of not following the treatment regimen of the team. She advised her on allowing her parents back into her life. They brought her into the world and want the best for her, narrated to her the efforts her parents made in locating her whereabouts, as well as the involvements of Ella, Elizabeth, and herself.

Francine was patient with Gina who got better by the day. She became her adviser, therapist, counselor, and "friend." As one of her doctors, Gina listened to her but was adamant as usual. Francine knew it would take time to break into Gina's psyche. She had been almighty Gina for a long time. Breaking into her psyche to see reason as a normal person would be like pulling a tooth without an anesthetic agent. Gina was a hard nut to crack. The nuts in her brain had solidly fused together over the years, and her thoughts were different from normal ways of thinking. Madeline and Benjamin made daily visits, sometimes twice, but Gina avoided them and had nothing to do with them. They sat in silence during the visits. Benjamin requested a private room for Gina and made sure she was comfortable.

The hospital made sure social workers visited her daily and made provision for therapists who visited and counseled her on the importance of sobriety. With all hands on deck for a speedy recovery for Gina, it baffled them that she behaved irrationally sometimes. All efforts of the team to get more insight on her emotional well-being was rebuffed by Gina. She shared nothing on her mental health status, though evident to all that she was not mentally stable and needed psychotropic drugs. Gina refused all drugs prescribed to treat her mental health diagnosis. She took all other medications but not the psychotropic ones. Ella and Elizabeth visited Gina while Francine was on duty. They learned about her hospital admission through Madeline. Gina was ashamed but happy to see them.

They looked different, cleaned, and articulated. It was a moment of "sadness and joy." They could not believe how emaciated Gina looked. It reminded Elizabeth of how she looked when she was rescued at the nightclub. As she looked at Gina, she wept inside and could not weep visibly as it would embarrass all of them, especially Gina. She vowed in her heart to do everything in her power to salvage Gina. The visit lifted Gina's spirit. They sat with her, shared jokes that made her smile, and eventually laughed. They, however, avoided everything to do with drugs, alcohol, or what culminated in her disappearance.

Madeline and Benjamin walked inside as Gina laughed. They were happy to see her in such a state of mind and hoped for more sunshine to come her way. Francine joined them when she was less busy. Gina had a room filled with visitors. She lightened up, even to her parents. Francine was happy and knew the ice had been broken. When all the visitors left, Francine returned to Gina's room and asked how she felt amid the people who loved her. She shared with her the importance of a support system, the love and happiness that filled the room when the visitors were around, and the negative consequences of living in isolation. Gina kept quiet and nodded her head severally to confirm Francine's statement.

They sat in silence for a moment. She looked at Francine as if she were probing her intentions toward her. Francine kept mute but had her eyes fixed on her. With the four-eyed intently fixed, she gave a wry smile. She explained to Francine how her nightmare started through the request for a designer handbag. The flashback of that night enveloped her brain like a daydream in an instant. She narrated the events in detail, the argument, and the gun she pointed at her parents. She bolted out of the house, the clubbing, drugs/alcohol use, the encounter with Ella at the mall, her vendetta for Francine, the accident, monies paid in millions by her father to settle cases out of court, and her eventual prison term. Everything came in a flash! She struggled with her emotions, but they got an edge over her. She cried like a baby. Francine listened attentively, did not utter a word, expressionless, and never judged but empathized. Francine knew she had narcissistic personality issues. She had studied her for years. Help should have been long before now. Gina had always felt special and superior to others, always occupied with fantasies that were not attainable, self-conceited, exploited others, including her friends and parents, grandiose in nature, and arrogant. Gina stopped talking, cleaned off her tears, pulled in the mucus in her nose, then blew it into a napkin. She waited a few minutes and continued. She discussed her incarceration, what she went through, lessons learned, and the desire to change and turn her life around for the better. To her dismay, her life turned upside down when she returned home to the news of her paternity. She initially thought it was a joke, an April's fool in the middle of the year. When they confirmed it was not a joke, her world crashed! She was too devastated and annoyed with her parents, herself, and the world. She contemplated suicide on occasions and thought of murdering her parents, but the fear of returning to prison for a long time hindered her action. She impulsively almost committed murder. Her best option was to leave the house to avoid a bigger problem.

Francine was dazed and confused with what she just heard. All she could do was hold her hands. The information was too much to digest. She pulled her into a warm embrace while she sobbed profusely. The pain in her eyes and the emotion in her voice showed she was heartbroken. Francine felt broken for her too. Empathy and compassion got the best of her amid sobs. She explained to Francine that she never thought she could make it alive. When she collapsed by the roadside, she heard her homeless partner screaming her name. To her, it felt like she was in a faraway land despite his proximity to her. His voice echoed in her ears until she no longer heard him. He left her when she became unresponsive. She thought she had died and saw some heavenly bright lights that depicted she was on another planet. She was truly grateful to be alive, alive to embrace and give life another chance.

When she calmed down, Francine told her that mistakes happen in life. Blunders we commit out of ignorance or miscalculation are unintentional errors in judgment that people later regret. We all make mistakes; nobody is above it because nobody is perfect. We are all working towards perfection. Everyone including herself is a work in progress, and we do not stop working on ourselves until we die. Nobody wants to intentionally do the wrong things, we all strive to do the right thing, but situations do happen. She encouraged her to hear her parents, most especially her mother out. Knowledge of the history behind her mother's story would shed more light on what transpired, and she encouraged her not to allow her mother's mistake(s) to define her. Living in misery because of her mother's mistake could debar her from reaching her designed potential and rob her of her goals in life. She should pull herself up, forge, and stride ahead. Forgiveness is divine, harboring malice destroys the heart, and ill health makes life meaningless and hurtful. When you forgive, you release the offender and yourself, most especially yourself. Unforgiveness keeps a person in bondage. Francine's speech hit a cord in Gina's heart. Her response seemed short and simple, but it worked. It worked like magic because of

Francine's true compassion, kindness, and selfless attitude. It felt like a heavy load was lifted from Gina's shoulder, as if ice-cold water was poured on the burning fire in her heart. Her heart felt light. She just shared the burden that laid heavily on her heart, which she had never shared with any soul, and the irony of it was that she shared it with her "perceived enemy." *Is it true that verbalizing helps?* She thought in her mind. It was clear. It just helped her. She felt like a new person. Gina thanked Francine and asked why she was kind to her despite all the evil actions she meted on her.

Gina immediately asked Francine for forgiveness. She smiled and told Gina she forgave her a long time ago. Gina looked at her in awe. Francine laughed when she saw the awed look on her face and explained to her that she learned about the power of forgiveness many years ago, and it made life's burden easy to carry. Forgiveness liberates. It is good tonic/medicine for the soul. We must learn to forgive even when the deed was grave. Learn to be each other's keeper. You cannot be each other's keeper when you harbor grudges or hatred. We would all pass through this planet only once. We should help each other and extend hands of support to all because no one would pass through this earth twice, only once. The opportunities we have should be beneficial to society. Togetherness and oneness liberate. Solitary destroys! We need one another. No one is an island. We should not live life in a vacuum. Togetherness makes the world go round and makes it a better place to live. Francine asked Gina if she remembered the song "I shall pass through this earth but once." Gina nodded. They sang together. Gina began to cry again. Francine wiped her tears, bear-hugged her, and whispered something into her ear that made her laugh. They laughed aloud together before Francine exited the room and left for the day. Gina tossed and tossed on her bed that night;

in fact, she murdered sleep. She was able to think deeply about her life, future, and way forward.

Gina made a call to her parents the following morning. They were surprised to receive a call from her. They visited her in the evening. She was welcoming and in good spirit. Her prognosis was much better, thanks to the doctors and the medications. Her appetite was back and had started eating healthy again. They had a lengthy discussion. Madeline explained everything in detail and was surprised that Gina listened, not only listened but listened attentively and asked questions. They were amazed when she responded that she forgave her for the mistake and asked Benjamin if he had forgiven her mother wholeheartedly. When he responded in the affirmative, she then apologized for her behavior and excesses. She explained that she shared the situation with Francine and got liberated by her wise counsel. It puzzled them how fast and effective Francine's discussion worked on Gina, appreciated her love, concern, and effort. Gina told her parents that she would love to do another DNA with Kyle, would love to meet with him after the result, would need more information about his medical and family history, and would want the situation kept as a family secret until she wanted it otherwise. They willingly agreed, happy to have their daughter back. The surrogacy situation was left in the cooler for the moment. The information might backfire and return them to the hurdle of stalemate they just crossed. Her optimistic attitude was notable. They were not willing to mess with it or push their luck too far.

Benjamin reached out to Kyle at the parking lot of the hospital and shared the good news of Gina's change of attitude and her request for another DNA. Kyle obliged immediately and would submit to any laboratory of Gina's choice, happy that a line of communication had opened between them and Gina. The DNA was done swiftly, and the result confirmed that Kyle was her biological father. Gina wanted to meet with him one-on-one, wanted to know who he was, at least have some level of interaction with him. Madeline and Benjamin agreed in principle that Gina should decide if she wanted Kyle or Benjamin. The thought of losing a child he had nurtured all his life frightened Benjamin to death, but Gina would have to make the ultimate decision. Kyle's view on life had changed since the day Madeline and Benjamin visited him with the news of Gina's existence. He never planned to father a child because of his family's history of severe mental health illness. It was too much burden to put on another individual. He planned to put an end to his lineage, but with Gina in the picture, his lineage had gotten extended in a mysterious and miraculous way that he never intended but now thankful for. He was now in a dilemma after he received the one-page paper that indicated he was "99.99 percent the father." Kyle who had promised to let Madeline and Benjamin remain Gina's parents had sleepless nights after he received the report. He was, however, a man of his words. His words could be taken to the bank, a man of integrity to the core. He, however, would not let Gina down if she chose to be with him. The ball was in Gina's court. Kyle, Madeline, and Benjamin had to wait on Gina's decision. The waiting period was tormenting, to say the least.

CHAPTER 15

A New Era

Ella completed her university studies and took over Carol's businesses fully, while Carol took the backstage to enjoy her marriage and nurse the twins. She alternated between caring for the twins and the florist stores. She was also on the board of her mother's NGO. Besides, she was in a flourishing relationship that might lead to the altar soon. Ella used her academic skills to translate the florist stores into cash cows, milking money in millions for the company. She introduced interior designs and decorations into the business and learned the craft and techniques from her mother. Ella was an adaptive person and good with her hands. Carol did a wonderful job redesigning their home when she returned from prison. She also transformed the new home Baron bought into a masterpiece.

Her skills and gifts of transforming and designing seemed out of this world. Amelia was good with the paperwork aspect and always a ready hand. She was meticulous and well-organized, and she gave her daughter and Ella the utmost support. Her health had improved tremendously. Her strength doubled. Her cancer had gone into total remission and had been cancer-free for years. Ella's staff had increased tremendously. Her leadership trait was highly commendable. She had been free from drugs and alcohol for years, and her mental health had stabilized. She followed her regimen of meetings and doctor's appointments seriously.

She was in a good shape in her romantic relationship, which had gotten the full backing of her parents and Amelia. She kept in touch with her circle of friends and created time to meet with them despite her very busy schedule. She recently won a big contract for the interior design and decoration of a five-star hotel that just got remodeled. The contract was big and would be a good advertisement for the company when completed. With the contract, she had to employ more hands, thereby creating job opportunities for many in the community. Carol's initiative was highly applauded in the community. She became a focal point, her story was referenced at gatherings, and her case was a second chance opportunity well utilized. At a gala night organized to honor achievers in the community, she told the large gathering that having an inheritance to fall back on was not the important factor. A heart of giving was of the essence. She would have devised means to give back to the community even if she were from a poor background. Serving humanity after serving a punishment was key to life. It showed she learned something good from her mistake. She had learned a great lesson in serving humanity, extending a hand of support to others, and putting a smile on another person's face. The lives touched, the turnaround in people's lives, was worth all the millions in this world.

*****

Elizabeth had the fastest turnaround. Within months of reuniting with her parents after leaving Ariel's Turnaround Center and the mandated court-ordered treatment, she had gotten her life back on track. She threw away her stinking thinking attitude and replaced it with positive thinking. She gained admission into the community college and began a good relationship with Jason and his children who saw her as the big sister. She never missed her counseling sessions, attended AA/NA meetings, took her medications as prescribed, and had not missed a single doctor's appointment. The experience of what she went through in the hands of Ralph had been meticulously kept in the deepest part of her heart. She had no courage to disclose or narrate the hell she went through to her parents. Bethena would have a heart attack to know that her daughter went through such bizarre experience while Jason would insist on finding and prosecuting him.

Bethena and Jason nursed her back to life and spent money on her health, but money could not treat her damaged emotions, which was for her to fix with years of counseling. The horrible experiences had scared Elizabeth's life; she never deserved the horrendous situations she went through if she had planned her life well. The lessons she refused to learn at home were handed to her a billion-fold outside without complaint. Jason loved her so much, showered her with praises and encomiums, and treated her like an egg. Jason became her biggest support but a firm disciplinarian, never accepted nonsense from anyone. She reciprocated accordingly, this time genuinely. Ella in strict terms told Elizabeth that their friendship was contingent upon a drug and alcohol-free life. Negative peer influence had been detrimental to her and made her run a rat race in the wrong lane of life. It got her messed up, fight for survival, fight the almost unending war with addiction. To win the war and stay conqueror, she needed to be firm, strict, and unapologetic to anyone. If she refused to get on the fast-moving train of sobriety, she would be left behind.

As for Francine, she knew her terms and stand. She was a machete and not a sword, a one-way traffic. Her position on doing the right thing had never wavered. Her motto had always been a capital *no* to drugs and alcohol. If Elizabeth wanted a better future, the season of a carefree, lackadaisical era must end. She needed to rebuild her name, life, and family name. She was not getting younger. Her mates had settled in different spheres of life, doing good, progressing daily. As for Gina, she was still a work in progress. She had issues with ego, anger, envy, hate, jealousy, unforgiveness, pride, lying, ignorance, prejudice, addiction, and mental health disorder. She had so much on her plate to deal with. The earlier she worked on all the issues, the better for her. All the issues are workable if she became dedicated to working on them. Her fear of losing both ways would be a task for her to surmount—a high mountain to climb but also doable. She needed to deal with her doubts and not allow her ignorance to rob her of a good future. Mental health is a disease that could be treated with medications, but medications cannot treat character defects. She must work on her defects and flaws diligently to achieve her desired goals in life, if at all she had any. However, time will tell.

*****

Francine was on duty the day Gina was discharged from the hospital; her parents were on hand to pick her up. Francine had a long talk with Gina the previous day, and they shared extensively some of her character defects. Francine was amazed that Gina attested to her flaws and pointed them out herself. It made it easy for them to discuss. Forgiveness was the most important topic due to the issue on the ground. Gina agreed to forgive her parents and move on; after all, there was nothing she could do to reverse it. She just had to accept it as her fate, a cross to carry. Francine encouraged her to seek counseling for her mental, emotional, and addiction issues to avoid a relapse. Her health would be in jeopardy if she relapsed. Gina agreed.

Gina's parents were full of thanks to Francine who in turn encouraged them to find a good therapist for Gina. Her situation needed prompt counseling sessions. Francine hugged Gina and encouraged her to put into action all they had discussed. Gina was happy to be back at home. She had a long bath, ate, took her medications, and rested all day. Madeline and Benjamin were happy once again, but how long the happiness would last was much to be desired. The surrogacy issue was pending. Benjamin and Madeline had to tell Gina as the arrival of the children was fast approaching. Benjamin went straight to his study when they returned home. He called Kyle to inform him that Gina was back at home and that he could come to see her. Kyle's phone went straight to voice mail. It was unlike him, so he left a message on his cell phone. Kyle did not call for two days. It got Benjamin worried, so he called back. Kyle collapsed at work and was rushed to the emergency room. A series of tests were recommended to ascertain what went wrong. He apologized to Benjamin when he told him he had called two days earlier and explained what happened to him. Benjamin promised to check on him at the hospital. He would stay a few days on admission to do more tests. It shocked Madeline to hear that Kyle was in the hospital. They saw him not too long ago, and nothing seemed amiss. Madeline and Benjamin discussed Kyle's admission to the hospital with Gina and if she would love to visit him. She gladly accepted to their dismay. They agreed to visit him together. Madeline and Gina dashed to the store and got flowers and balloons to take along with them to the hospital to visit her father.

Kyle was happy to see them. They were the only people he could refer to as family. He had nobody but acquaintances, no friends, or wife. He was not a bad person. The stigma of his mental illness made him stay away from people. He mastered his diagnosis well, learned the signs and symptoms, and managed it perfectly well with medications. It would be difficult for a layperson to know he had a mental illness. He dressed well, was always physically neat, and kept his home and office clean. He was friendly with his neighbors and offered help to them when needed and held in high esteem. No one knew he had any form of mental illness.

He held his job and position well, had been in the same government organization for years, and rose within the ranks. Seeing Gina in good health lightened him up. He sat upon his bed, beckoned to them to sit after pleasantries, and jokingly asked if he could hug Gina. She was happy to hug him too. The flowers were placed on the bedstand, and balloons were tied to his bed rail, giving the bare room a facelift. He could not really explain his ailment. The results were yet to be back. He looked stable and healthy. Nothing to show he was seriously sick. Gina kept looking at him, seizing him up at close range. Her mind kept racing with varied thoughts. Flashbacks of the story her mother shared about how she was conceived erupted in her mind. Strangulating him came as a flash in her thought, seemed like a daydream. She quickly erased the stinking thinking from her brain. He is her biological father, she thought, had promised herself to always do the right things. She got up from her seat and hugged him again. It was a shock to all of them but were all happy.

Gina promised to visit him the following day alone. She needed to spend "alone" time with him, know him better, and ask him questions if it was fine with him. Kyle told her she was free to come anytime she wanted; he would tell her all she needed to know. They spent a long time with Kyle who was happy to see them, most especially Gina. She looked beautiful unlike the haggard Gina he saw weeks ago on the hospital bed. Ironically, he last saw her in the hospital, and she saw him again on a hospital bed. Madeline and Benjamin engaged the services of a therapist who was able to see Gina immediately. From her analysis, Gina needed to see a psychiatrist as soon as possible. Gina had no full knowledge of the history of her biological father's mental health diagnosis. He looked normal to her, but she needed to meet with him for full disclosure. Madeline and Benjamin also had no full details. All they knew was that he had ongoing mental health issues that he inherited. It would be better for Kyle to personally tell her all she needed to know. Kyle was happy to see Gina the following day. She looked even healthier than the previous day. He sat by the window when she entered, got up, hugged her, and beckoned her to sit by the window with him. Gina's ears were itchy. She was eager to know who Kyle was, everything about him. Kyle cleared his throat, paused, and looked at Gina. His eyes caught the birthmarks. Gina looked at them too. She got the marks from her father, very obvious and conspicuous. She touched and played with it as they discussed. Kyle told her he knew she needed information and promised her he would tell her the whole truth and nothing but the truth. Gina sighed and thanked him.

Kyle explained to her that he was an only child. His parents never introduced him to any family member. They married early and moved from a very remote area that he could not recollect to the city to find greener pastures. His father worked as a handyman, and his mother was a stay-at-home mum. She inherited her bipolar disorder from her lineage. As little as he was, he knew they fought and quarreled a lot. His father was really good with his hands, got a lot of jobs, made money but would spend his money on drugs and alcohol and would return home broke. He had no friends but had mistresses who took money from him. His addiction and attitude pushed his mother who had post-partum depression after his birth to sink deeper into her untreated depression. Her depression got worse due to his father's attitude and incessant fights.

One day, after bouts of quarrels and fights, she threw him down the stairs in anger, and he was seriously hurt. His leg got tangled by the staircase, and his groin became seriously swollen. No medical attention was sought for him for several days. When she eventually did, the doctor declared that he would not be able to father a child because of the damage. The incident attracted the police who arrested them. When they saw the mental status of his mother, she was Baker Act to a psychiatric hospital, assessed, and placed on psychotropic drugs. A child protection officer took him to foster care while his father was detained. He reunited with his father when he regained his freedom. His mother was discharged two weeks later. She returned home, but the fights, cheating, alcohol, and drugs, never stopped. She stopped using her medications because the side effects were too much for her to bear. Without the medications, she progressed gradually from depression to manic to schizophrenia. Her condition went speedily out of control. She would fight for no reason, break things, cut herself, suicidal, and would sometimes harm him with the belief that she was caring for him. She would fight with the neighbors for no justifiable reason and became a burden and a nuisance in the neighborhood. One day, she hit his father so hard that he almost died. When the police arrived, they took her back to the psychiatric hospital, and he visited her, but the visit stopped when he was transferred to foster care. She was institutionalized till her death. His father became his only custodian but not for long. He would drink himself to a stupor, get high on drugs, and leave him alone at home for days. He was very lonely because the neighbors would not let him play with the children in the neighborhood because of the stigma of mental illness. They believed he would act out on their children like his mother. He stayed indoors mostly. A neighbor called the child protective service to report he had been home alone for days. They picked him and sent him to a foster home. His father never came back for him. He learned that he died of liver cirrhosis.

Kyle looked at Gina who had become emotional. He asked if she wanted to hear more of his sad tale. She nodded in the affirmative, and Kyle continued. His foster parents loved him, and he got an abundance of love he did not receive from his birth parents. They were privy to his family history, so they made sure he got a psychiatric assessment early. By the time he was twelve, he was already on psychotropic medications. He hated the way he felt with the medications. The side effects were horrible. The stigma of his mental health disorder would shame him if his classmates knew, so he treated himself by substituting his prescribed medications with drugs and alcohol and hid it from his foster parents. He became addicted to the substances, and his foster parents were unhappy with him. They pulled him out of school and started homeschooling him. He was brilliant. They thought peer influence was the factor, but there was no peer. It was the side effects of the medications that pushed him into drug use.

He finished high school with flying colors and got admission into the university. His foster parent died when he was in the university, rendering him homeless. He had manic episodes and managed them with drugs but eventually finished well. He got a job in the town where Madeline and her family lived and started attending the church Madeline's father pastored. The pastor liked him so much, took him as his son, frequented his home, and treated him like an insider. The pastor started a sobriety ministry in the church because of him, was loved by all, and did handyman jobs for the congregants, volunteered at the maintenance department in the church, but his mental outbursts limited him. He loved Madeline and expressed it to her severally, but her heart was for Benjamin. He loved the pastor's family and desired a family like his but without children. He wanted someone from a good family that would love him the way he was. Madeline fitted his heart's desire. Weeks before Madeline's wedding, one thing led to another, and the unexpected occurred. It was as if a force propelled them. They could not explain how it happened. It was not intentional. He believed he could not father a child. It was the first time for him. They regretted it instantly, ashamed, but thought the incident would endear Madeline's heart to him. Madeline was one of the best human beings anyone would wish for in this world. He apologized and was sorry for putting all of them through this situation. He punctuated his story with the fact that Madeline was never a wayward lady. What happened was a mistake, a total mistake that was never supposed to happen, never intended.

Gina got up, stretched her legs and body, and looked out of the window for a while. Kyle kept his eyes focused on her, unsure of what her thoughts were. She sat down again and asked him to continue. Her affect was flat, unhappy, unexplainable; Kyle hesitated but continued. He was sad when Madeline married Benjamin two weeks later. He attended the wedding. It was the worst day of his life. He left town that night and never returned. He relapsed on drugs, became seriously depressed, had a mental breakdown, could no longer function on his job, and lost it. Weeks turned to months, and he progressively became full-blown manic, was Baker Act, institutionalized for more than one year in a psychiatric hospital. He went through rehab and counseling. He was treated for dual diagnosis and eventually stabilized on his medications. Since that admission, he turned his life around and had not had an episode since then. He moved away after his discharge and never contacted Madeline or any member of her family until they came to find him. He explained that he never got married, had no children, and had a longtime live-in lover who was always in and out. He preferred it that way. As for his job, he got a job with the government when he became fully stabilized, had been in the same organization for over two decades, and rose within the ranks. He bought a house and already paid off his mortgage and cars; he was not as rich as Benjamin but extremely comfortable in his own way. He had been clean and sober for over two decades also. Kyle appealed to Gina to forgive him and Madeline. What occurred between them was beyond them. It was unexplainable. He never wanted to procreate. He wanted to put an end to his lineage. Madeline also never wanted a child for reasons best known to her, but Gina came to this world through two unwilling parents. Her procreation was deemed fate-linked. Whatever that "fate" intended to achieve might evolve to her eventually. All she needed was to embrace her fate and make the best of it.

Kyle had tears rolling down his cheeks by the time he finished his story. Gina was sobbing also. He held her hands, told her that he loved her, and believed there is no mistake in God's dictionary. God intended for her to be in this world despite the mistake they committed. He wanted her to see her existence as a design by a power higher than them. He would love to be part of her life but would hate to usurp the only life and family she knew all her life. He had promised to allow Madeline and Benjamin to be her parents but would like to be part of it in a way if Gina would permit him. Gina thanked Kyle for telling him the truth about himself. What he said correlated with what Madeline and Benjamin told her though not in full detail. She was happy they told her the truth. She had a lot of thinking to do, and just as Francine told her, she could do nothing to reverse the situation. All she had to do would be to embrace and make good of it. They sat in silence for about ten minutes. Gina broke the silence, told Kyle she loved him, and gave him a bear hug as they wept together in silence. She then poured her heart out to Kyle, the demons of addiction and mental health that plagued her, if she knew what she just learned, she would have embraced treatment a long time ago, that her underlining mental illness precipitated her outbursts, behavior, and attitude. Addiction was a big problem, mental health a bigger problem, and both were fundamental problems. Every problem, however, has a solution and expiration date if we work on it. Recovery works if one walks the work. She will work and walk the walk for her sanity and benefit. With medications, she would surmount her mental illness the way Kyle surmounted and managed his mental health prognosis and dealt with his addiction. Her prognosis has been revealed to her through lineage and heredity. She will use medications and counseling to fix them. Her purpose and passion from henceforth would be to work on her problems. She spent more time with Kyle. They had dinner together before she left for the hotel to meet her parents who were eagerly waiting for her.

Madeline and Benjamin were worried when Gina spent more time than expected to return, not that they did not want them to bond but unsure of how Gina would receive the story. They were happy when she returned and seemed to be in a good mood and told them she stayed to have dinner with Kyle. They were happy at the development, happy that Gina felt relaxed with Kyle to the extent of having dinner with him, a development in the right direction for all of them. She shared all Kyle told her with them, fully convinced that all she had gone through was due to the imbalance in the brain chemistry that she inherited from the genes of her biological father, the addiction, and the mental health diseases that ran in his lineage. They encouraged her to think and digest all the information from Kyle and the way forward. She needed to decide what she wanted, and they would abide by it and give all the needed support, but foremost, she needed to follow suit with her counseling and psychiatric appointments so that her treatment and rehabilitation process could begin in earnest. They reiterated to her that she would forever remain their first child.

Gina and her parents visited Kyle again before returning to their home. Gina called Francine the following morning and told her she would like to meet with her as soon as possible. They met after work, and Gina told her everything without any omission. As usual, she listened attentively and asked Gina what her thoughts were on the information presently available to her. Gina told her that her story pointed to hereditary. She ought to have realized her problems early, but ignorance, ego, and pride debarred her from the right thought process. The way forward would be a total turnaround in her life. With her issues laid bare before her now, the onus rested solely on her to do the right thing. Her first line of action to get back on the right track would be to start her therapy sessions in earnest and have a psychiatrist diagnose and recommend medications to treat her diagnosis and get into treatment for her drug abuse. Francine was happy with her decision. She explained the issues of hereditary to Gina from a medical point. She also added that she needed to normalize the relationship with her parents and Kyle. They both have a history that binds them together and encouraged Gina to follow Kyle's footsteps. He mastered the symptoms of his mental illness, followed the doctor's prescribed regimen, and had been stable for over two decades. Likewise, he had been clean and sober for over two decades. He made the decision to choose a better life, worked on his addiction, and stayed away from drugs and alcohol. Gina should adopt the strength of Kyle and do the same. She should allow Madeline, Benjamin, and Kyle to give her all the support she needed to overcome her issues, and she would be there to lend her support as much as she wished. Francine promised her story and paternity issues would forever be confidential. Gina thanked her profusely for her attention and encouraging words.

Gina began her counseling sessions, worked diligently with her therapist, listened attentively during sessions, and asked questions. She bore her heart out to her therapist and left no stone unturned on her attitudes, behavioral traits, atrocities, criminal activities, and hereditary. The only thing she did not discuss was the issue of her paternity and discussed her mental hereditary in detail but left out the source of it. Her therapist started with the cognitive behavioral therapy technique. She needed to learn how her behavior had jeopardized her decision-making, thinking process, and values in life. Other techniques such as psychoanalysis and psychodynamic therapies, guided self-help, interpersonal therapy, and dialectical behavioral therapy to identify and change negative thinking patterns were helpful to her. She was very thorough with Gina during individual therapy sessions. Her lifestyle changed drastically for good. Her stinking thinking gave way to positive and reasonable thinking.

Mental health was a genuine issue, but not all people with mental health disorders partake in disruptive and criminal activities. Hers was at a higher level due to the negative traits she personally imbibed. Her entitlement attitude and the wealth she was born into made her believe she was worth more than her true worth. Privileged children believe that money answers all things and could buy them the world, but most times, they end up ruining their lives and the lives of others around them. Gina met other entitled individuals like herself at the group therapy sessions. At a group session, she listened to a client whose story was like hers, so close to home. By the time he shared the horrors, aches, disgrace, and pains he caused for himself and family, everyone present shed tears. Shame and disgrace were not in his dictionary. He did whatever he wanted not minding the consequences. His addictive brain got used to shame and erased conscience from his heart. Gina saw herself in him, and the similarities were obvious; unfortunately, his mother died due to his addiction and atrocities. Gina thought that could have been her story too. She almost killed her mother with her behavioral and addictive excesses. He had been in and out of prison severally, had ruined his family economically, and caused them so much horror. He was a privileged child that squandered the resources of his family as she did. Gina's sob at the session became the turning point in the right direction. She saw herself in him, and he became her mirror during that group session. Most times, we do not realize how hurtful our actions are to others and even to ourselves. We can unlearn distorted behaviors when our thinking patterns and habits change. Attitudes get better through understanding unhelpful behavior; we need to work diligently to change bad behaviors by thinking thoroughly before action.

Gina's psychiatrist was a seasoned professional with years of experience and had written medical journals that had given her prominence. Gina armed with the true story of her birth was able to give her the true picture of her mental health disorder and had gotten enough information from Kyle and his family history. The first set of psychotropic medications her psychiatrist prescribed were not helpful. The side effects were terrible and made her situation worse. Her parents and the therapist told her to give the medications time for clinical effectiveness. At the next appointment, she explained her experiences and how she felt. Her doctor encouraged her to continue for one more appointment. If the side effects persisted, she would change the medications. Gina discussed her medications with Kyle who shared his experiences and told her it took a while to get the medications that benefited his issues also. What worked for him might not necessarily work for Gina. He told her some of his medications and how long it took for them to get him stabilized. All said, she needed to persevere. The psychiatrist changed, altered, and they worked eventually. Gina was happy. Her disposition changed, and she was happier, levelheaded, and on the right track.

Kyle was surprised when he received a stage 2 prostate cancer diagnosis. The news devastated him seriously and had no inkling that something was wrong in his body. He did his annual physicals yearly and had no other illness besides his mental health diagnosis. He fainted on the job again and was rushed to the hospital. It was not the news he wanted to hear; his plan was to be in Gina's life even if it would only be from afar. He asked the doctor questions. He made him understand that his prognosis was fair and could be effectively managed; he needed to start chemotherapy immediately. He called Benjamin and told him about the prognosis. It broke his heart. He promised to pass the information to Madeline and Gina, knew it would affect Gina terribly because she had taken a liken to him, which they were happy about. Benjamin and his family rushed to Kyle's bedside; he just finished a chemotherapy session when they arrived. He was not looking or feeling too good but was happy to see them. Kyle needed rest; his nurse told them they had to return later in the evening so he could rest from the torturous chemo session. They obliged, hugged him briefly, and left. He slept off as soon as they left. The chemo was very alien to his body. He woke up a few hours later and threw up until there was nothing left inside of him. The nurse gave him medication to make him comfortable. He could not fall asleep again and was restless and uncomfortable when the Wiggins returned. The nurse told them they could see him only for a few minutes. Their presence cheered him up. They stayed for a few minutes as agreed with the nurse. When they returned the following day, he looked better and felt better. They were able to chat and cheer him up. Kyle discussed the effects the chemo had on him. He described it as a wicked and torturous alien residing in his body. They all laughed at his description, and Gina realized how humorous Kyle was. They visited again in the evening before traveling back to their city. The Wiggins called daily to check on Kyle. Gina called at least three to four times daily to talk to him. Their discussions were always positive, qualitative, and soul-lifting. They made his day worthwhile.

Kyle shared more information about himself, his struggles in life, and how he was able to overcome his "demons."

He explained to her how difficult it was for him to become stabilized on his medications. His doctor tried various drugs/combinations until he was able to get the exact medication that suited his diagnosis and worked perfectly for him. At a point in his life, he contemplated suicide but quickly realized that death was not an option. Committing suicide was to concede and give up. Challenges are meant to be faced squarely, not run away from them. Testimonies abound only when you overcome a trial. Trials don't kill. They strengthen us. He fought his demons hands down. Gina should do the same. He also shared the efforts he made to become truly clean and sober. He persevered and was fully dedicated to the struggle, worked on his issues one day at a time, and managed to erase the pains as much as he could. Both diagnoses were a big pain to his existence. They made him go through excruciating pains, but he never stopped working on them. That was how he was able to live his life and build his career. He told her she must struggle to overcome as he did. It would be an uphill task, but she must do it. Looking back would be detrimental. Giving up would make her a failure. To tap all her potential in life, she must overcome her addiction and bring her mental health under control. Gina enjoyed talking to him. He was full of wisdom. His experiences in life and about life were worth tapping into. He was such an encourager, a living example. He encouraged her to call him anytime, and the calls were therapeutic to him, and so was it to Gina. They enjoyed talking to each other. It got them closer. There was no downtime talking to Kyle. He was so humorous and down to earth. Gina took all the encouraging words of Kyle to heart. He understood her situation perfectly. He had walked the same path before and understood the terrain perfectly.

CHAPTER 16

Reunion

Madeline and Benjamin discussed the surrogacy with Gina. To their amazement, she was happy that she would have siblings. She asked questions about the surrogate and told them she would love to decorate the nursery as her personal contribution to await the arrival of the twins. Her mother told her they had bought most things needed for the nursery but waited until after the discussion with her. Gina's acceptance bothered them initially because they expected resistance or resentment. She, however, disappointed them and did the opposite of what they expected. Gina had changed. She was no longer the old Gina they knew. Her therapy sessions had made a significant impact on her. She discussed the surrogacy issue with her therapist who was happy for her and explained that the arrival of the children would be a positive turning point, and her involvement in caring for the young souls would teach her values of life, responsibility, and love. Gina purchased blue and pink paints and painted the nursery before Madeline and Benjamin returned home. She did an excellent job; they could not believe their eyes nor fathom Gina's skill because she had never applied herself to do anything before. She inherited the handyman skill from Kyle. The room was painted with artistic pictures on the wall in the right places. They were amazed. She sent the pictures to Kyle who was impressed with the beauty of what she accomplished. All the things bought for the babies were personally fixed and positioned by Gina; it took her two days to finish. She showed the pictures she took to her therapist and psychiatrist; they were impressed. Such actions are good for recovery. It helps keep her mind focused on other things instead of drugs and frivolities.

The surrogate mother would be due soon. Gina met with her, and they bonded immediately. She explained her pregnancy issues, and they laughed hard. She was an amiable, beautiful woman with blond hair, the same hair color and features as Madeline and Gina, same height, skin, and eye color. Madeline went to great lengths to find her. She had a clean slate of health, had never abused substances, and never smoked cigarettes. She was in her early thirties with two children of her own, a university graduate who opted to put smiles on the Wiggins's faces, it would be her first and last surrogacy. She liked Madeline and Benjamin though the pay was impressive. The contract was signed and dotted; the babies were one hundred percent Wiggins. She would allow Gina and Madeline in the labor room, initially did not want Benjamin to be present but later changed her mind. Gina was happy and thanked her for the honor. Gina shopped for more toys and items for the nursery, decorated the room tastefully, ready for the awaited bundles of joy, and went through the list for the nursery daily to ensure everything needed was in place. She was ready to become a big sister.

The babies arrived at exactly thirty-eight weeks gestation; they came out beautiful, a boy and a girl, healthy, cute as a button. Gina was the happiest. She witnessed a woman in labor and the birth of her kid brother and sister. The boy came out first and the girl a few minutes later. The surrogate was in labor for about six hours. She had an epidural injection that made the labor almost pain-free, but Gina knew it was not an easy task for her to carry the pregnancy or go through the labor. The surrogate shared her experiences with morning sickness at the inception of the pregnancy and the desire to eat like a glutton. They had become "friends," but the surrogate intentionally did not discuss anything about her personal life with Gina. Even when she asked, she made sure the relationship was as platonic as ever. She was on contract with her parents and made sure it was left as such. She gained weight, which she planned to shelve after the delivery. Madeline and Benjamin were on top of the moon. They took pictures with Gina and the babies, but the surrogate politely declined any pictures with them. The babies got a clean bill of health, and the surrogate and babies were discharged the following day since there were no health issues or complications with any of them. She handed the babies to the Wiggins, wished them and the babies well, hugged Gina and the new parents, hopped into a taxi, and left. Her contract was over. The surrogate was however a wonderful woman who went beyond with her kind heart and love for the Wiggins. She knew the importance of breast milk for babies. She had not started lactating when she was discharged. When she got home, she decided to pump as much milk as she could daily, froze, and sent boxes of frozen breast milk to them from an undisclosed address for three months. The Wiggins twins had breast milk, enough to last them for a whole six months to a year. The arrival of the twins was the best thing that happened in the Wiggins household. Things had changed for the better. Their only heartache was Kyle's illness.

Kyle was discharged after his health became stabilized. He was to continue the rest of his chemo from home. Gina shuttled between Kyle's place and her parents. She devoted time more to the twins and made sure she talked to Kyle at least twice daily to be sure he was doing well, and took his medications on time. On her part, she took her recovery seriously, attended her counseling sessions, both individual and group, never missed her support group meetings and psychiatric appointments, and was ready to return to school. Her busy schedule scared the Wiggins. They were afraid she might relapse because she was doing too much at the same time. Not getting enough rest could be a disaster for a relapse. She promised her parents, Kyle, and therapist that she would be fine, and she was truly fine. She was able to cope under the enormous pressure. Her tenacity seemed to be out of this world. She had a determination so real that she sometimes doubted if she was once the toxic, disgusting, and loathing Gina. Her recovery was intact, solid as a rock. She identified that she was her obstacle, the main clog in the wheel of her progress, and her shambolic and mismanaged attitude had caused untold damage to her and her loved ones. She was ready to exchange her chaotic and disorganized life for a life of decency and order. She reaped the negative consequences of jealousy, hatred, bitterness, and envy. She lived on her parents' successes, forgetting that living only on success is key to failure. Success could become ephemeral if not improved and worked upon. Her life was never close to perfect. She misused the successes she got by birth with so much impunity. She was repugnant, became her cancer, forgot that she could not run from her shadow but could make her shadow a replica of an impressive and positive inner trait if she wished. Her parents who she abhorred so much became her greatest supporters, Kyle inclusive, but the greatest honor belonged to Francine who never gave up on her despite her odious character. Francine eventually became her savior and supported her to become a new creature.

Gina left her therapy session early. The group session was shorter than expected because the therapist had to leave for an important assignment. Gina had never missed a session, unlike the others. Leaving the group session early was an opportunity to get home on time to be with the twins. She called Kyle on her way home; he shared his latest prognosis with her. The development was not what Gina wanted to hear. She felt bad that Kyle's health was not improving as fast as she expected imagining the pain he was going through. They briefly discussed his current prognosis, but the medical terminologies were big jargon, abstracts for a layperson like Gina to understand, Francine would know what they meant. Kyle changed the topic and asked Gina about her sessions and recovery efforts so far, Gina shared that if she had the knowledge she had presently, she would have lived her life differently. It was always good to have something and not need it than to need it and not have it. Knowledge is power. The statement is a hundred percent true. Knowledge of a subject matter is a good liberator, thanks to those who invented education and learning. Without knowledge, we will all be in the dark. No one is a perfect reservoir of knowledge; we learn from one another, iron sharpens iron, and two minds are always better than one. She lived her life like an accursed individual due to total ignorance, lack of knowledge, and devoid of good decisions. She was deaf to the voice of reason and wisdom and lived as a lost soul on the highway called self-destruction. She could go on and on. Kyle encouraged her to leave the past behind and forge ahead with the hope of a better tomorrow, allowing redemption and knowledge to wipe away her ignorance. What she needed was not regrets but a change in strategy, to proffer the best methods to solve her problems and work on varied methods diligently because the only person that could effect a change in her situation was no other person but her. She needed to be truthful to herself, not fake it. An individual can lie and fake situations to others but would know within himself/herself that it was a fake and a lie. Gina used to be a perfect liar, lied to the extent that her lies became absolute truth in her brain. She parroted truth negatively to her advantage, but all that had changed. She no longer twisted the truth. She narrated and discussed her issues with utmost truth, commitment, and loyalty to Francine, her parents, Kyle, her therapist, psychiatrist, other clients in therapy, and whoever needed to hear her story.

The twins grew like grass. Bigger, healthier, happier, source of joy and happiness to the Wiggins. Kyle was happy for them. He often asked for video chats to see them and loved them as if they were his flesh and blood. The Wiggins were totally involved with nursing the babies. They employed nannies, and Gina competed in caring for them. Madeline had turned a new leaf. She dotted on the babies and loved them with all her heart. She refused to allow the mistake of being an absentee mother and a workaholic to repeat itself. Volunteering at the children's section of her father's church when she was growing up made her believe she was not cut for mothering and motherhood. Her mother being the pastor's wife stayed mostly at the children's ministry and made Madeline volunteer at the department all the time. It was not an easy one for her. She hated the cries and attention the babies always needed. All she wanted was to enjoy her marriage with no children. Madeline saw the experience as exasperating and hard. It bothered her what the mothers went through at home with those babies. She vowed in her heart not to have babies, but faith had it otherwise. To make it even easier and better, she was now a stay-at-home mother. She left her high-powered job when her health woes occurred, all thanks to Gina. Benjamin insisted she become a "full-time house engineer." The surrogate mother disappeared from their lives. Her contract was over. She relocated far away from them with her family and had no contact with them. She, however, sent pumped, frozen breastmilk as often as possible out of her own personal volition. Whether they used them or not was left to the Wiggins. They appreciated her kind gesture immensely but were not able to thank her. All contacts they had no longer worked. Her generosity was out of this world. People like her are hard to find. To her, it was not about money. It was about putting smiles on the faces of other people. She was a woman filled with the milk of beneficence and human kindness.

Francine, Ella, and Elizabeth made it a point of duty to support Gina in her recovery process. They were her greatest encourager and made sure she followed through with her appointments. Occasionally, they met for lady's outings, shared ladies' stuff, and encouraged one another. Francine's marriage agreed so much with her. She radiated, glowed, looked every inch happy, peaceful, and contented. Her marriage to Craig had so much bliss. They loved each other passionately, understood each other, and operated on the same frequency. Francine was not pregnant. She intentionally went on birth control pills after her marriage because she wanted to enjoy "alone" time with her husband, have fun, and explore. Marriages are not only for procreation but primarily for companionship, savoring, and enjoying life with your spouse. She was under the age of thirty and still had time. Pregnancies at the age of thirty-five and older are geriatric pregnancies. The term seemed funny to all of them.

All Francine devoted her life to before marriage was study, study, and study hard. She had minimal fun and focused only on her goals in life. As for her grandmother who wanted great-grandchildren immediately after Francine's marriage, she would have to wait a little longer. Francine jokingly told her grandmother that waiting for her great-grandchildren would make her live longer. She must be alive to see and enjoy them to the fullest. Her grandmother told her that she wanted to personally hand over the child(ren)'s envelope the way she did on Francine's wedding day, so she should hurry up. Francine laughed her heart out and told Grandma to chill. They laughed more! Francine loved her mother-in-law the way she loved her parents and grandmother. She treated her with the highest degree of respect. Craig's mother reciprocated with more love—pure, undiluted love. Francine refused to be a hater of her mother-in-law. She was not in the league of ladies who prayed not to marry a man whose mother is alive or prayed for the mother-in-law to die. She cherished, loved, and adored her a great deal. Craig loved Francine the more for her disposition, love, and respect toward his mother. Who wouldn't? A home where love resides and reigns would enjoy peace. Ladies like Francine are rare at this age and time when ladies wished the mothers of their spouses dead with other family members to virtually disappear from the face of the earth. Craig's mother was a rare gem, a unique personality with distinct and amiable character, beautiful in and out. No wonder Craig was a wonderful person, a good husband, filled with love and admiration for his wife. An apple does not fall far from its tree was the best way to describe Craig and his mother, the love, goodness, and kindness in their nature were enviable.

Thanksgiving was by the corner. Many accomplishments to be thankful for in all the households, good and marvelous things had occurred over the years. Good health, marriages, recoveries, graduations, births, new and thriving businesses, growing charitable organizations, and more. Preparations were in top gear for the turkeys and merriments to follow. Francine asked all the families to celebrate together. She shared that the togetherness would reinforce the needed support for those working or dealing with one issue or the other. "Let us have a reunion during this Thanksgiving, be under one roof thanking and blessing God for the many marvelous breakthroughs we have all experienced in the last few years," she wrote to all the families. Everyone bought into the idea. Jason was happy at Francine's idea. He responded that he would love for them to converge at his place because he had lots of space that would accommodate everyone. Francine shared the information, and they agreed, everyone agreed to bring a portion as a personal contribution. They all converged at four in the evening, Amelia, Carol, Baron, Ella, and the twins, Francisca, Francis, Francine, Craig, grandma and Craig's mother, Benjamin, Madeline, Gina, the twins, and the hosts, Jason, Bethena, Elizabeth, Jane, Judy, and Jason Jr. It was a full house! A field day for all the twins to run and crawl around. They created fun for everyone. The reunion made the families bond more with each other. Francine was the rallying factor, had the impetus, zeal, and the great idea that allowed love to become infectious. Love covers a multitude of issues; negative things happen in people's lives due to the absence of love. Pure and true love heals situations, turns situations around, brings newness to shattered lives. It changes lives in ways difficult to explain or describe. There was an abundance of food, a show of love and fun. Alcohol was not available, and great fun could happen without alcohol. Jason and Bethena were the perfect hosts. They made sure comfort was at its peak for everyone irrespective of age.

Francine did it again. She sowed goodness that germinated more goodness in the heart of everyone.

*****

Gina called Kyle to wish him a Happy Thanksgiving early in the morning and shared with him that they were all meeting at Jason's place for Thanksgiving dinner. Kyle was not invited due to his peculiar situation; he was happy for all of them, though he would be alone. Gina ordered food to be delivered to him from a restaurant in the city where he lived. The restaurant specialized in preparing healthy meals for people with serious health issues. Madeline and Benjamin discovered the restaurant and organized with the hospital's nutritionist for the best nutrition for Kyle. He was alone, had learned to be his best companion, mastered the art of reading as his passion, and his neighbors loved him and sent him portions from their Thanksgiving dinner. Gina looked forward to the reunion. They all seemed to be on the same page and would be a meeting like no other for everyone. The discussions, actions, and fun blended seamlessly, even the sets of twins became inseparable friends, blended as if they lived together under the same roof. Love was personified in the hearts of everyone present. It was a reunion like no other. No one wanted it to end. They cleaned up together, tidied up, and dropped the trash into the bins before they called the party over. The love shared that day was enduring.

*****

Two years into Francine's marriage, she called her grandmother to share the good news she had waited so long for. She told her she was pregnant. Grandma's joy knew no bounds. She screamed and danced around the house all by herself. The news was long overdue. She waited for Francisca and Francis to return so they could see how elated she was. Francine called to inform her parents too. Francine told all her friends about the result when the test strip had indicated "positive" but would let them know when her gynecologist confirmed it. She took herself off birth control only a month ago. A scan would confirm the sex of the baby, but that would be later. She wished the pregnancy would be a set of twins. She loved twins. It would be a rapid result/answer to her prayer. A set of twins would mean no more pregnancies. The scan showed Francine was pregnant with a set of twins, but the sex of the twins would have to wait a few months. Francine was ecstatic, an era and season of twins for all the families. She loved twins, saw them as adorable, loved to dress them in the same attires, and roll twin prams around. What a joy! Craig was the happiest of all. His mother was overjoyed. Francine's pregnancy was so easy. From day one to the day of her delivery, she had no issues, no morning sickness, throwing up, overeating, or undereating. She made pregnancy seem easy. She went about her daily activities with ease, never missed a day at work, slept well, and rested well. The scan showed she was expecting a set of boys, identical twins.

Gina painted the room blue for the arrival of the boys. Ella and Elizabeth decorated it, and a big baby shower was planned for Francine. She was well worth it. The shower was attended by all the beautiful lives she had touched, her colleagues at work as well as friends and colleague of Craig. She went into labor at exactly forty weeks gestation. She put to bed naturally within two hours. She shared that the two hours were the longest hours of her life. The pain was extreme, excruciating, and torturous but refused epidural injection.

She wanted to experience the pain of motherhood as experienced naturally by others. The boys came out screaming at the top of their lungs. They were beautiful and handsome rolled into one. They stopped crying as their bodies touched Francine's. It was a moment of joy and she shed tears of joy. Gina, Ella, Elizabeth, Craig's mother, and Francisca who witnessed the birth with Craig shed tears of joy too. The tears momentarily turned into laughter. Francine's delivery room was full, filled with love and joy from those who mattered most to her. The nurses cleaned the twins, checked all vitals, and gave the parents a good report. The pediatrician would visit them in the morning, and they might leave in a day or two. Francine's grandmother's wish had happened. She was alive to see her great-grandchildren, two beautiful identical boys, and her bundle of joy arrived at last. When Francine got back home, she had more hands to support and help with the boys. Craig took his annual leave to coincide with the birth of his children. He was good with babies, with the midnight blues, making it easy for Francine.

Kyle's health turned worse. His cancer suddenly returned and rapidly spread all through his body and organs like a wildfire. The cancer was already in remission when it returned with a grave vengeance. He managed and maintained his health well since the diagnosis, but with cancer, no one can be too sure. He was well, used his medications as prescribed, followed through with all his doctor's appointments and advice, and returned to work. Things looked normal. He was dazed when his doctor told him the unwelcome news, but he took it with great stride, a good heart, and an abundance of courage. He was not scared of death but feared the bouts of chemotherapy he would go through again. Gina was sad to hear the news. She thought her father was out of the woods, but the opposite was the case. Cancer was such an unpredictable disease, a silent killer that permeates the body and system without any knowledge by the individual being destroyed. Gina feared losing Kyle. She had grown fond of him. The daily discussions meant a lot to her. She found it easier to share issues of life with Kyle than with Benjamin. Kyle always had a listening ear. Benjamin was too busy, addicted to his job, had no time for talks, his law firm, and the court cases were demanding. He was extremely tired and fagged out by the time he returned home. After dinner, he would be at his study getting ready for the following day and would sometimes fall asleep in the study due to excessive fatigue. Gina had a drug addiction, and Benjamin and Madeline had a work addiction! Kyle called Benjamin after sharing the shocking news with Gina. He was devastated. He shared the information with Madeline. They traveled to him immediately and spent the weekend at his bedside. Their arrival and presence meant a lot to him. They were the only family he had in the entire world, no other known relatives.

Gina was happy that her parents supported Kyle a great deal. They had a sincere love for him and supported him with all their hearts. They were always available and spared no expense in caring for him. The fact that Kyle was an only child with no known relatives bothered her. She knew Kyle was not happy that he had no relations and was happy to have Gina as the only relation known to him. Gina normalized relations with her uncle, aunties, and cousins on her maternal side. She had matured, changed her attitude and lifestyle, and her relationship with her family and extended relatives had improved tremendously. She wanted to avoid the aloneness Kyle experienced in his life. Gina had turned her life around, had been clean and sober for years, and almost done with her first degree. She had decided to become a licensed social worker. She needed to give back to others the way she got help and support for her addiction and mental health disorders. Her final examinations and graduation were by the corner. Kyle's health status was a bother to her and had caused her anxiety in recent times. Kyle's oncologist told him he had a few months to live. He was at peace with the information and homegoing. He was tired of the pain, suffering, puking, chemotherapy, and sleepless nights. Dying early was not his wish, especially with the existence of Gina and the bond and love they had formed, but there was nothing he could do to change his fate. Gina spent more time with Kyle as he was nearing his end. He was happy that Gina showed him so much love and affection. Benjamin and Madeline came on weekends to spend time with him. Gina graduated in flying colors. Madeline and Benjamin were proud of her and threw a surprise graduation party for her.

Francine was happy that Gina proved her worth and ability to truly regain all the glory she lost in the past. Kyle was too weak to attend Gina's graduation but was thrilled that she finished well. The weekend before his death, he made a moving appreciation speech to Gina and her parents. Kyle shared how appreciative he was to Benjamin as they all sat around his bed. He thanked him for giving him a family he never had and yearned for all his life. Benjamin proved the power of forgiveness to him, the power to be a true husband and father, showing pure undiluted love. Fatherhood was not just donating a liquid but being there, always available. Fatherhood was doing the needful physically, psychologically, emotionally, and materially. It was seeing the child smile, cry, crawl, take the first step, walk, ride the bicycle, all the trivial things of life that meant a lot in a child's growing years.

He forgave Madeline, never hated her, and even loved her more. He never turned his back on Gina despite all her previous excesses and had even shown him pure affection and love, became the brother he never had, stood by him, and did not hate him for what happened between him and Madeline. He became his greatest confidant, nursed him in his ill health, and treated him as a family even to the end. Not many people could have the heart he had and exhibited. He thanked him profusely. Kyle turned to Madeline and thanked her, calling her a rare gem, a worthy example. They made a mistake, but in retrospect, he had realized that the maker of life designed it. Both wanted no children, but the Maker proved them wrong.

He encouraged Gina to emulate her mother. She was a well-brought-up woman who loved and treated people with love and kindness. It endeared him to her. Marrying another person almost made him commit suicide. She was a woman any man would want. Benjamin was lucky to be her husband. He thanked Gina again for turning her life around. Sobriety is key, and she must guard it with all her might, must continually work on her mental health. Thanked her for being a kindhearted woman like her mother, and exhibiting all the traits Madeline had. Her mental health exposure robbed her of her good traits for a long time. Thank God for recovery, she can now soar like the eagles with her good heart, traits, and deeds. He took Gina's hands, put them into Benjamin's hands, and told her, "These are your real parents, not me. I might be your biological father, but he is your real father. I will keep the DNA result a secret between us. I will take the information to my grave. Please keep it within the family. You are an unusual design, God's own exceptional design. God had a reason for your existence. I do not know his reason. I pray he reveals it to you. In all the years with my in-and-out live-in lover, she never got pregnant in the morning and miscarried in the evening, never pregnant for one day. I never used any form of precaution because I believed my doctor when he told me I would never procreate, so God has a purpose for you in this world." His speech began to slur. He lifted his left hand, signaled to Madeline to bring her hand, joined her hand to the others, looked at Gina with his weak and pale eyes, and said, "I pray that the purpose for your existence is achieved in your life." The word "life" began to slur as he breathes his last breath. Gina began sobbing profusely as the nurse who was monitoring the machines from the nurse's station came in. She told them he was gone. He already signed a "do not resuscitate" order.

She covered his head after she confirmed that all the vitals had stopped. Kyle before his death told them to be happy; his death must be celebrated, not mourned, because God surprised him in many ways in the last years of his life, and he was thankful to Him. His sorrows turned to joy. God gave him a daughter, a new family, love, and happiness. Kyle schooled Gina on the importance of happiness. He said, "Happiness is contagious. Do everything in your power to be happy. You owe it to yourself. Do not let anything or anyone take it away from you. Happiness is medicine for the soul. Your soul needs this medicine to thrive." Kyle requested immediate cremation and the urn given to Gina and her family. Kyle requested Madeline's father to preach at his funeral. He gave a short sermon on "God's design and ways." God does whatever he wanted with individual lives, His ways are not our ways, and His designs are different from our plans. His last will and testament gave 80 percent of all he had to Gina and the Wiggins twins. He willed the remaining 20 percent to the psychiatric hospital that treated him for his mental health issues. Gina mourned Kyle. It affected her. She had to attend grief therapy sessions to overcome her grief, was exhausting, knew she needed help to avoid a relapse. She remembered Kyle's speech on celebrating his life instead of mourning him. It was difficult for her not to mourn him. He was a good man and father, and it took time for her and her family to get over it. Francine was the only one who knew about Gina's paternity. She did not share the information with Ella and Elizabeth. Gina kept it a secret from everyone. It was the wish of her parents that it be kept away from the public and prying eyes of the press. Ella and Elizabeth noticed that Gina seemed depressed and anxious. She told them she was all right and attributed it to preparations for her finals and subsequent graduation.

*****

Ella's fiancée proposed, and she said yes! Carol, Baron, and Grandma were happy for her. Ella requested a small wedding attended by only her loved ones, friends, and their families. She had learned to be prudent, appreciated the value of money, no longer squandered money, and would rather use it to benefit humanity than squandering it. She met her fiancé at Francine's wedding. He was one of the groomsmen, a close friend of Craig, who graduated from the medical school Francine and her husband attended. The wedding was exactly three months after the proposal. A beautiful wedding with aesthetic flower arrangements and details, it became the talk of the town. Ella invested money in wedding decoration to highlight their floral and home decor business. Pictures of the flower arrangement/decor were uploaded online. It was the perfect advertisement for their business.

People who saw the pictures booked for events and decorations afterward. It became a moneymaking bonanza for their business. Ella had added event planning to the list of services rendered at the company. Her family was so proud of her, a great asset to her family, businesses, including the

NGO. Amelia paid for her wedding dress; it was beautiful to behold, and everyone in attendance wowed at her wedding dress and the details. Her brother and sister also became a focal point. They were adorable as members of the wedding train. They loved Ella to death, enjoyed being with her, and would cry anytime she was leaving the house; in fact, many people believed she was their mother because of the age gap. Ella and her husband had their honeymoon on an island with tourist attractions. They rested during the day, did sightseeing in the evenings, attended operas, or went to the movies. They dated for a while before marriage and understood each other perfectly. Ella's wedding spurred Elizabeth's boyfriend to propose. Incidentally, Elizabeth caught Ella's bouquet at the reception. Everyone chorused that it was their turn and her boyfriend jokingly said he agreed. He was also one of the guests at Francine's wedding. It was an answered prayer to her soliloquy at Francine's wedding. He proposed two weeks later, and the wedding would hold in six months. Jason and Bethena were overjoyed, more than excited. They were willing to spare no expense for the wedding, but to their disappointment, she opted for a small wedding also. Her fiancé worked as a senior partner at one of the big law firms. He was a brilliant chap with enormous prospects. His brilliance had given him name recognition and access to the high and mighty in society at his early age.

*****

Elizabeth had changed immensely; she had been clean for a long time, and her personal disposition toward her parents, siblings, and friends had changed for the best. She loved and adored Jason's three children and treated them as her siblings. Jason's three children were on her wedding train.

They were happy for her and planned the wedding with her. It was small, sweet, and attended by the people who loved and mattered to them. Jason had his pilot fly them to the Bahamas in one of his private jets for their honeymoon. They had a swell time for the one week the "moon" lasted with extra "honey" reserved for the blissful journey ahead in their union. Elizabeth was happy to be married, just as Francine told her when she wished for a wedding, her time came at the appointed time. Everyone has an appointed time. No matter how fast we wished for a particular thing, it would only come when the time is ripe. Gina was happy for her friends who had back-to-back weddings. Ella and Elizabeth got married within nine months. She was not in any relationship and wished for one. Francine read her mind as she sat starring into space, lost in thought. She went and sat beside her, whispered into her ears that her time would be sooner than expected. Gina was surprised that Francine knew her thought and smiled, looked at Francine, and thanked her for the lives she had touched. She told Francine, "If not for you, Ella and Elizabeth would not be open to this great happiness and joy. You are a wonderful person, a special breed." Francine pulled her hand gently and led her to the dance floor where her thoughts evaporated for the moment.

"Today might be your lucky day," she whispered again. "You might be lucky to get a date."

*****

Gina got a job at Ariel's Turnaround center. The therapists who counseled her a few years back were happy to see her return fully changed and sober. A few of the former clients were amazed to see her return to give back from her wealth of personal and professional experience. Her story became an inspiration to those who had turned the door of the center into a revolving door. She planned in her heart to use her knowledge to liberate them, turn them around for good, if not all, at least some. If she could do it, they could too. Addiction is a disease that holds people in bondage. Dual diagnosis is worse, and to detach from both is difficult but doable with great determination. She is a living testimony that everyone can do it. It took all her zeal, effort, and sincere support. Carol was happy to have her on her staff. Gina was happy to have an income she could call her own, her personal sweat, and remuneration. She allowed her parents to manage all Kyle left for her and the twins. With her input, the monies were invested in an interest-yielding account, which she hoped to use to start her own rehabilitation center. Gina used her time at work to fill the gap in her grief. She went through brief therapy sessions to overcome the grief of Kyle's death.

*****

Elizabeth returned from her honeymoon and resumed at one of the companies owned by Jason as entry-level staff. The salary was more than juicy though. Jason wanted her to begin from the lowest cadre and work herself up the ladder. He did not give her a high-level position because he wanted her to learn on the job and acquire experience at all the levels and positions. He could give her an executive position but knew it might set her up for failure and make her feel superior over the people she met on the job. He knew she would one day hold the highest executive position at the group of companies, but climbing through the ladder would equip her effectively in the long run. She exhibited an excellent work ethic, and Jason was overly impressed with her performance. Her husband was a pleasant soul who did everything to support her sobriety. He was a social drinker who went to the club occasionally. He stopped drinking and resigned from his social club to support his wife. He was an incredibly positive individual who believed that if a person views an issue from a positive perspective, problems of life would be avoided and reduced to the barest minimum. He went into partnership with one of his classmates soon after the wedding. They formed a new law firm with billboards that displayed their pictures all over the city. Everyone was happy with his tall success. He planned to go into politics, and Elizabeth could become the first lady someday. Her husband was brilliant and exudes success. The great transformations in the life of Elizabeth were worthy of emulation. She went from a total junkie to a fully sober, repentant, and responsible adult. The way she treated, loved, cared, and related with her siblings and parents showed she was a changed and totally refined woman. Jason and Bethena knew she was ripe and matured for marriage when she got married and knew she would do them proud.

*****

Ella's grandmother fell and hit her head on her dressing mirror. She woke up in the morning, felt a bit dizzy, and before she could get her gait upright, she fell. Carol rushed to her room when she heard the big thud. She was groaning on the floor. Carol dashed to the phone and called the ambulance. Amelia believed she was all right and asked her not to call the ambulance, but she insisted. She was transported to the emergency room after being checked by the paramedics. She seemed all right to them but was still transported to fulfill all righteousness. At the hospital, a series of tests were ordered, but suddenly, her health became a cause of concern for her family. Her speech started to slur, and before the result of the tests were back, she slipped into a coma. Her situation puzzled them. There was no illness. She was in good health at the office the previous day and did her usual daily tasks without any trouble or hindrance. The doctor waited for the results. Nothing to show the reason for the coma. They started a series of palliative treatments, but her organs started shutting down drastically. Her situation was unexplainable, and she died a week later. It was so sudden, not expected. She had cancer years ago; the cancer had been in remission for a long time. There was no cause for alarm, and her death took all of them unawares. The grief was colossal, vast, and painful, seemed they would not be able to overcome it. The therapists at her foundation rallied around them. Gina was highly supportive in their grieving process, and all the therapists did their best to give them grief counseling.

Amelia's homegoing occurred days later. The funeral service was short, beautiful, and attended by all loved ones. Ella's eulogy was touching. She described her as an angel that walked this earth. Amelia was truly an angel. When she changed her lifestyle for the better, she truly did. She was not perfect and had her share of problems but worked on them and was able to overcome. She was love personified, loved with all her heart, showed that life is love and love is life, and became a mother and grandmother in a million—the best anyone could ask for. She was a good accountant when it came to money matters. She was not one by profession but invested the money she inherited from her late husband like a pro, used the money to make more money, made more money from her inheritance, a financial guru in her own right. Highly organized, meticulous, and good to a fault with paperwork and record-keeping, she left a shoe outrightly difficult to wear by anyone. Her eulogy was long, with bouts of outright sobbing, but she carried everyone along.

Carol's eulogy came after Ella's. She was unable to hold herself up. Tears were running down her makeup-less face like a river. She could not finish reading her eulogy, was too distraught, and Francine led Carol off the podium when it was visible that she could no longer stand upright. Baron read the rest of her eulogy as well as his. Amelia was fully prepared for the inevitable. She knew death could come anytime, but the time for her was sudden. She had her last will and testament prepared a long time ago and updated it often. She left everything to her daughter, granddaughter, and the twins. She took cognizance of the great-grandchildren she was unable to meet and made provision for their inheritance. The healing would be long. She left a big vacuum that nobody could fill. Amelia was a matriarch like no other. Her sudden death was a total and rude shock. Ella and her family got support from loved ones. Francine, Elizabeth, and Gina led the way. The show of love and support was mammoth. The whole community stood for and by them. Their charitable work and support for humanity made them the doyen of the community. They sympathized with them and showered them with empathy.

At the remembrance service for Amelia one year later, Ella had her baby girl in attendance. She became pregnant two months after her grandmother passed. She wished she were alive to see her pregnant, give birth, and nurse the baby. She named her after her grandmother, the first great-grandchild she was not opportune to meet. Carol planned to immortalize her mother and named a nonprofit organization after her as she did for her father. This time, it would be to support children's welfare. She had enough money to do it. To her, what was the essence of money others do not benefit from? Her whole life was about doing good. The hurt of their loss had started wearing off, and Amelia's charitable deeds alleviated their pains. They visited the motherless home in the community and made donations on her behalf. Carol promised the home a yearly donation to commemorate her mother's anniversary.

C H A P T E R 1 7

Walk the Talk

Francine was the president of the alumni of her high school. She planned a reunion for the year they graduated. It was a day everyone looked forward to. Notable among those who would attend were Gina, Ella, and Elizabeth. it would be the first attendance for Gina and was eagerly looking forward to it, hoping to use the occasion to relaunch herself, redeem her image, and allow people to see the new reformed Gina. Francine read her welcome speech and introduced those attending for the first time. When she introduced Gina, she got a standing ovation. Francine's introduction of Gina itemized her impact on humanity, especially in the addiction and mental health field. It amazed those who knew Gina as an addict that she had turned her life around even to give back to those who threaded the destructive path she once trod. She was not alone in her destructive and notorious ways. She had Ella and Elizabeth as her accomplices, but everyone knew she was the one in charge. She called the shots. The attendees at the reunion who saw her subdued and approachable were greatly surprised. It was soothing to all of them. A changed life was a welcoming situation any day. Francine encouraged all in attendance to have an enjoyable time with love, smile, laughter, dance, and merriments. She explained to them that they all needed to imbibe a "smile" as a form of diffusing tension. A smile solves problems, laughter lightens the heart, and dance depicts the inner joy inside an individual besides the exercise it gives to the body and joints. Gina told Francine she would like to address the attendees. She permitted her but told her to make the speech short.

Gina thanked Francine for allowing her to make a speech at such short notice. She spoke with a tone most were not familiar with. Her irksome, irritating voice had given way to a pleasant subtle voice pleasing to the ears. She narrated that she was stupid, showed all signs of stupidity, and thrived on stupidity until her stupidity caught up with her. She attested that she was full and pregnant with nefarious atrocities for many years, and they destroyed her big-time. She had no reason for doing all the evil things she did. Inferiority complex and envy overtook her and robbed her of valuable experiences, exposures, and enjoyments she was to have while in high school. She turned herself into an island and then a monster, unreached by words of wisdom and reason, seared her conscience with a hot iron. She confessed that she learned her lessons the hard way, all thanks to Francine who never gave up on her, who showed her that life was more than the negative vices she wrapped herself with. She poured encomiums on Francine. Her words and praises for Francine made the whole group honor Francine with a standing ovation that lasted minutes to acknowledge and appreciate her. Gina, in her final submission, apologized openly again to Francine and all her classmates, the people she hurt in the past. It was a restitution long overdue. To them, she looked every inch a changed person, but looks could be deceptive.

She paused, about to drop the microphone, changed her mind, and continued, "Now that I work as a therapist in the field of addiction and mental health, I have come to realize how difficult it is to win the battle against addiction, mental health, the almighty dual diagnosis. It is an unseen, unending war fought by an unseen army that never lets go or forgives. The weapons of this unseen army are targeted at a person's brain. It robs the mind, conscience, and ability to make positive decisions. The brain is shackled, fogged, and imprisoned. To get the shackles off, acceptance, dedication, and determination are needed by the individual while reinforcements, support, and counseling are vital from loved ones and professionals in the field. I am a living witness. I have been there, done worse things anyone could think of. She paused for a moment. There was dead silence in the hall.

She turned again to Francine. "I have wronged you beyond words or what anyone could imagine, to be factual, while we were in school. I adored your meekness, gentleness, brilliance, personal disposition toward all and sundry, your beauty, dress sense, looks, and hairstyle that adorned your self-expression, in fact, everything about you. I wondered why a person should have all those attributes. They hurt me deeply and made me hate you with great passion. I hated you for being too good, too nice. Instead of adoring you in a positive way, I allowed my ego to get in the way. It took the best of me in the negative direction. I turned myself into a terrible hater who eventually and unfortunately drowned in the hatred I personally orchestrated, birthed, and created. I was the one who suffered, not you. There were no moral justifications for what I went through, my personal pains and sufferings."

"I thank and appreciate you for showing me that evil does not prevail, and that good always wins. You showed me the right part that led to my liberation. On behalf of myself and my co-conspirators, I tender my unreserved apology again from the depth of my heart. I am sorry. Kindly accept my apology. Let us be kind to one another. This is a new Gina. The Gina you knew before, you will never see again."

Elizabeth and Ella joined her on the podium (the co-conspirators). Francine was rooted to her seat. All eyes turned on her. She was short of words but emotional. Tears was dripping down her beautiful makeup face. She got up, went to the podium, and gave Gina a bear, tight hug, and beckoned Ella and Elizabeth to join. It was an impressive remarkable sight. All the attendees got up for Gina, gave her a standing ovation, and clapped endlessly for her. She was not able to continue her speech because the show of love by her classmates was endless. Her speech touched the core of the heart of the audience. They milled around her and hugged her, happy that she won the battle against hate, ego, and jealousy that she purposely birthed at last. It took great heart and courage to ask for forgiveness in a public place. Her courage impressed everyone, and she broke her shackles at last, free indeed, though she was still a work in progress.

After the massive show of love and support for Gina by all present, Francine picked up the microphone and thanked Gina for the moving speech, courage, and apology to everyone including herself. She told her she forgave her a long time ago and had never harbored any form of animosity toward her or any of her conspirators. She loved her like any other person in the room and had always extended the same portion of love to all irrespective of who they were. Doing good and helping others was her natural innate attribute. If there was a need and she turned a blind eye, her conscience would not let her rest. She went further to discuss the values of love and support. Love covers a multitude of negative things while support was therapeutic. We all need the support of one another—support from family, friends, acquaintances, classmates, neighbors, and more. We must be each other's brother/sister from another mother. With support, we can overcome issues and problems. A problem shared they say is half solved. The burden is no longer the individuals alone. Help comes from places you least expect. The love extended to Gina was natural with no strings attached. She expressed to her that she loved and would always love everyone come rain, come shine. All anyone needed was to just call her.

Francine's vice took the microphone from her and expressed happiness at the speeches. He reiterated that they could never over flog issues surrounding love, support, togetherness, and kindness. They all needed to learn the rudimental skills of an unrepentant giver of love and support like Francine. He appreciated Gina for accepting responsibility for her actions and thanked her for the courage to share, apologize, and take responsibility for her actions. It takes great guts most especially in public. He admonished everyone including himself on the great lesson of courage and responsibility from her speech. Accepting responsibility is a bold step in admitting guilt when we err. Taking responsibility is contingent on working on a change. Be truthful to yourself. Do not wish to be someone else. Change is the only thing that is constant. It impacts knowledge from diverse areas and angles. Learning and change do not stop until death comes knocking. With that said, they hit the dance floor. Gina danced with so much joy, as if the leftover demons in her got released by the force of the restitution she made. She was a great dancer and danced with an aura of happiness and freedom. One of her classmates who had a crush on her while in high school before she became a "monster" rekindled his love for a relationship a few weeks after the reunion. He was in awe at the new Gina that spoke from the heart.

He saw a new perspective, a totally changed individual, visualized the genuineness of a changed person willingly working on a new lease on life. Gina got hooked at last, thanks to the power of restitution, rehabilitation, and recovery, and all thanks to Francine. It truly ended well; nothing was ever too late. A turnaround could happen at any time in the life of an individual. Change could happen to the worst offender. Life offers chances, second, third, fourth, as many as life could give, but readiness to accept the "chances" matter. With breath still in our nostrils, opportunities, chances, learning, and changes abound. Stagnancy should be avoided in life. Problems are never permanent, and challenges are inherent in life. Change and chances lead to new beginnings and prospects that we must strive to embrace and welcome. Chances and opportunities change the world we live in with the strategies we implore to make life worth living. It is never ever too late to change and become a reformed individual. We make mistakes, imbibe wrong choices, have dark pasts, not proud of past decisions or birth circumstances. Whatever the situation, they are not definers of our life and future. A person's reactions to life's conscious effort through readdressing, reassessing, and daily improvement would place a person on the right pedestal to success. It can never be too late unless a person makes it too late.

ABOUT THE AUTHOR

Adetoun Adenrele Afolabi, fondly referred to as Ms. Ade, holds a first degree in English (BAEd), a master's degree in adult education (MEd), and a graduate certificate in addiction and substance abuse counseling. She is a certified master-level addiction professional (MCAP), with an IC&RC Alcohol & Drug Counselor (ICRC-ADC) certification. She was once a presenter and producer on television, a schoolteacher, and later a senior inspector of education. During this time, her interest to become a writer developed and was cultivated. She later became fascinated with the importance of therapy resulting in a career as a co-occurring therapist followed by an access-to-recovery care manager. She became passionately empathetic with individuals experiencing mental health, substance abuse, and the many challenges that come with dual diagnosis. With the COVID-19 pandemic and societal lockdown, a seed for this book came to the fore, and was born. Ms. Ade is married with children and grandchildren.